Altar Call in Europe

*Billy Graham, Mass Evangelism, and
the Cold-War West*

UTA A. BALBIER

Oxford University Press is a department of the University of Oxford. It furthers
the University's objective of excellence in research, scholarship, and education
by publishing worldwide. Oxford is a registered trade mark of Oxford University
Press in the UK and certain other countries.

Published in the United States of America by Oxford University Press
198 Madison Avenue, New York, NY 10016, United States of America.

Library of Congress Cataloging-in-Publication Data
Names: Balbier, Uta A., author.
Title: Altar call in Europe : Billy Graham, mass evangelism, and the Cold-War West /
Uta A. Balbier, King's College London.
Description: New York : Oxford University Press, [2022] |
Includes bibliographical references and index.
Identifiers: LCCN 2021022711 | ISBN 9780197502273 | ISBN 9780197502280 |
ISBN 9780197502259 | ISBN 9780197502266 | ISBN 9780197502273 (epub)
Subjects: LCSH: Graham, Billy, 1918-2018. | Evangelistic work—Europe—History—20th century. |
Revivals—Europe—History—20th century. | Europe—Church history—20th century. |
Billy Graham Evangelistic Association.
Classification: LCC BV3785.G69 B25 2021 | DDC 269/.2092—dc23
LC record available at https://lccn.loc.gov/2021022711

DOI: 10.1093/oso/9780197502259.001.0001

1 3 5 7 9 8 6 4 2

Printed by Integrated Books International, United States of America

For Max and Jan

Contents

Figures

Abbreviations

BBC	British Broadcasting Corporation
BGEA	Billy Graham Evangelistic Association
CDU	Christlich Demokratische Union Deutschlands
CMS	Church Mission Society
DM	Deutsche Mark
DPA	Deutsche Presse-Agentur
MP	Member of Parliament
NAE	National Association of Evangelicals
SED	Sozialistische Einheitspartei Deutschlands
YFC	Youth for Christ
YMCA	Young Men's Christian Association

Introduction

The day before Harringay Arena opened its doors for the Greater London Crusade of 1954, Billy Graham prayed. Despite his celebrity status as the rising star of American evangelicalism, the challenge Graham was about to embark upon—to revive Christian Britain, a country over which secularization was looming large—was formidable. Yet any worries Graham may have harbored would prove misplaced: between March 1 and May 29, he preached to 2,047,333 people, and 38,447 answered his altar call—numbers that would not be exceeded until his marathon Madison Square Garden crusade in New York three years later. Even in Germany, a country with a less established revival tradition than Britain, Graham's pulling power was immense: he drew 80,000 to a single revival meeting at the Olympic Stadium in Berlin in 1954. When he returned to Germany in 1960, his three-city crusade attracted 649,000, of whom 16,636 answered his altar call. These numbers were impressive, and the Billy Graham Evangelistic Association (BGEA), whose job it was to calculate and disseminate them to a voracious press, knew they were evidence of a remarkable evangelical success story.[1]

These figures are even more striking considering the different political, economic, and religious landscapes in which these revival meetings took place. The United States was firing itself up for the so-called American Century, surfing a postwar boom that transformed the economic lives and consumption patterns of millions, especially among the white middle class. Germany and Britain, in contrast, still lived in the shadow of conflict, their towns and cities bearing the scars of war, their citizens only recently relieved of the hardships of food rationing. While Britain briefly flashed a few final imperial hopes and aspirations, Germany approached its future burdened by wartime guilt and postwar separation. Churches on American soil embraced the suburban lifestyles of their followers and the anticommunist impulses of their politicians. Across the Atlantic, the Anglican Church attempted to assert its leadership in the postwar re-Christianization of Britain. German churches, meanwhile, were forced to confront their role in the moral catastrophe of war and genocide. And then Billy Graham entered the scene—a

Altar Call in Europe. Uta A. Balbier, Oxford University Press. © Oxford University Press 2022.
DOI: 10.1093/oso/9780197502259.003.0001

young, handsome, American evangelist, dressed in a sharp business suit and with a distinct southern drawl, who proved that there was a way to unite Christians in nations faced with such diverse social, economic, and religious experiences.

The success of his revival work in such seemingly different settings—London, Berlin, and New York—raises three important questions: What were the common issues about the future of faith, ecumenism, and seculari-zation that Graham allowed Christians on both sides of the Atlantic to inter-rogate? How did common transnational discourses around Cold War culture and consumerism manifest themselves in the way Graham was perceived in these different localities? And what transatlantic flows of people, practices, and ideas tied these questions and discourses together in the preparations for, and the aftermaths of, Graham's revival meetings? This book aims to an-swer these questions.

When Billy Graham stepped off the cruise liner *United States* in Southampton, England, in February 1954, he was, at the age of thirty-five, already a recognized evangelist in the United States. Graham's first national campaign in Los Angeles in 1949 had been his springboard, its success down to many factors. Importantly, there was the twin approach that was typical of all Graham's events—strong support from local churches backed by a cre-ative and energetic marketing campaign. Publicity for the Los Angeles mis-sion was boosted by its show-business location: the downtown revival tent attracted Hollywood stars, some of whom joined the thousands who con-verted, in a celebrity-focused strategy that would remain part and parcel of Graham's revival work until his final crusade in New York in 2005. And Graham himself would no doubt have said that it was the power of the prayers of thousands of Christians that played a big part in his breakthrough. But perhaps more than anything else it was the support of the media mogul William Randolph Hearst and his propagation of Graham's message of na-tional revival, Christian restoration, and anticommunism, that propelled the young evangelist to national fame.

Through extensive coverage in his network of newspapers and radio sta-tions, Hearst catapulted Graham into the headlines. Soon he was attracting huge audiences to crusades in all corners of the United States. Each event encountered specific local challenges, whether dealing with the strong Catholic presence in Boston in 1950 or, in the same year, negotiating Jim Crow laws that required segregated seating in Columbus, South Carolina. And yet Graham's revival meetings were always packed because, even when local conditions called for changes to an event's orchestration, Graham's core message and its basic structure remained the same. There were the mass choirs, the large audiences, their heads jointly bowed in prayer, and Graham's compelling preaching. And at the climax of every meeting came Graham's altar call, asking those present to come forward to publicly commit their lives to Christ as the choir softly sang "Just as I Am." That journey of commitment, taken by the thousands who stepped forward in that final act, was the same one that Graham himself had taken at the age of sixteen, in a revival tent not far from his parents' farm near Charlotte, North Carolina. Graham's own walk down the sawdust trail came in response to a call from the revivalist Mordechai Ham; from that moment, in 1934, Billy Graham considered himself reborn.[2]

Graham's early life gives us some insight into his religious growth. When Graham answered Ham's altar call, he had already been raised in a Christian household, yet he embraced the idea of the altar call that would constitute the spiritual climax of all of his own future crusades. By denominational affiliation Graham was a Southern Baptist, the church in which he was ordained in 1939. His education also sheds some light on Graham's faith: he dropped out of the fundamentalist Bob Jones Bible College in Cleveland, Tennessee, after just a couple of months and switched to the Florida Bible Institute in Temple Terrace. While homesickness, or even the weather, may have played some part in his decision to leave Tennessee, Graham's move to Florida meant he would turn his back on Jones's brand of exclusive, authoritarian fundamentalism for good, and side with a significantly more malleable and culturally open version of fundamentalism that would become known as neo-evangelicalism.

In 1940, Graham found his academic home at Wheaton College in Illinois, where he later graduated in anthropology. Graham had left the American South and he would soon embrace the world: in 1944, he joined the new evangelical Youth for Christ (YFC) movement as vice president and the organization's first full-time staff member. Graham's affiliation with the YFC saw him preach at mass revival meetings for the first time, including before sixty-five thousand people at Chicago's Soldier Field in May 1945. Under the YFC flag, he embarked on his first trip to Europe in 1946, followed by another a year later. Graham would remain committed to Europe as an important mission field for the following two decades before shifting the focus of his ministry to the global South.

Graham's crusades in London, Düsseldorf, and Berlin in 1954 built on those earlier YFC European trips, although the political, social, and economic landscape had changed considerably. Recent historiography on transnational US evangelicalism has examined the activities of American evangelical missionaries who found themselves confronted by the physical ruins and spiritual despair of immediate postwar Europe: much of their work involved raising funds to rebuild churches and organizing relief work, in addition to the core spiritual mission of hosting revival meetings.[3] But when Graham returned in 1954, it was the Cold War that was at the forefront of Europeans' anxieties, alongside their continuing hopes for a post-war economic recovery. And like the United States, Britain and Germany were also witnessing a revival of Christianity. Appreciating the convergence of these social, economic, and geopolitical contexts helps us to understand the success of Graham's revival work in London, Berlin, and New York, as much as a transnational reading of his crusades allows us to gain a deeper appreciation of their spiritual underpinnings.

The Transatlantic Postwar Revival

Billy Graham has always been a central figure in the seminal works on America's postwar revival by scholars such as Joel Carpenter.[4] In comparison, his presence in the historiography of postwar European Christianity has been decidedly uneven. On the one hand, the British historian Callum Brown acknowledges the importance of Graham's Harringay mission as a factor in Britain's religious revival of the 1950s: the celebration of the Christian identity of Britain, the revived energy of local churches, and the prominence of religion in public media all came to the fore during the spectacular staging of Graham's London crusade.[5] In sharp contrast, when Thomas Grossbölting published the translated version of his compelling history of religious life in Germany after 1945, Graham's German revivals are only mentioned in passing.[6]

The reasons for the different prominence given to Graham in these three historiographies are manifold: Graham never turned into a religious and national "icon" in Europe as he did in the United States, where he is still remembered as "America's pastor." The three countries inherited a different revival tradition: the United States and Britain were closely linked from the eighteenth century onward, but the significantly smaller German pietist communities would only define themselves as *evangelikal* at a much later date.[7] While evangelicalism was a powerful social and political force in England until the end of the nineteenth century, and still is in the contemporary United States, the German evangelical milieu never gathered sufficient numbers to gain power and influence, thanks partly to its tendency toward a more outer worldly theology.[8] Yet it was not only these different historical traditions and circumstances that shaped the perception and memory of Graham's revival work. It was also the very different historiographical answers to the fundamental question of what constitutes religious life in the first place.

Brown considers Graham's role important because religious life for him does not manifest itself solely in church attendance or the institutionalized rituals of belonging. The postwar Christian revival in Britain, Brown argues, also revealed itself in the sacralization of national and political discourses and in the everyday spiritual activities of ordinary Britons. And in all of these, Graham's missions featured prominently.[9] However, those who deny Graham's influence in Europe argue that his revival work did not have a lasting impact on church membership or attendance, because what he offered was genuinely foreign to local churches.[10] They point to contemporary critics who often focused on what they considered the nontraditional elements of Graham's revival work—the spotlights, the business suits, and the sale of soft drinks—all of which seemed to suggest that his meetings were more American-style entertainment than a genuine religious offer. Someone who converted at a Graham crusade might have easily found him- or herself lost at the next Sunday church service, without the thousand-voice choir and the emotional vibrancy of the altar call.

Indeed, Graham's revival work in Britain and Germany did not lead to an increase in church membership. But in this case, numbers fail to tell the full story. For those working on the ground on Graham's revivals it was not simply about packing their churches with new members. Undoubtedly they hoped for a few new faces in the pews, but more importantly they believed Graham's mission would energize their churches in a way that would allow them to resist the looming process of secularization just a little bit longer. In that sense, Graham's religious offer was inextricably linked to local church life in London and Berlin because it invited local ministers, evangelicals and evangelists, and ordinary Christians to interrogate important questions about the future of faith, ecumenism, and secularization. This book argues that, in this way, Graham's revival work constituted a significant rite of passage in German and English Protestantism, just as it did in the United States.

To fully capture this impact, we first have to reconceptualize the writing of the religious histories of the 1950s, to break down the artificial boundaries that have prevented a comprehensive understanding of the transatlantic revival. These are the boundaries between the national and the transnational, between the sacred and the secular, and between religious institutions and everyday religious life.

Simon Green creates a clear boundary between the religious revivals taking place in Britain and the United States: "The periodical literature of the time offers countless examples of just how much more impressed contemporaries were by the very different dynamics of organizational change observed across the Atlantic. America was the real home of Anglophone religious revival in the 1950s."[11] The numbers clearly support Green's interpretation, yet they fail to capture the multilayered exchanges, connections, and flows that crossed the Atlantic in both directions and at whose crossroads the crusades in London, Berlin, and New York were located. German ministers attended the events at Harringay to witness and learn; British evangelicals provided the organizational blueprint for the New York Crusade; and there was a lively exchange of missionary practices across the Atlantic on a range of subjects, including the organization of prayer groups, film screenings, and bus rides. Not least, there was Graham himself, who considered Europe a stepping stone on a path that would eventually see him transformed from a nationally recognized evangelist into an international evangelical superstar.

Of course, national particularities remained and others were reinforced, but studying the postwar transatlantic revival through a transnational framework allows us to highlight similar responses across different religious landscapes to the increasingly rapid modernization of lifestyles. European religious historians and sociologists tend to overlook these similarities when they overstate the linearity of the secularization process and the artificial dichotomy between secular Europe and religious America. Here I am building on Hugh McLeod's observation that "it is wrong to assume that the religious histories of Europe and the United States are fundamentally different, or that Americans have been consistently 'more religious' than Europeans." Consequently, McLeod argues that assumptions about the different secularization paths the United States and Europe embarked upon in the 1950s should be reconsidered.[12]

The challenge of bringing together the religious historiographies of the United States and Europe in the 1950s also requires rethinking national assumptions about what religious life actually encompasses. The German historiographical tradition of church history (*kirchliche Zeitgeschichte*), in particular, has thrived on the assumption that religious life takes place almost entirely in a realm defined by the administrative, social, and cultural roles of the churches. Despite the creative productivity of German church historiography, it still largely focuses on the religious actors and theological debates within the established churches.[13] This perspective leads the historian of German evangelicalism Gisa Bauer to argue that Graham had no impact on religious life in Germany, not even within the evangelical movement.[14]

However, by broadening the understanding of the different cultural and social forces at play, such as Cold War discourses, consumer aspirations, and everyday religious practices of ordinary Christians, one gains a different view of Graham's contributions. Of course, Graham consistently worked with and through established churches: he would only come to a city if the local churches invited him and pledged their support. But his work also created its own spaces, communities, and practices that could not easily be categorized as religious in the traditional institutional sense—and as a result German church history probably underplays Graham's role. In their very nature, these spaces, communities, and practices challenged what American sociologists such as Meredith McGuire describe as the "artificial character of the dichotomy between sacred and profane."[15]

In Graham's revival work there was virtually no boundary between the sacred and the profane. After all, how could anyone draw any meaningful line between the sacred and profane in the highly organized bus rides that offered secular convenience to the modern religious pilgrims or the catchy marketing campaigns that blended secular entertainment with religious themes? While this led some European critics to dismiss Graham's faith as too shallow, too entertaining, and too inauthentic, many ministers and ordinary Christians on both sides of the Atlantic saw Graham's faith as an invitation to question their own expectations about the interface between the sacred and the profane. This spirit of inquiry and the enthusiasm with which Christians explored a religious world beyond the organization and ritual of church life was a powerful ingredient of the 1950s transatlantic religious revival.

The stories in this book are therefore the stories of ordinary Christians who embraced Graham's revival missions with or without the support of official churches. They are the stories of the people who lived and made the Graham crusades—how their motivations, their practices, and their everyday lives created their own religious worlds, and how those worlds were shaped by the interplay between the Graham organization, their churches, and their own initiatives and desires. In exploring all these forces, this book builds on the observation of those writing lived religious history, that "while we know a great deal about the history of theology and (say) church and state, we know next-to-nothing about religion as practiced and precious little about the everyday thinking and doing of lay men and women."[16] While the concept of lived religion has already enhanced our understanding of the complexities of Catholic faith in Germany and Britain after World War II, the equivalent Protestant experiences, thoughts, and practices remain comparatively underexplored.[17]

Furthermore, by focusing on everyday religious lives we add an important layer to our understanding of the inner functioning of the crusade machinery and at the same time provide insights into the hidden spiritual dynamics of the 1950s. For example, by highlighting the powerful role of praying women and the ecumenical nature of the many joint bus rides to the crusades, this book reveals the extent to which new types of spiritual experiences were taking place outside established church structures. Indeed, the ease with which ordinary Christians experimented with religious practices that combined faith with a modern lifestyle is not only one of the strongest features of the transatlantic revival, but also among the most important religious behaviors that European churches failed to instrumentalize in their own battle against secularization.

The religious history of the 1950s offered in this book asks us to consider what constituted the religious life of Christians on both sides of the Atlantic and questions how they imagined the future of their faith. In giving a voice to evangelists, members of evangelical faith groups and free churches, ordinary Christians in the official churches, their ministers, and theologians, it enhances our understanding of the depth, breadth, and content of contemporary debates about secularization and the modernization of religious life. Once one moves beyond the obvious observation that the United States and European religious landscapes developed distinctively different forms in the 1950s and 1960s, one realizes that they nonetheless responded to and were shaped by similar political challenges and economic, social, and cultural changes. For this reason, European Christians, publicists, and politicians were always likely to join their American brethren in debates about two inextricably linked phenomena: the spiritual Cold War and the interplay between consumerism and religious life.

The Transatlantic Spiritual Cold War

In recent years analysis of Graham's revival work has increasingly surfaced in American historiographical debates beyond the religious realm, especially in discussions about the role of religion in the Cold War. Scholars such as Jonathan Herzog, Jason Stevens, and Raymond Haberski have established a close connection between the religious revival of the 1950s and Cold War culture, based on the assumption that Christianity was an effective defensive barrier to communism and a guarantee for democratic and moral order.[18] This Cold War revival, which increased the prominence of religious symbols and narratives in US political and popular culture, was administered through religious and state actors who jointly created, funded, and operated what Herzog called the "spiritual industrial complex." Graham's crusades feature prominently in the historiography, connecting the worlds of high politics, institutionalized religion, and everyday faith.

The political-ideological terrains Graham encountered when he visited London in 1954, and Berlin and Düsseldorf a few weeks later, did not look that different compared to the US case. In both countries there were the signs of a spiritual Cold War worldview: Britain had demonstrated its identity as a Christian nation in all its pomp and pageantry during the coronation of Queen Elizabeth II in June 1953.[19] Germany, meanwhile, was led by a Christian Democratic Party: debates about the country's belonging to the Christian Occident featured prominently in contemporary political and intellectual discourses.[20] Politicians and religious leaders in both countries, just like their American counterparts, were more than willing to frame their anticommunism in religious language. The idea that Christianity could provide the foundation for the future functioning of the Western democracies flourished on both sides of the Atlantic.

While Graham successfully rode this ideological wave, he also expanded its reach: during his crusades he made these discourses accessible to ordinary Christians and non-Christians, helping them to locate their place in the imagined Free World. It is this important element of how the discourses surrounding the spiritual Cold War were opened to ordinary Christians and citizens, beyond the institutionalized framework of churches and political parties, and the role this therefore played in their everyday lives, which has been largely overlooked in current historiography.

Deeply bound up with American evangelicalism's role in the spiritual Cold War was its commitment to free market capitalism, as compellingly shown by Darren Grem, Sarah Hammond, Darren Dochuk, and Kevin Kruse,[21] and the spread of neoliberal and consumer culture, as observed by Bethany Moreton.[22] Graham's crusades provide a unique prism through which to explore the interconnectedness of consumerism, business, and evangelicalism both in his performances and in everyday religious life. Testaments to these connectivities were prayer groups held in cozy living rooms, pilgrimages to the crusade that also included a Manhattan River cruise, and flashy marketing printed on the back of bus tickets. On both sides of the Atlantic, consumerism and Christianity embraced in the minds and lives of those who prepared for and took part in Graham's crusades.

Yet in no area is the chasm between religious life in Europe and the United States perceived as wider than Christianity's relationship with the world of business and consumerism.[23] After all, even today there are no megachurches in London or Berlin that could match the American model. The reality, of course, was rather more complex. The British business historian David J. Jeremy has demonstrated a multifaceted interplay between business culture and Christianity in the United Kingdom, albeit to a much lesser degree than in the United States.[24] While British Christian capitalists were traditionally more concerned with taming capitalism, there was a small circle within the British business community willing to throw support behind Graham's revival work and its celebration of the American Way of Life. And although Germany was a different case again, with a complete absence of financial support for Graham's campaigns from local businesses, the German evangelical community nevertheless learned the importance of professionalism, numbers, money and efficiency from Graham's organizing team.

And Graham did not just inspire and attract Christian businessmen—he also educated Christian consumers. Graham's crusades in London and Berlin revealed how British and German Christians, like their American brethren, struggled with the impact of consumerism on their religious worlds.[25] Not only were there the demands for rigorous business and marketing structures in the organization of a Graham crusade, but Graham himself was perceived as being *the* American white middle-class consumer. Graham was the embodiment of the American Way of Life: his smart looks, mode of travel, and passion for golf were all important ingredients of his appeal to Europeans, who had barely left the painful days of postwar austerity. Graham's revival meetings created a religious community that valued these common aspirational class features.[26] And they also fashioned an overlapping political community committed to the ideals of the Free World, in which prosperity was as important as freedom.

Graham's crusades, therefore, provided important spaces to shape the identities of Christian consumers on both sides of the Atlantic. The vast marketing campaigns addressed his followers as fellow consumers. And consumer culture impacted the everyday running of the crusades at a local level, from the way prayer groups were conducted to the transport arrangements for visitors. Hence, my work builds on James Hugnut-Beumler's analysis of the transformation of American religious life in the context of suburban living, increased mobility, and new prosperity.[27] Furthermore, it examines the transatlantic dimensions of this process to show how a spreading consumer culture challenged traditional communities of faith, and how the churches in Britain and Germany responded to these new identities and desires.[28] Ultimately consumerism helped shape the identity of Graham's followers, who consumed a faith that was marketed and sold to them in the United States and in Europe.

This study connects the passionate debates in the United States and Europe during the 1950s about the opportunities and pitfalls of a faith that embraces consumer culture instead of resisting it. It points to the European yearning for a more accessible faith, which was already so clearly visible in the dynamics of suburban religiosity in the United States. In doing so, it reveals the artificial exceptionalism of the US historiography, fueled by the absence of comparative perspectives, which suggests a uniquely American relationship between consumerism and religion. There is no doubt that the intensity of the interplay between consumerism and religion in the United States was never matched in Europe, but European churches still used Graham's crusades to experiment with practices that originated from their combined religious and consumer identities. Moreover, the link to consumerism offered European church leaders, who were deeply troubled by the spiritual legacies of war and the fast-eroding authority of their churches, a distinctive way of engaging with emerging popular practices and new popular culture. Spirituality, consumerism, and religious life ultimately had different trajectories in the three countries—but these emerged through a common engagement with each other, sparked not least by the influence of Graham. This book demonstrates how Cold War anxieties, spiritual desires, and economic ambitions blended during a religious revival that shook established and non-established churches, and thus impacted deeply not just postwar spiritual life, but everyday culture in "the West."

The Question of Belonging

Graham clearly created an international awareness that a transatlantic revival was underway in the 1950s, and he certainly turned America's spiritual Cold War into a global one. But was he also able to shape a transatlantic community of evangelicals? Press reports as early as 1954 referred to the fluid and imagined community of "those Christians who heard Graham preach in Boston, Albuquerque, London, Copenhagen, and Düsseldorf."[29] By 1966, a German journalist was writing of a "global congregation" (*weltumspannende Gemeinde*) of Graham's followers. One German scholar even goes as far to argue that German evangelicals only began to define themselves as evangelical (*evangelikal*) through their engagement with Billy Graham and American evangelicals during the World Congress on Evangelism in Berlin in 1966.[30] Graham himself, with his accustomed humility, would probably have denied that this was the case. After all, he made it quite clear that he never wanted to establish his own church or denomination: he just worked with different local churches wherever his revival work took him. This book, however, will argue that the German observers do have a point. A Western evangelical community took shape in the dynamic interplay between structures and methods implemented by the Graham team. Local ministers and ordinary Christians engaged with these creatively and energetically. Even if this process was not without tensions, they created a Western evangelical community based on a shared style, on a constant flow of communication, and on emotional belonging.

The bourgeoning field of the transnational study of US evangelicalism has shone a light on networks, media, and emotions, through recent works by Melani McAlister, Heather Curtis, David King, and David Swartz.[31] Evangelical international organizations such as World Vision, Campus Crusade for Christ, and the BGEA flourished after World War II and shaped tight transnational networks that were, in Swartz's words, "pluralistic, participatory, and multidirectional enterprises."[32] Their success was based on the ability, as shown by Curtis and McAlister, to create a transnational sense of belonging and care.[33] This deeply felt compassion for fellow Christians and Christians-to-be who lived thousands of miles apart has been a driving force behind the shaping of evangelical humanitarianism and global aid initiatives.[34] Moreover, it has allowed evangelicals who understand themselves as "being one body in Christ" to generate a global community of evangelicals.[35] What sets this book apart from the global breadth of the works by Swartz and McAlister is its focus on evangelical exchanges that took place within the Western political, social, and cultural context. It does not directly address the impressive rise of an Americanized evangelical Christianity in Africa and Asia, but aims to enhance our understanding of this distinct Western gospel of personal salvation, free enterprise, and democracy that first spread to postwar Europe before sweeping the rest of the world.

In contrast to their African and Asian brethren, the British and German Christians to whom Graham reached out were not threatened by famine, war, or natural disaster. Yet from the perspective of the BGEA they lived under the very real shadow of impending secularization and moral decay. That was a discourse that American neo-evangelicals successfully established after World War II and that mirrored Graham's preaching in America. Thus, Graham's warnings about the threat of secularization, spelled out so vividly in London, Berlin, and New York, tied together his followers on both sides of the Atlantic. He did not just generate a shared awareness of the threats to Christian life through his preaching, but also stirred Christians into action: Americans donated to his campaigns in England; British evangelicals fundraised for his revival work in Germany; and ordinary Christians prayed for the success of Graham's crusades around the world.

Through the crusades, evangelical Christians in the West joined hands and hearts in a transatlantic battle against secularization and in support of America's spiritual Cold War. And the BGEA provided the organizational framework to allow Graham's followers to imagine themselves as "one in Christ" and to belong to one evangelical Western community that acted as a bulwark against secularization and the communist threat. The association's publications provided an important channel of communication: these included conversion narratives, books, including Graham's *Peace with God*, and journals, such as *Decision*. All were available in German as well as English. Glossy images and powerful, firsthand accounts of lives changed allowed evangelicals in Britain, the United States, and Germany to imagine themselves as members of the Billy Graham family.

Yet no means of communication was as vigorous as prayer.[36] Organized through prayer partner letters and prayer chains, encouraged by the Graham team, and administered through local churches, prayer connected the different international audiences. At the same time, prayer became a very social act in which individuals "ritualized their beliefs" as members of the emerging Billy Graham community.[37] The publication of crusade images and the shared conversion stories shaped a common "evangelical style" across national borders.[38] Graham's missions seeded this transnational evangelical community. It might have been imagined, fluid, and intangible, but it manifested itself in the preparation of the crusades, at the meetings themselves, and in the memory of many of those who participated.

1

Reviving Religion

Billy Graham's Early Crusades in the Religious Landscapes after World War II

On March 1, 1954, American evangelist Billy Graham took to the pulpit at Harringay Arena in London to open his twelve-week Greater London Crusade. The thirty-five-year-old evangelist, who had already become a household name in US evangelicalism, prepared himself to address the audience present of between eleven and twelve thousand. Many more had been turned away. The big numbers at this revival event were certainly a tribute to a shrewd public marketing campaign and the fact that a thousand churches across the country had urged their congregations to attend. But their meaning ran deeper: those present were looking for a genuine religious offer in an increasingly secular environment; they came looking for a fresh and modern faith that could still attract people in future decades.

Those present on the first evening and during the coming weeks experienced a revival service that, from preparation to content, was little different from those Graham and his team had held in Los Angeles, Boston, and Albuquerque before, with one minor concession to the tastes of the hosts, as a correspondent with *Time* magazine observed: "Graham slowed down his usual machine-gun delivery for the benefit of British ears and moderated his usual platform prowl in deference to British dignity."[1]

The sermon, with its emphasis on the dangers of secularism and materialism, echoed Graham's familiar American themes. Musical director Cliff Barrows led a two-thousand-voice choir with the efficiency and melodic rigor of the American meetings. Hymns such as "Blessed Assurance, Jesus Is Mine," "All Hail the Power of Jesus' Name," and "Guide Me, O Thou Great Redeemer," sung to the tune of the Welsh hymn "Cwm Rhondda," which would become the crusade's anthem, turned the secular arena into a sacred space. After a forty-five-minute sermon on John 3:16, Graham made the altar call, which, on that first night, was accepted by 178 people. Exactly as in the United States, each inquirer was led to a counseling room, where

Altar Call in Europe. Uta A. Balbier, Oxford University Press. © Oxford University Press 2022.
DOI: 10.1093/oso/9780197502259.003.0002

they received a free copy of the Gospel of John.[2] Graham's revivalist offer had crossed the Atlantic.

The Greater London Crusade, like Graham's US revival meetings, set new standards for fundraising, local organization, and mass promotion. Even more so, it stirred fresh discussions about the identity and role of evangelism, ecumene, and secularization. Graham's revival meetings in the United Kingdom, the United States, and in Germany, where he visited after his time in London, provided an important focus for discussions about the transformability and future of Christian faith that crossed denominational and confessional boundaries. With both critics and supporters of Graham's religious offer often sharing membership in the same church or denomination, these revival meetings broke up and blurred religious boundaries and identities, allowing new religious alliances and communities to form. Graham's revival meetings took place during the seismographic shift in the religious landscape "from a culture of obligation and duty, to a culture of consumption and choice," observed Grace Davie for the British case.[3] Through the debates Graham's crusades stirred, they made this shift possible and visible, and accelerated it, in Europe and the United States.

Whether Christianity could survive in modern societies, with their increasing focus on choice and individualism, was a pressing question on both sides of the Atlantic. Yet there remained important differences regarding the dynamics and possibilities within the religious landscapes and the position and impact of evangelical Christianity within the three national religious contexts. Evangelical Christianity had been a highly influential force politically and culturally since the nineteenth century in Britain and the United States, but while it would sustain its societal impact in the United States after World War II, its broader cultural role kept fading in the United Kingdom. The German evangelical movement, on the other hand, traditionally only populated a marginal realm of the religious landscape and remained close to invisible in political and wider theological debates. While British evangelicals thrived not just within the Free Churches but also within the Church of England, German evangelical Christians found it significantly harder to live their faith and conduct their missions inside the established Protestant church and often preferred an institutional home in the Free Churches so as to remain among coreligionists.[4] Neither of them were able to operate in a religious landscape as dynamic and fluid as the American one.

The different role that evangelical Christianity played in the politics and culture of the three countries, and the position that it possessed in the religious landscapes, influenced the way in which Graham was perceived in the 1950s: while he set out in the United States to become "America's pastor," he remained a religious outsider in Germany and at least a religious stranger in the United Kingdom.[5] But Billy Graham did not intend to come to Europe as an evangelical Christian: Graham's offer was to transcend the deep structural differences between faiths in the countries he visited. This forced religious leaders and congregations alike, from all denominations, to engage with this offer, raising the question how they positioned themselves toward him and the religious offer of a modern, revivalist Christian faith he represented.

Graham's offer arrived timely in all three countries, which experienced a unique revivalist buzz in the aftermath of World War II. Yet the degree to which a revival took place in Europe is much contested. William McLaughlin was among the first scholars to argue that a religious revival took place in the United States after World War II. McLaughlin defined a revival as a period when "theological and ecclesiastical reorientation coincided with an intel-lectual and social reorientation in such a way as to awaken a new interest in the Christian ethos which underlies American civilization."[6] That was certainly the case in the early Cold War United States; however, ecclesias-tical and social reorientations tied to questions of national identity were also taking place in the United Kingdom at the same time. Thus, Callum Brown argues compellingly for a revival taking place in the United Kingdom in the early 1950s, in which the events at Harringay "both reflected and reinforced discursive and institutional Christianity."[7]

German scholars such as Thomas Grossbölting acknowledge as well a new dynamic in German Christian circles after World War II, in which important initiatives to re-Christianize the country took place. In the light of declining church membership, German Protestant churches engaged in new mis-sionary efforts and created new public forums to discuss and celebrate faith, such as the Protestant Academies and the biannual Kirchentag, established in 1949. Yet Grossbölting sees "the lustre of the religious spring" fading when one confronts it with the hard data of church statistics and the churches' very own hopes regarding the spiritual maturity of their old and new members.[8] And the German religious landscape, marked by a distinctive absence of his-torical religious revivalism, just seemed to look too different to speak of a revival taking place.

Yet focusing on Graham's revival work on both sides of the Atlantic allows us to move beyond this established focus on transatlantic differences. Instead it enables us to access the world of a transatlantic revival that took place in the 1950s and even touched Germany, where the Christian churches also had to reposition themselves in relation to societal, cultural, and theological changes. The political, cultural, and religious circumstances of this revival could not have been more different; but the hopes and anxieties articulated during the revival, the willingness to leave traditional denominational and confessional boundaries behind, and the genuine search in religious circles for new religious styles and practices could not have been more similar. And they all traveled with Billy Graham across the Atlantic.

A New Religious Offer

The story of Harringay and the consecutive European tour that took Graham to Germany began at the American West Coast, where Graham launched a revival meeting in 1949 that would catapult him to national stardom. When Billy Graham's revival meeting opened its tent doors at the junction of Washington Boulevard and Hill Street, just south of downtown Los Angeles, on the afternoon of September 25, 1949, its success was no accident.[9] Church membership had reached an all-time high after the end of World War II. Polls revealed that nearly 95 percent of Americans believed in God and 90 percent of the public still engaged in the private practice of prayer.[10] Church building flourished in the prosperous economic climate; sales of Bibles skyrocketed, and religious publishing in general enjoyed unprecedented popularity. The postwar baby boom contributed to growth in church membership, with even mainline Protestant churches embracing the evangelistic fervor of the decade.[11] Secular newspapers fueled the revivalist atmosphere by running articles on the seemingly insatiable enthusiasm for religion under headlines like "High Tide of Faith."[12] Evangelical organizations, like the YFC, had already shown they could attract thousands to events in large stadiums, such as the revival meeting that took place on Memorial Day, 1945, at Chicago's Soldier Field. "For evangelists it was like being a stockbroker in a runaway bull market," wrote Graham biographer William Martin in describing the spiritual atmosphere of the decade after the war.[13]

While the traditional Protestant fundamentalist milieu bristled with renewed energy, it also experienced significant transformation with the rise of the neo-evangelical movement. The traditional fundamentalist milieu, revealed in all its otherworldliness during the Scopes trial in the 1920s, now split into a remaining otherworldly minority and a broad new neo-evangelical movement, which combined traditional fundamentalist faith, such as the belief in the inerrancy of the Bible, with new "effectiveness, growth in numbers of adherents, and public image."[14] Furthermore, in its engagement with the world, this neo-evangelical movement also found a strong political voice. It quickly established new organizational structures, with the foundation of the National Association of Evangelicals (NAE) in 1942 and the opening of Fuller Theological Seminary in 1947. While key figures such as Carl Henry and Harold Ockenga, the pastor of the Park Street Church in Boston, were among the early driving forces, Billy Graham's revival campaigns contributed significantly to the popularization of this new evangelical brand, turning it into a real spiritual experience for thousands of future American neo-evangelicals.

Graham's first Los Angeles crusade reflected and perpetuated many of the inclusive characteristics of the rise of neo-evangelicalism, which had blurred the lines between the religious and civic realm and had underscored concerns about the future of religion in a growing mass culture. The campaign was organized by Christ for Greater Los Angeles, an interdenominational organization dedicated to revival work in the region and supported by a thousand regional Protestant churches, reflecting the breadth of the evangelistic passion of the times. Graham traveled to Los Angeles with his own team, including his musical director, Cliff Barrows; baritone George Beverley Shea; and fellow evangelist and later vice president of the BGEA, Grady Wilson. Other evangelistic heavyweights such as Jack Shuler and Bob Jones appeared as guest preachers. Lasting just under two months, the revival meetings at the so-called Canvas Cathedral were attended by 350,000; three thousand converts were registered and thousands more rededicated their lives to Christ. Thanks to the support of two media moguls, William Randolph Hearst and Henry Luce, Graham's revival work gained national attention, with headline-grabbing stories about the conversions of the war hero and former star athlete Louis Zamperini, the wiretapper and mob affiliate Jim Vaus, and the radio star Stuart Hamblin. Operating alongside this media coverage was an extensive and sophisticated promotional campaign. From the colorful campaign posters and lapel microphones to people listening to the transmitted sermons while sitting in their cars outside the traditional revival tent, it was a campaign embedded in the 1950s urban culture of Los Angeles, an American culture that had been fully embraced by the hundreds of church organizations and evangelists involved in its organization.[15]

While being embedded in the religious, social, and economic changes of the immediate postwar period, Graham's crusades also displayed their roots in older evangelical traditions. His message could not have been more traditional, with its focus on crisis, repentance, and personal conversion and his constant call for revival. The fact that the secular and religious press drew comparisons to Billy Sunday located Graham firmly in this American revivalist tradition. Graham himself underlined it even more when he closed his revival by preaching Jonathan Edwards's familiar sermon, "Sinners in the Hands of an Angry God," verbatim.[16] The newspapers highlighted the fusion of old and new: pictures of the young preacher behind a shiny microphone were presented alongside more religious images of listeners kneeling in prayer and singing hymns and of a young couple walking up the sawdust trail.[17] These photographs suggested the continuing existence of traditional forms of religious practice beneath the flashier layers of the revival.

The deeply religious core of many of the conversion experiences was not lost on contemporaries. News stories about some of the conversion experiences emphasized more of these partially hidden spiritual depths. The *Los Angeles Times* published a feature by its religious editor, William A. Moses, about a preacher from Yucca Valley, Reverend Edward Garver, who had taken time off from his community church to work as a night watchman at the revival tent. It seemed there was more to the job than simple security. "Above the rustle of the tent flaps and intermittent sound of traffic, Eddie heard the shuffling of feet in the sawdust, sobs in the darkness," wrote Moses.[18] Evidently, some of those who attended the revival meeting during the day found themselves drawn back to the tent during the night as they agonized over making their decision for Christ. Garver, according to the *Los Angeles Times*, would comfort those who found themselves sleepless with an aching conscience and in need of joint prayer. By removing the masses, the choirs, and the microphones from the description of this particular conversion moment, the article highlighted the genuinely religious core of Graham's missionary work. Graham's first mission, in short, thrived on a balanced orchestration of evangelical tradition and modern missionary techniques.

Graham's preaching in Los Angeles reflected the new outlook of the neo-evangelical community and the religious landscape more generally. A banner on the side of the revival tent promised "dynamic preaching," a phrase picked up eagerly in newspaper coverage. In his preaching, however, Graham himself declared the apparent dynamism of the religious landscape to be shallow. He contrasted polls that indicated that 95 percent of Americans believed in God with the reality that only 8 percent of the citizens of Los Angles went to church more than once a year.[19] With these numbers, that sounded quite exaggerated, Graham was warning of the increase of secularization in the United States without actually using the term.

By questioning the authenticity of the current revival taking place in the United States, he echoed the critique of public intellectuals such as Reinhold Niebuhr and Will Herberg, who suggested that during this high tide of religious zeal, it was becoming increasingly hard to distinguish between faith in God and a more general commitment to American culture expressed through tropes and practices of faith. Religion had fallen captive to American culture to such a degree that faith seemed to have turned into a secular end in itself, as in the words of Reinhold Niebuhr: "The 'unknown god' in America seems to be faith itself."[20] Many of the public critics of the 1950s revival zoomed in precisely on Billy Graham's revival meetings, as vast national celebrations with a religious theme.[21]

Graham aired his grievances about the state of churches that he saw as functionally efficient but spiritually empty.[22] But he did not stop there: the increase in divorce rates and the spread of the modern vices of sex, drink, and gambling all pointed to a societal moral degeneration that he blamed on declining faith. His laments over religious and moral decline within and outside religious institutions went beyond the mere recitation of unpalatable facts—they constituted nothing less than an evangelical battle cry, used to stir his followers into action.

The appeal of Graham's message to Americans grew consistently in the aftermath of the Los Angeles crusade. Revival meetings led by Graham in New England attracted about 160,000 participants. In Portland, Oregon, and Atlanta, Georgia, an estimated 500,000 attended several week-long revival campaigns.[23] In 1951, Graham and his team held major crusades in Fort Worth, Texas; Memphis, Tennessee; Seattle, Washington; and Greensborough, North Carolina. Around the time of Graham's 1952 revival meeting in Washington, DC, a campaign that placed him in America's political center, the idea took shape to take his evangelism to Europe, a continent Graham had visited several times before.

Preparing the Ground

Graham's early ventures to Europe had been in his capacity as vice president of the YFC: first during a six-week tour of Britain in spring 1946, followed by another six months of missionary work beginning in October 1946. Graham highlighted his knowledge of Europe in his opening sermon in Los Angeles, referring to the experience of destruction caused by World War II and the menace Europeans now faced from the threat of communism. He continued: "Many of these people believe that God can still use America to evangelize the world."[24] Graham's concerns reflected a broader trend in the evangelical community in the postwar years. In 1947, *United Evangelical Action*, the organ of the NAE, published several articles on the state of civic and religious life in Germany. Harold Ockenga's reports from Berlin warned of a political and spiritual vacuum in which German youth seemed to be trapped after the end of the Third Reich. He emphasized the importance of education and religion in the future democratization of Germany.[25] Under the alarming headline "Will the German Nation Be Lost for God?" the YFC president, Torrey M. Johnson, declared America responsible for bringing a new revival to Germany.[26] The National Socialist secularization project, the destruction of war, and the ethical implications of the Holocaust had turned the homeland of Martin Luther into a mission field.

The American view of the British religious landscape was hardly more favorable. Echoing reports issued by the Church of England's Commission on Evangelism, *United Evangelical Action* bemoaned the state of religion in Britain, which was marked by emptying churches and declining moral standards.[27] Johnson of the YFC pointedly remarked: "We sometimes think Chicago is bad, but I tell you Chicago is a gospel meeting compared with London."[28] As a result, American neo-evangelicals involved themselves in relief work and missionary campaigns in Europe, often traveling alongside the US Army. These connections between British and American Christians gave Graham the confidence to declare at the end of his Los Angeles campaign that people in England and other countries had followed his crusade on the Pacific coast.[29]

Though some European evangelicals may have been aware of the impact of Los Angeles, it had certainly not made significant headlines. Instead, it was Graham's personal connections, established during his earlier YFC work in the United Kingdom, that finally got him an invitation in 1952 to hold large-scale revival meetings in London. He also benefited from a general tendency in the British Evangelical Alliance, one of the main organizing bodies for evangelical activity, to encourage closer connections with the United States after the war.[30] As in the United States, Graham did not bring a revival to the United Kingdom, he stepped right into it.

When Graham launched his first mission in the United Kingdom, he entered an existing hotbed of evangelical activity, nourished through an evangelical renaissance in the postwar years reminiscent of that in the United States.[31] From an American perspective, religious life in Britain may have looked in decline, and it certainly did not match the membership levels seen in the United States, but organized Christianity in Britain actually experienced a remarkable growth between 1945 and 1956, a growth that exceeded the dramatic documented increases of the nineteenth century.[32]

The appointment of Geoffrey Fisher as the archbishop of Canterbury in January 1945 marked the Church of England's transition from dealing with the immediate aftermath of war—the disruption of communities and social anxiety—to facing up to the challenge of a postwar society and new world order. New evangelistic ambitions were outlined in the church's 1945 report, *Towards the Conversion of England*, which called for a spiritual resurgence within the church and outreach to those who were unconnected to it. To achieve these ends, the authors suggested new liturgical forms, new community-based structures, including diocesan groups and Christian cells, as well as the use of modern missionary methods, in particular the use of mass media, marketing, film, and literature. Graham's revival style seemed to fit this bill perfectly. Yet the leadership of the Church of England was initially reluctant to grant its support. The financial and organizational risk of running a revival campaign for several weeks, led by a relatively unknown American evangelist, appeared too high.

British evangelicals, whose movement saw a striking renaissance after World War II in response to the same challenges of impending secularization, seemed significantly better positioned to take on the challenge of bringing Graham to London.[33] Methodists, Congregationalists, and Baptists were launching evangelistic campaigns in the early 1950s, but probably more important for the growth of the evangelical movement was its increasing participation and visibility within the Church of England.[34] Evangelicals clearly left their mark on the *Towards the Conversion of England* and articulated the contributions they were planning to make to the life of the Church of England in another report published in 1950, *The Fulness of Christ: The Church's Growth into Catholicity*.[35] Evangelicals such as John Stott, appointed as rector of All Souls Langham Palace in London in the same year, gave the revival of British evangelicalism a face; organizations such as Inter-Varsity Fellowship, drawing together evangelical university students since 1928, gave it momentum and structure.[36] In addition, the opening of evangelical study centers and the appearance of major evangelical publications, particularly Bible studies, reflected and fueled the evangelistic atmosphere of the early 1950s. Evangelicals such as John Stott had good reason to dream "of renewed cultural influence, of an age where church and society might be united again in a Christian moral order."[37]

The British Evangelical Alliance simultaneously went through important changes while joining in the evangelistic renaissance. It appointed new members such as Rev. Hugh Gough, who became honorary secretary in 1946, and Gilbert Kirby as the Alliance's general secretary, in 1947. Roy Cattell joined as secretary in 1949. The young nondenominational evangelist Tom Rees helped set up Hildenborough House as an evangelical conference center where Graham stayed overnight in 1946 on one of his missions with the YFC to Britain. Rees also attained a degree of celebrity with a series of revival meetings in the London area.[38] All of them became driving forces behind Graham's first London crusade and took over the organization of what would become one of the most elaborate revival events in British history, after Graham addressed a meeting of six hundred churchmen and laypeople at Church House in Westminster in March 1952.

The organizing committee of the London crusade gathered for the first time on January 23, 1953. It was composed of leading evangelicals who were also recognized religious, military, and political figures and influential businessmen. They included Rev. John D. Blinco, a Methodist minister who would later join the BGEA as an evangelist, Rev. Arthur W. Goodwin Hudson, later bishop of Sydney, and John Henderson, a Scottish Conservative politician, member of Parliament, and president of the International Council for Christian Leadership. Later, the Rev. Hugh Gough, bishop of Barking, who was influential in promoting the campaign within the Church of England, joined the committee as well. Major General Donald J. Wilson-Haffenden acted as chairman of the committee.[39]

The committee was established by the British Evangelical Alliance and acted on behalf of the BGEA, the body that would take over the proceedings once the crusade opened.[40] By May 15, 1953, individual subcommittees to organize prayer, publicity, film, counseling, and finances had been set up. These acted in close cooperation with their American counterparts, and several exchange visits took place. Jerry Beavan, Graham's public relations manager, met the London executive committee for the first time the same month and attended another session six months later, accompanied by Graham's musical director, Cliff Barrows, who gave early instructions on the musical arrangements to the London organizing committee. After November, Beavan attended all executive committee meetings to ensure that the crusade would follow American standards.

The London organizers themselves were keen to learn from their American brethren. In August 1953, Rev. J. D Blinco, Rev. A. R Gough, and Rev. A. W Goodwin-Hudson from the London organizing committee attended the Syracuse crusade in New York State, where they also met Graham and several members of his team. They were especially impressed by the success of Graham's altar call and the streamlined follow-up work that ensured that new converts and those who stepped forward to indicate a rededication of their Christian faith would be delegated to a local church. Gough, the bishop of Barking, published an enthusiastic report about his experiences in Syracuse in the *London Crusade News*, in which he again underlined Graham's spiritual authenticity: "I am convinced that many of the misgivings that British people seem to have concerning Dr. Graham would immediately be removed if they could see him and hear him as I did. His sincerity and humility are beyond question. God is using him to the winning of tens of thousands of Americans; and these conversions are due not to the human talents which Graham undoubtedly possesses, but to the power of the Spirit of God within him."[41]

Rev. Frank Colquhoun, another UK committee member and editor of the *London Crusade News*, attended Graham's Detroit crusade, sending his committee colleagues regular reports. The close ties between the British and American organizers were evident in the idea to reuse the artificial tabernacle built for the Detroit campaign. The proposal was to dismantle the tabernacle, ship it across the Atlantic, and erect it on an empty bomb-site near St. Paul's Cathedral. The plan was later dropped on financial grounds.[42] Instead the organizing committee decided to rent Harringay Arena, a vast event space that usually hosted sports events and circuses. It was there that Graham addressed his first audience, on the evening of March 1, 1954. In the following twelve weeks, he would preach to around two million people, and the organizers would record 38,400 conversions at the revival events. Its organizers advertised and celebrated the Greater London Crusade as an example of the possible modernization and future of faith, such as through an advertisement in *The Times* of London: "Surely something new is needed—not a new message, but a new method, a new technique, a new voice."[43]

What happened at Harringay made headlines in the United States. The American religious and secular press studiously followed Graham's first campaigns in Britain. *Moody Monthly* dedicated an entire issue to Graham's London crusade, while the *Christian Herald* also ran a series of reports.[44] The secular press was no less interested. *Time* magazine followed every step of Graham's campaign in Britain, from the celebratory welcome at Waterloo, to the early misgivings expressed in the British press, to a detailed report on the massive response to Graham's altar call, which the editors found rather surprising considering the nature of "traditionally phlegmatic Britons."[45] The *New York Times* commented with pride on the opening night at Harringay: "There was no question about it—when he emerged into the cold-blue arc lights to begin his ministry he was the town's top attraction."[46]

Crossing the Channel

The new spiritual activity and activism north of the English Channel did not go unnoticed in the rest of Europe. Major national and regional newspapers in Germany, where Graham would later take his campaign, also covered the events at Harringay in depth, informing readers of the success and sincerity of Graham's missionary effort. Even though they saw the modern revival meetings as a somewhat manufactured and orchestrated commodity, they nevertheless respected them as part of the long revival tradition dating back to John Wesley and George Whitfield.[47] Even if some headlines suggested journalists were at odds with some presentational aspects of the mission (a *Frankfurter Allgemeine Zeitung* story, for example, was headlined "With Bible, Microphone, and Cowboy"), they still introduced Graham predominantly as a sincere religious figure and established his credentials before his actual arrival in Germany.[48]

At the same time, German evangelicals also prepared the spiritual ground for Graham's arrival in Germany by introducing his specific revival style to Germans through several publications. Wilhelm Brauer, head of the *Volksmission* of the State Church of Westphalia, who would play a leading role in championing Graham's mission, published a book, *Billy Graham, ein Evangelist der neuen Welt*, containing testimonies about Graham's work by his campaign manager, Robert Evans, and Reverend Gough.[49] He also contributed to a brochure about the organization, atmosphere, and follow-up work in London that was published before Graham's arrival in Germany.[50] In the same year, the German translation of Graham's first book, *Peace with God*, came out, presenting to the German audience his faith and message.[51] The commitment to creating a positive image of Graham in Germany was even noticed by the American organizers, who observed that "the breakdown of prejudice in Germany, especially in Berlin—has been very striking."[52]

Yet strong prejudices remained in the German evangelical milieu, of which large parts sided against Graham. In contrast to its British partner organization, the board of the German Evangelical Alliance neither endorsed Graham's first German campaign nor participated in any of the preparatory work. Many board members of the Alliance, among them its chairman, Walther Zilz, shared Graham´s message, but unease with his methods kept them from unconditionally supporting him. For them, Graham's campaigns were too worldly, too modern—in a nutshell, too American—a perspective that would stay a dominating theme in German evangelical circles throughout the 1950s.[53]

The task, therefore, of organizing Graham's first visit to Germany fell to the German Evangelist Conference (Deutsche Evangelistenkonferenz) and its enthusiastic chairman, Wilhelm Brauer.[54] Brauer took part in the Harringay revival meetings, together with other German evangelicals such as Paul Deitenbeck, a youth minister and evangelist, and Erich Sauer, head of the evangelical Bible school Wiedenest, who even joined Graham on the platform in London. Harringay was a formative and inspiring experience for Brauer, who said afterward that it was in London that he realized the deep spiritual hunger of modern men for salvation.[55] Brauer saw men suffering from an existing *Weltangst* in the masses, a deeply felt inner loneliness, a yearning for answers behind technological progress, anxieties he all associated with the process of secularization. Brauer did not trust the traditional church structures and methods to create a revival that all churches in Germany would profit from. Therefore, he turned to the American missionaries for help.[56]

Leading representatives of the Evangelical Church in Germany, such as the bishop of Berlin-Brandenburg, Otto Dibelius, and bishop of Hannover, Hanns Lilje also trusted Graham more to modernize German faith than they did their own organizations.[57] That German churches failed in stopping their decline was proven through numbers: in 1949, forty-three thousand new members joined the Protestant church, but twice as many left.[58] In 1952, for the first time, more members died or left the Catholic Church than joined through birth, conversion, or entry.[59] Religious communities disintegrated, and church membership declined in what looked like the unstoppable process of secularization in Germany. In response, the focus for both the evangelical community and for the evangelical churches shifted to a stronger commitment to mission and outreach.[60]

Dibelius and Lilje were both involved with mission among the German people, the so-called *Volksmission*.[61] Familiar with the lively American religious landscape, through their involvement in the international, ecumenical movement, and willing to experiment with approaches being practiced abroad, both men were frustrated by what they saw as the stiffness, rigidity, and bureaucracy of Protestant church life in their own country. They saw a church in desperate need of the courage to experiment with new religious forms and missionary approaches and to adapt to the beginning of the modern, media age. New forms of religiosity and community, including the visibility, communication, and display of faith, were openly discussed in German Protestantism and Catholicism in the 1950s and found their manifestations in annual public festivals (Kirchentagen), and the opening of religious study centers, the Kirchliche Akademien.[62] German Protestants were also exploring ways to communicate faith in new ways, through film, plays, and journals; Lilje in particular campaigned publicly for a new relationship between churches and the media.[63] He now insisted that Graham's mission highlighted the churches' need to learn how to use media and modern marketing methods.[64]

Due to this ongoing commitment to mission and the active search for new forms of evangelism in German Protestantism, it is not surprising that both of Graham's first revival meetings in Germany, in Düsseldorf on June 25, 1954, and in Berlin two days later, attracted thousands and were supported by the Evangelical churches of the areas. Church superintendent Heinrich Held, the head of the Evangelical Church in the Rhineland, led a prayer of the fifty thousand at the Rhine Soccer Stadium in Düsseldorf, signifying the Evangelical Church's backing of the event. The event closed with the saying of the Lord's Prayer. After the ending, around five hundred inquirers visited the mission tent next to the stadium.[65]

Proceedings in Berlin at the Olympic Stadium followed the same format as Düsseldorf—only the hymns were changed. There was communal singing of the eighty thousand present, a performance of trombones and a solo by George Beverley Shea. The head of the Inner Mission in Berlin, Dr. Theodor

Wenzel, opened the event, and Bishop Dibelius of Berlin-Brandenburg offered the benediction before they joined in the closing hymn "Ein feste Burg ist unser Gott," a hymn that symbolized the core of German Lutheranism and tied the event closely to the national religious tradition.[66] The event made an international splash and was reported in the *New York Times* the next day.[67]

As in Düsseldorf, the layout of the stadium did not allow people to step forward after the altar call, so Graham asked them to just get off their seats (figure 1.1). Half those present stood up to signal their Christian rebirth. By noon the next day, fourteen thousand people had followed up that simple act of standing by getting in touch with the organizing committee to indicate their willingness to participate in further Bible study and to profess their commitment to leading a Christian life. By the following week that number had increased to sixteen thousand.[68]

These were impressive numbers indeed, but the real impact of Graham's mission, his mark on the religious landscape of Germany, as well as that of the United Kingdom and the United States,—was his ability to stir important debates within traditional church structures. His contemporary John Cogley, the editor of the Catholic periodical *Commonweal*, commented on Graham's revival meetings, "There may be more to be learnt about the state of contemporary religion from their criticism than from the nightly crowds gathered (at the revival meetings)."[69] Graham's crusades offered a focus for discussions about the state and future of Christian faith in Europe and the United States in the aftermath of World War II.

Talking Faith

In the United States and Europe, the secular press both covered and contributed to Graham's rise to evangelical stardom. In the early days of the Los Angeles revival William Randolph Hearst encouraged positive press coverage of the young preacher, whom he saw as a central figure in leading America back to morality and Christian values after the social disruption of World War II and the menacing threat of the new Cold War. Articles covering the Los Angeles crusade contained three key themes: the youthfulness of Graham, indicating the freshness of his religious offer; the innovativeness and technological sophistication of his religious mission; and the looming social and political crisis to which Graham seemingly provided an answer. Articles made reference to Graham's good looks and the fact that he

Figure 1.1 Billy Graham preaching at the Olympic Stadium in Berlin, 1954 (Bettmann/Gettyimages)

had not yet turned thirty. Richard Reynolds of the *Los Angeles Daily News* rejoiced: "That old time religion has gone as modern as an atomic bomb."[70]

Before Graham arrived in Europe there might have been some initial odd voices warning of Graham's "hot-gospeling," but these quickly receded, particularly after the first event at Harringay, which the newspapers described as quiet and demure.[71] This first impression opened room for unexpectedly positive press coverage, often highlighting the freshness and modernity of his religious work in a fight against secularization. *The Times* quoted from the *British Weekly* in explaining Graham's attraction in the eyes of the British clergy: "His appeal is to the people we have not been able to move."[72] Heddy Neumeister, a reporter for the conservative *Frankfurter Allgemeine Zeitung*, said Graham's revival meetings revealed a deep longing in the modern masses to familiarize themselves with the Christian faith in ways that exceeded the traditional Sunday service. Neumeister saw Graham playing a leading part in reawakening the spiritual life of the country.[73] This assessment was mirrored in the national and regional press, which usually commented favorably on Graham's committed, sincere, and refreshingly simple preaching style. Graham opened up new ways to communicate faith.[74]

The surprisingly consensual view on Graham's revival work in the secular press was contrasted by fierce debates in religious circles. Here his revival meetings stirred much broader discussions about Graham's contested fundamentalism, the modernity of his methods, and his actual ability to reach those outside traditional church structures, which blurred denominational, hierarchical, and intellectual boundaries: critics and supporters of Graham often belonged to the same churches and denominations; they could be equally found in the conservative milieu and on the political left wing. Graham was criticized and praised at the same time by Baptists, Methodists, Catholics, and Protestant fundamentalists and in this important way Graham facilitated a conversation that freed participants from traditional religious structures, enabling a new religious community to take shape, one committed to an ecumenical and universal approach to the transformation and modernization of faith.

To just give a few examples: while Carl McIntire's fundamentalist magazine *Christian Beacon* criticized Graham's techniques and beliefs for years and with a vengeance, the fundamentalist periodical *Moody Monthly* reported favorably about the Graham crusades in an article published as early as in January 1950.[75] When Graham announced his 1958 San Francisco crusade, the Californian fundamentalist Baptist leader G. Arch Weninger asked his followers not to cooperate with Graham's campaign team, prompting one member of his congregation to write to *Christianity Today* reassuring the Graham-friendly periodical that not all Baptists in Weninger's flock shared his views. Another letter from the public relations officer for the Presbytery of San Francisco commented that, even though his denomination had pledged its support for the crusade, "said action was not by any means unanimous."[76] Even the Catholic Church, usually known more for dogma than debate, to whom Graham reached out explicitly, did not develop a clear-cut attitude toward Graham's revival work. Favorable Catholic assessments were published during Graham's earlier crusades, such as the one in Washington in 1952.[77] And indeed, during the New York Crusade in 1957 there was the sense among Catholics that their church had given Graham's campaign work "a mild sort of approval."[78] Yet Rev. John E. Kelly, director of the Bureau of Information of the National Catholic Welfare Conference, defended at the same time the exclusiveness of the Catholic Church as Christ's true church. The notion of choice, so prominent in Graham's rhetoric and in evangelical rhetoric in general, was rejected by conservative Catholics, from whose perspective choice did not exist in the realm of faith.[79] Although thousands of Catholics attended Graham's meetings all over the world, they did so with their priesthood divided between those urging them to go and those urging them to stay away.

Critical voices surrounded first and foremost Graham's faith and theology. Ironically, what appeared too fundamentalist to liberal Protestants was not fundamentalist enough for the most conservative circles of the evangelical communities in Britain, Germany, and the United States. The battles between Graham and leading American Protestant fundamentalists such as Carl McIntire and Bob Jones Sr. filled magazines such as the *Christian Beacon* and the *Sword of the Lord*, became manifest in the exchange of pamphlets and letters, and are well documented in the historiography.[80] Even though Graham defined himself as a Protestant fundamentalist, fundamentalists pointed out that his outreach to Catholics and cooperation with liberal Protestants went against the grain of Protestant fundamentalism. In particular his practice of sending those who had responded to the altar call to a church of their choice for the follow-up work was a thorn in the flesh of Protestant fundamentalists. They openly questioned the authenticity of Graham's faith and the religious legitimacy of his campaigns.

Graham's campaigns exposed a similar rift in German and British evangelicalism. As much as the spiritual and theological openness of the Harringay campaigns attracted many British, it repelled many on the conservative wing of British and German evangelicalism. Martyn Lloyd-Jones, the pastor of Westminster Chapel, who would later encourage evangelicals to leave the Anglican Church, clearly distanced himself from Graham during the Greater London Crusade.[81] In Germany, the debates about Graham's mission reflected the country's unique evangelistic and pietist past. German evangelicals were distinct from their British and American brethren—the movement was significantly smaller, maintained an otherworldly profile, and found cooperation with the Evangelical Church often difficult. Indeed, it is hard to speak of an existing evangelical community in Germany at this time.[82] In their identity, brought to light in the way Graham's revival work was discussed, these German evangelicals were closer to American fundamentalist circles than to most British and American evangelicals. Like American fundamentalists, they feared Graham's missionary style would seriously deplete the religious core of evangelistic work.[83] He might be able to fill stadiums with thousands of enthusiastic participants, but at the same time he made a religious offer that appeared increasingly ecumenical and secular. Despite these concerns, the German Evangelical Alliance restrained itself from publishing any critique that would compromise Graham's mission.[84] Zilz even joined the organizing committee for Graham's first German campaign in 1954, if only to keep a close eye on the events. Graham posed a particular challenge to the fundamentalist wings of the Protestant milieus in Europe and the United States. Debates about his crusades were clearly used to discuss, navigate, and confirm the increasing tensions between a more inclusive, modern evangelicalism and a more theological and methodological conservative fundamentalism.

A similar conflict took also place in the British Methodist milieu, where the debates about Graham focused as well on his theology or lack thereof. Many Methodists deployed strong words against Graham, who was criticized less for his methods than for his theology. Rev. Bryan H. Reed, secretary of the Methodist Youth Department, condemned Graham's fundamentalist approach and in particular his pronounced literalism.[85] Reed received backing from the president of the Methodist Conference, Dr. Donald Soper, who expressed fears that Graham's preaching took the church three hundred years backward, although it cannot be ruled out that Soper, a pacifist and socialist with a significant social gospel agenda, had several other reasons to oppose Graham's rather outer-worldly gospel of personal salvation.[86] Both Reed and Soper were concerned about the direction in which new converts could be taken—a direction that could potentially lead to a growth in traditional, exclusive, fundamentalist churches. The much broader question burning in Methodist circles was whether much-needed revivalism and painfully achieved critical theology were actually compatible.[87]

Many Methodists, however, saw the future of religion resting in the hearts of the faithful and not in the minds of the clergy. The controversial future president of the Methodist conference, Dr. Leslie D. Weatherhead, said that it was not Graham's fundamentalism that mattered, but his ability to reach the people that traditional church structures had missed. For Weatherhead, "The theology comes much later."[88] Many readers of the *Methodist Recorder* shared this opinion, pointing out that Methodism's own revival efforts of the early 1950s had failed.[89] Often uneasiness and admiration mixed in the same statement, such as in the words of Rev. Herbert Price, chairman of the Methodist Church for the Manchester and Salford District, who wrote: "However critical we may feel about American high-pressure salesmanship and Hollywood glamour, . . . I think that Christian people will say, 'God bless Billy Graham.'"[90]

In the United Kingdom, the debates surrounding Graham's mission reflected the existing tensions in an increasingly fragmented evangelical milieu that dated back to the interwar years.[91] While Graham's campaign led to much soul-searching in Methodist circles, British Baptists were more than happy to fully embrace a preacher whom they perceived as one of their own.[92] Baptist ministers who attended the meetings were more willing to overlook Graham's literalism than their Methodist brethren. During the Harringay campaign, Graham met with leading British Baptists, including the president of the Baptist Union of Great Britain, Arthur Henry Bonser, and vice president, Principal R. L. Child, and attended the London Baptist Association Meeting and the Annual Assembly Pastors' meeting.[93] The editor of the *Baptist Times,* Rev. Dr. Townley Lord, undoubtedly saw Graham as an ally in the battle against increasing secularism.[94]

The discussions about Graham's faith and the future of faith in the United States and Europe did not just split churches and denominations, but also crossed church hierarchies. Many ordinary Christians felt compelled to express their attitudes toward Graham publicly and quickly—often more so than church officials or intellectual theologians. Some of the crusade participants grabbed pens and wrote to newspapers, church periodicals, and their ministers to comment on Graham's work, initiating lively debates. "Billy Graham is a question posed to the Church," wrote Heinrich Giesen, the theologian and general secretary of the German *Kirchentag*, accordingly, in a critical article published in *Kirche und Mann* in August 1954.[95]

Giesen himself did not hold back in his criticism: he clearly judged Graham's mission politicized and his beliefs simplified and outdated. The article caused an uproar. Three months later the periodical had received so many letters that the editorial board published a summary of the collective response. The letters from Graham's supporters exposed a wide gap between the Evangelical Church and the Free Churches. Readers complained that the Evangelical Church could not grasp Graham's merits because its judgments were based on its own assumptions about faith and conversion. Those assumptions, in the eyes of some of the contributors, were clouded by intellectual and institutional hubris, which were far from essential Christian beliefs, such as role of the Holy Spirit in personal conversion.[96] Here German Christians sounded like their British brethren: some weeks earlier, one Anglican had complained of "the dry sawdust of academic correctitude" existing in the religious landscape.[97]

In Berlin, where the Evangelical Church strongly supported Graham's campaigns, the debate in the *Berliner Sonntagsblatt, die Kirche* took a different spin. The church magazine had published a highly sympathetic special issue on the Berlin crusade in 1954, prompting a backlash from its readers. This time ordinary Protestants felt obliged to air their skepticism about Graham's focus on personal conversion and to attack his theological simplicity.[98] In contrast, other readers did not perceive Graham as backward but instead as the transition point between Germany's pietist past and the American future of evangelism: "It was evangelism conducted in the style and content of the Old World with the tools and through a man of the New World. "[99] A similar debate unfolded in the *Church of England Newspaper*, where the admiringly official line on Graham's revival work inspired several letters to the editor criticizing Graham's style and theology.[100] Conflicts between editorial boards and laymen and laywomen also emerged in the United States, where Graham's theology and mission was openly discussed in, for example, the Methodist *Zion's Herald*, as shown by Andrew Finstuen.[101]

It was not only the faithful masses that threw themselves into the debate over Graham's revivalism. His campaign work also attracted the attention of important public intellectuals and theologians, who used their analysis of Graham's evangelical contribution to position themselves in the ongoing debate about the future of religion in the United States, the United Kingdom, and Germany. The theologian Paul Tillich attended a talk given by Billy Graham in 1954 at the Union Theological Seminary, shortly before joining the Harvard Divinity School. Afterward Tillich expressed admiration for Graham's seriousness but still questioned his methods. He acknowledged Graham's dedication to convert people but called his means to doing so "primitive and superstitious.[102] Even though his assessment was harsh, it was surprising that one of the leading theologians of the century would be interested in the mission of the young evangelist in the first place. Reinhold Niebuhr was no less harsh in his public comments about Graham's style of revivalism, despite the fact that both often argued "from a common theological anchor" focusing on original sin.[103] Niebuhr criticized in particular Graham's simplistic gospel and its shortcomings on social and moral responsibility.[104] Despite Niebuhr's frequent and eloquent attacks on Graham, the theologian repeatedly emphasized his respect for the young preacher's sincerity, echoing Tillich's assessment. The fact that Niebuhr and Tillich seemed to have few problems with Graham's personal faith suggests that both theologians used him as a focus for a much broader critique of the state of American religion in the 1950s.

German theologians echoed the concerns of their British and American colleagues when questioning the reach and meaning of Graham's conversion practice. Helmut Gollwitzer, professor of theology at the University of Bonn, who attended Graham's first German press conference, doubted in particular Graham's ability to really reach the unchurched. Even so, he admitted that his impression of Graham was much more positive than he had initially expected.[105] Theologian Helmut Thielicke echoed Reinhold Niebuhr's criticism of Graham when attacking him for focusing too strongly on the individual-centered doctrine of salvation.[106] The Catholic theologian and public intellectual Walter Dirks not only questioned Graham's ability to reach the unchurched, but interpreted his mission as leading the churches away from the core principles of conversion. He saw conversion as arising out of real-life experiences, such as love or hardship, and through the experience of communion, not out of the emotionally charged atmosphere of the revival meetings. He expressed concern that the churches were endorsing an easy way to future salvation through their support for the Graham campaigns, a concern that was shared in US Catholics circles.[107]

Graham was able to involve ordinary Christians, church officials, and theologians in important debates about the modernization of missionary practices and the liberalization of doctrines surrounding conversion and biblical inerrancy in an increasingly secular world, and the future of faith between traditionalism and liberalization. It speaks to the novelty and inclusiveness of the Billy Graham movement that the criticism did not break along denominational or even confessional lines: Despite the very different denominational traditions and fault lines among Christians in Germany, Britain, and the United States, the question of support or rejection of Graham's revival style increasingly cut across denominational and church lines. At a time of dramatic social, cultural, political, and economic change, Graham's religious offer enabled Christians to question traditional forms of religious belonging and paved the ground for new religious alliances and communities to form.

A New Community of Faith

It was not just the debates about Graham that allowed new alliances to form; Graham himself and his team made it clear that they aimed for an inclusive Christian community to arise from the crusade experience. The Graham-supporting periodical *Christianity Today* publicly bolstered Graham's attempt to break down the traditional dividing lines between a social gospel-oriented liberal Protestantism and a fundamentalist approach that aimed at a more personal evangelism.[108] When attacked by Protestant fundamentalist R. T. Ketcham, the national representative of the General Association of Regular Baptist Churches, for the Graham organization's involvement with secular culture, Catholics, and Jews, Jerry Beavan unmistakably explained to Ketcham in a personal letter: "In this type of evangelistic work we refrain from attacking Catholics, Jews or any other group of race, color, or creed."[109]

Even if this was true for the inclusive ecumenical character of Graham's revival work, Beavan's words glossed over the racial limitations and exclusivity of Graham's early revival work. Steven Miller has compellingly shown that despite the inclusive rhetoric of Beavan and Graham himself, the early crusades did not prove equally attractive to white and African Americans. Even Graham's crusades in the American South in 1950 in Atlanta and Columbia, South Carolina, had a low attendance by African Americans.[110] For many African Americans at that time, Graham as well as the NAE symbolized the whiteness of postwar neo-evangelicalism, which became most obvious in the fact that the organization failed to integrate African American evangelicals into its leadership, and in the beginning no African American denominations were included. Thus, in the words of Matthew Sutton, "For decades to come, the NAE consistently served as the face of male-dominated, respectable, mostly irenic, white evangelicalism."[111]

Moreover, the ground rules laid out at the beginning of the revival meetings by members of the Graham team seemed to create an atmosphere that excluded African American spirituality. At Madison Square Garden, for example, Cliff Barrows reminded the audience in the beginning that overly emotional outpourings such as applause or shouts of joy were not permitted: "And if somebody says something that makes you feel like shouting for joy, . . . for the sake of your neighbor, just make it a silent prayer deep in your heart."[112] This created an emotional atmosphere that could not have been further apart from the more expressive religious culture practiced in many African American churches. The underlying differentiation between healthy versus unhealthy emotionalism had a long tradition in the history of American revivalism and had turned many earlier revivals into manifestations and celebrations of a distinct, and exclusive, white evangelicalism.[113] Anthea Butler pushed this argument even further: "In order for Black evangelicals to belong, they had to emulate whiteness."[114]

The successful ecumenical character of Graham's revival meetings, however, became obvious in the different religious figures taking their seat next to Graham on the platform every evening at Harringay, Madison Square Garden, or Olympic Stadium, but was also expressed in several published eyewitness accounts of revival meetings.[115] The *Methodist Recorder* recounted the story of a Catholic priest sitting next to a Methodist minister finding common ground in their support for the American preacher.[116] Contemporary reports of the Graham campaign in Germany in 1955 confirm a deeply ecumenical atmosphere: Free Churches, the Evangelical Church, and the German Evangelical Alliance often stood shoulder to shoulder during the organization and hosting of the events.[117] At some meetings, the collection was taken by both Catholic and Protestant sisters. In Frankfurt, many Catholic sisters in habit followed Graham's altar call.[118]

Asked to write a comment on the Harringay events after the closing service, Rev. Dr. Irvonwy Morgan, general secretary of the London Mission of the Methodist Church, highlighted the ecumenical reality of the revival meeting: "What also impressed me was the fact that this campaign demonstrated, without dispute, the underlying spiritual unity of the churches, and the fact that men and women of different ecclesiastical and theological traditions can work together in harmony and love."[119] In Baptist circles, Graham also put the question of ecumenism on the agenda. Several letters to the editors of the *Baptist Times* dealt with the unifying character of the crusade meetings and used these to discuss possible cooperation and understanding across denominational boundaries. In the words of an Anglican who wrote to the *Baptist Times*: "Is not Mr Graham presenting the churches in this country with a tremendous challenge to unite in every possible way that they can, much, much more than hitherto?"[120]

These debates echoed in the world of the German Free Churches, where Brauer hoped to create a degree of harmony within the broader Protestant family by bringing together the experiences of the Free Churches, the Evangelical Church, and smaller groups such as the German Salvation Army.[121] Brauer's interdenominational vision clearly mirrored the developments taking place in the religious landscapes in the United Kingdom and the United States. After Graham's second visit to Germany in 1955, Brauer rejoiced that during the campaign "different Christian circles found each other in an active commitment to evangelical alliance."[122] The organizing committee for the campaign the following year had already signed up representatives of the different factions of Protestantism in Germany, among them the Evangelical Alliance, the Free Churches, the Evangelical Church, Baptists, and Methodists, as well as organizations that had grown as part of transnational religious networks, such as the German branches of the YFC (Jugend für Christus) and the YMCA (Christlicher Verein Junger Männer) and the Navigators.[123] Often the local evangelical base was so small they happily and successfully cooperated with the Evangelical church in the area, which at least for a short time eased the competitive environment in which Free Churches and the Evangelical Church existed.[124]

Graham's commitment to ecumene also gained him the support of leading church officials such as the archbishop of Canterbury, Geoffrey Fisher, and Bishop Otto Dibelius. Many Anglican bishops, clergy, and members of the church attended the revival meetings at Harringay Arena. They served on the organizing committee and as ushers and counselors and carried their evangelical enthusiasm into the pews of the Church of England. Anglican publications such as the *Church Times* and the *Church of England Newspaper* had reported favorably on the campaign. Even so, Archbishop Fisher could not bring himself to endorse the crusade—Graham's revival style and his fundamentalism remained essentially foreign to him. Thus, he positioned himself in friendly neutrality toward the London crusade.[125]

Several times members of the organizing committee, including Wilson-Haffenden and Joynson-Hicks, sent letters to Fisher urging him to attend one of the crusade meetings. As the final event at Wembley Stadium approached, Graham himself grabbed his pen and wrote to Fisher to ask if he would take the prayer at the closing service. He put particular emphasis on the fact that this would be an important gesture for the growing ecumenical movement in Britain and would seal the new unity among the British churches.[126]

Fisher's commitment to ecumenism, evident in his early speeches as archbishop, was well known, and so it did not come as a surprise when the archbishop of Canterbury did agree to speak the closing prayer and benediction at Wembley. Fisher's purposely neutral position had initially allowed the different churches to define their own position on Graham without being pushed toward one particular standpoint.[127] Now he was making a strong symbolic statement of the Church of England's recognition of Graham's mission.[128] Weeks later, the bishop of Berlin-Brandenburg, Otto Dibelius, another Protestant with a commitment to the ecumenical movement, would use the same gesture to underline the German Protestant church's acknowledgment of Graham. In a circular to the local churches of Berlin in 1960, Dibelius, again forcefully stated the connection between ecumene and Graham's mission: "In the age of ecumenism our hearts should be open when every now and again an impulse is coming from another country and another Church."[129] These words echoed one of the earliest defenses of Graham's work in Germany by Brauer, who highlighted the quintessential international nature of Grahm's revival work and Christian ecueme in response to anti-American criticism of Graham: "This is not Americanism, but Christian alliance, ecumene in the innermost sense."[130] The street-working evangelist Brauer and the leading Protestant bishop, Dibelius, found common ground in their view on Graham. This new alliance went far beyond Graham's invitation to different faith groups outside the immediate evangelical milieu: it arose straight from the debates taking place during the planning of the crusades and during the crusade meetings themselves.

Conclusion

In Los Angeles, Graham had embarked on a national revival mission: within five years the project had turned international. Graham's early engagement in Europe during his YFC days had left a mark on Graham as a preacher and a Christian. It is no surprise that he often referred to Europe in his early preaching, and that he also felt an urge to return to the old continent. What comes more as a surprise are the open arms with which he—an American, evangelical revival preacher—was received. Graham was welcomed in the United Kingdom and Germany because religious revival was already in the air, demonstrated through new initiatives to evangelize and position religion in the secular world after the war, undertaken not just by the Free Churches but also by the Evangelical Church in Germany and the Anglican Church.

The degree of the revivalist fervor certainly differed and was more pronounced in the United Kingdom with its established transatlantic revival tradition that dated back to George Whitfield and Dwight Moody and on which Graham was able to build his mission. And yet the debates surrounding Graham's revival meetings in London, Düsseldorf, and Berlin highlighted similar questions regarding the search for a more modern, easily accessible faith; the need for re-Christianization after the Holocaust and the social upheavals of World War II, and in the light of increasing secularization; and the meaning of ecumene in a rapidly globalizing world. Graham's appearances tied these debates together across the Channel and the Atlantic through national religious and secular media outlets that followed every step he took and explained to their audiences the important role that Graham played in a shared transnational commitment to a return to religion. In doing so, they created an awareness for an ongoing transatlantic revival in which Britons and Germans took part when attending Graham's crusades.

During this revival, the evangelical organizers of the crusades played their part in laying the groundwork on which a transnational evangelical community could form. Through exchange visits and under the guidance of the American team members, they learned not just to run the crusades in exactly the same style in different locales and national contexts, but also to identify as members of Graham's international ministry. The following chapters will explore in depth how belonging to Graham's mission challenged and transformed national evangelical identities and the extent to which individual practices of faith, such as prayer, allowed German and British evangelicals to grow even further into this transnational community of faith.

Graham stepped into religious landscapes already committed to reform and evangelism, and that is one of the reasons why his revival meetings were not perceived as cultural aberrations, but as serious rites of passage. Graham's revival events were firmly embedded in the local religious landscapes of the United States and Europe. They symbolized freshness and offered an array of modernization possibilities for religious life. At the same time, they stirred and provided focus for important discussions about ecumenism, mission, and secularization. The contemporary discussions among theologians and minsters about the future of faith in all three countries became accessible for ordinary Christians and non-Christians through Graham's crusade meetings. Those provided important forums for them to position themselves with respect to a new religious offer that was perceived as more modern, and in the moment of the altar call allowed them to make an individual choice.

Graham rose to international triumph at a time of a transatlantic revival that occurred in the aftermath of World War II in Europe and the United States. It was Graham's revival work in the United Kingdom and Europe that truly propelled Graham to evangelical stardom both in America and abroad. As John Earl Seelig of the Dallas Baptist Association observed after the first week of the Harringay revival: "The London Crusade already has received more publicity here than the Dallas Crusade received during the entire time."[131] *The Times* of London echoed this assessment when observing that Graham "has had to come to London to command the attention of the United States press as a whole."[132] Graham had left the United States as a national celebrity; he now returned as an evangelistic superstar.

His reputation grew alongside the neo-evangelical movement, which to the present day forcefully shapes US politics and culture. His impact in the United Kingdom and Germany, however, was different. Graham might have been able to contribute to Britain's short-lived "return to an older evangelical discursive state"[133] during the 1950s, but in Germany there never existed an evangelical cultural and social force comparable to Britain's. And, needless to say, the thousands of Christians who flocked to the stadiums in London and Berlin would find themselves caught in an ever more rapid process of secularization after the late 1950s, which sets their religious experiences distinctively apart from those Christians living their faith in the United States. Clearly, neither the Anglican Church nor the Evangelical Church in Germany was able to fully utilize the impulses and dynamics articulated during Graham's revival meetings in their battle against secularization; only evangelical circles that are still firmly present and growing in both countries were willing to embrace Graham's religious offer.

These significant differences in the religious trajectories from which American, British, and German Christians came to Graham's revival meetings, as well as the different directions in which they left them, makes an interpretation of the religious similarities and conjunctures that the 1950s crusades brought to light even more important. For a short decade, American, British, and German Christians, all bound together by the experience of World War II and the Holocaust, shared in a joint commit-ment to re-Christianization, evangelism, and the search for a more modern faith. In all three societies, Graham provided the forums to explore new re-ligious identities and communities beyond traditional denominational and church structures and hence accelerated the erosion of traditional religious structures, communities, and obligations. In the history of secularization, Graham's attractiveness in Germany and the United Kingdom highlights the missed opportunities of the British and German churches: their members asked for a modern faith that those churches were neither willing nor able to provide. Moreover, those touched by Graham articulated their new com-mitment to religious choice. But the religious market able to accommodate and fulfill these yearnings did not exist in Germany, and it only existed in a confined part of the denominational spectrum in the United Kingdom. Only in the United States were those touched by Graham integrated in, and in turn energizers of, churches across the denominational spectrum. The next chapter will explore the complex roots of this rising Christian commitment to choice in the experience of accelerated consumerism in Europe and the United States after World War II.

2

Selling Religion

The Business of Revivalism at
the Early Billy Graham Crusades

Graham sold God with the drive and panache of a former salesman. None of his revival meetings demonstrated this better than his 1957 New York Crusade. With a budget of $900,000, it would remain until the end of his ministry his most lavish campaign. $300,000 went into marketing materials alone, including radio and print advertisements, 650 billboards, thirty-five thousand window signs and forty thousand bumper stickers, which blanketed the city and its suburbs.[1] Two large billboards were set up along Broadway—one on the corner of Forty-Second Street and the other at Forty-Sixth Street—bringing the crusade right into the heart of Manhattan's glittering, neon-lit theater and tourist district.

The campaign advertising slogan was powerful in its simplicity: "Hear Billy Graham." As Jerry Beavan, Graham's PR manager, pointed out, Billy Graham had been a fully established brand since the mid-1950s: "When you see an advertisement for a Cadillac, it just says Cadillac and shows you a picture. Billy is like a Cadillac. We don't have to explain."[2] The Cadillac himself slotted perfectly into this powerful business machine. The New York press described Graham admiringly as the iconographic 1950s salesman of religion. "He describes the goods in plain terms, lets you see them and decide on them," the *New York Telegraph* observed: "He is a wise and practiced salesman of a commodity he truly believes should be in every home."[3]

Graham's salesman demeanor stood firmly on the traditionally close relationship between business and faith in the United States. American churches had pitched their religious offers since colonial times in a deregulated religious market; and businessmen in return used their church membership to boost their social and moral credentials.[4] The relationship grew even tighter in the course of the nineteenth century when, as John Corrigan has marvelously shown, evangelicalism adopted the rhetoric of business contracts in the course of the mid-century young businessmen's revival, during which

Altar Call in Europe. Uta A. Balbier, Oxford University Press. © Oxford University Press 2022.
DOI: 10.1093/oso/9780197502259.003.0003

prayer and conversion were discussed and worded more and more as business transactions.[5]

All these American evangelical traditions shaped Graham's ministry, with one probably standing out: the close ideological alliance between evangelicalism and free market ideology, which had come to life in response to Roosevelt's New Deal policies during the Great Depression.[6] In fear of the New Deal's collectivism and the administration's extended reach into personal lives, ministers and preachers in alliance with businessmen, who also openly opposed the new social and political order, promoted instead the close interplay between individual salvation and economic order in the United States: "If any political and economic system fit with the religious teachings of Christ, it would have to be rooted in a similarly individualistic ethos. Nothing better exemplifies such values, they insisted, than the capitalistic system of free enterprise."[7] Their vision of a corporate and Christian America gained weight and momentum with the rising anticommunism of the immediate postwar years, postulated through preachers such as Graham and spread through those who financed and attended his crusades.

Graham, however, did not just embody yet another phase in the traditionally close relationship between business and revivalism in the United States, built on a shared belief in the righteousness of capitalism and the American Way of Life. He also adjusted that relationship to the unique cultural atmosphere of 1950s America by inextricably linking evangelicalism not just to business but also to consumerism. Even more so, he was the catalyst for important debates about the role of money and marketing in the future spread of faith. This was particularly the case in Europe, where business and faith were seen as separate entities that for moral reasons should not be intertwined. If Christians spoke up on economic questions in Germany and the United Kingdom, they mostly advocated a social and moral taming of an always voracious capitalism. In the words of the leading British Methodist and well-known Christian socialist Donald Soper, spoken in 1953: "I thank God for the welfare state."[8]

At the same time, in 1943, when the national gospel of corporate Christianity took form in the United States, the archbishop of Canterbury, William Temple, published *Christianity and Social Order*, a sound call for a strong welfare state and the protection of working conditions and workers' rights in a postwar Britain.[9] The Christian Democratic Union, founded as an interconfessional party in West Germany in 1945, and led by Chancellor Konrad Adenauer, also firmly rejected libertarian principles in favor of the establishment of a strong welfare state.[10] Yet, in a climate of increasing prosperity and with the breakthrough of consumerism on the horizon in mid-1950s Europe, Graham's corporate evangelism forcefully challenged traditional European assumptions about the relationship between faith, business, and consumerism at a time of increasing secularization and at the peak of American cultural influence in early Cold War Europe. Those wishing to make more and more consumer choices in an economic sense were less and less reluctant to consume a faith that was sold to them and based on choice.

Establishing an Evangelical Brand

Compared to New York, Graham's campaign in Los Angeles in 1949 started modestly. A marketing effort that included billboards, posters, newspaper announcements, and radio advertisements cost barely $25,000. The language of the campaign, however, was more extravagant, featuring invitations to experience its "Dazzling Array of Gospel Talent" and "Visit the Canvas Cathedral with the Steeple of Light."[11] With Graham not yet an established brand name in his own right, the posters instead highlighted the quality of the music and the intensity of the preaching, preparing the audiences for what to expect inside the revival tent. On stage, Graham was not yet the smooth salesman of religion he would become during the first half of the 1950s: he still wore flamboyant ties and socks that he would only later exchange for the serious gray flannel suit, worn by thousands of traveling salesmen across the United States.

One economic feature of his future crusades, however, was established during the Los Angeles campaign: the strong support of the local business community. The organizing committee of the Los Angeles crusade, Christ for Greater Los Angeles, which combined the efforts of several evangelical groups, such as the YFC, the Christian Endeavour, and the Gideons, was chaired by businessman Clifford F. Smith and backed by the local Christian Business Men's Committee. These Christian Business Men's Committees, originating in Chicago in the 1930s, were committed to defending their economic and social privilege by promoting a gospel that combined free market rhetoric, social conservatism, and Christianity.[12]

Leading figures from industry and finance were also important supporters of Graham's later crusades: the Texas oilman Sid Richardson sponsored the 1951 Fort Worth Crusade, and J. Russell Maguire, another oil-made man, was an early supporter of Graham's revival work.[13] In New York in 1957, Roger Hull, the executive vice president of Mutual Life Insurance Company of New York, presided over the crusade executive committee,[14] while further backing came from members of the Dodge, Vanderbilt, Phelps, Whitney, and Gould families.[15] Their support reflected the historic American alliance between progress, work ethics, and Christianity that dated back to colonial times and had significant racial underpinnings. All those white businessmen who supported Graham, as Darren Grem points out, could at least afford to be "passive towards racism and segregation because their station made it easy to be so."[16] In this respect Graham's revival work was attractive to them, as it did not question the social and economic setup of the 1950s United States; on the contrary, it clearly favored the free market order over the reform-oriented New Deal and the revolutionary communist counteroffer.[17]

Businessmen did not just fund Graham's revival work, they also actively bought into his quintessentially American brand of faith, with its commitment to individuality and commercial success. Such was obvious to Graham's outspoken critic Reinhold Niebuhr, who published a critical article on Graham's revival work in *Life* in July 1957.[18] Of the 250 letters that Niebuhr received in response, many came from Lutheran businessmen expressing open admiration for Graham's business-orientated evangelism. Their praise for Graham's clear focus on data and statistics was dismissed by Niebuhr as "the American penchant for numbers and success."[19]

The individual stories of those businessmen who converted at the crusades were seized upon by Graham's campaign team to highlight the corporate nature of the mission and to propagate the gospel of the free market. Several evangelical publications captured these conversions: *Revival in Our Time*, published after the Los Angeles crusade, prominently featured the conversion stories of North Carolinian leading lumber merchants Harry Reynold and Colonel Guy V. Whitener.[20] The *New York Crusade News* highlighted the conversion story of the oil executive Carl B. Anderson, who had made his decision for Christ during the Oklahoma crusade of 1956. The publication reported that Anderson's business had seen an improvement in efficiency after his conversion and that a new spirit of cooperation had emerged from the weekly devotions attended by his employees.[21]

These conversion narratives shared a common theme: they endorsed the practices of capitalism, acquiring wealth and growing businesses, while at the same time interpreting the meaning of economic success within the framework of Christian faith. Personal success was replaced by the image of working for God's glory. In the words of a successful Minneapolis car dealer: "I have made a deal with the Lord. . . . It is now His Business, not mine. I am only running it for Him."[22] The practices of business and success were wholeheartedly endorsed by Graham, as long as they were framed in a Christian mindset. And the business community in return was more than happy to fund his revival work.

Graham did not just stay rhetorically close to the corporate world: the increasing financial responsibilities and opportunities of his mission during the early 1950s saw the need for a more corporate structure within his own organizing team. Thus by 1950, Graham, his wife, Ruth, and his key associates, Cliff Barrows, Grady Wilson, and George Wilson, founded the BGEA with headquarters in Minneapolis. About the same time, the increasing reach of Graham's citywide campaigns made organizational and structural changes necessary. During the 1950 crusade in Columbia, South Carolina, the team hired Willis Haymaker, a former associate of Billy Sunday and Gipsy Smith, as central campaign manager, enhancing the professionalization of the campaign. By 1954, Graham's headquarters' staff had grown to 80 employees, and it increased further to 120 the following year. Income through donations steadily rose with Graham's rising media profile: he wrote a regular newspaper column, created a weekly broadcast program, *Hour of Decision*, and in 1950 set up a movie company, World Wide Pictures. By 1952, all team members received a fixed salary through the BGEA.[23]

As the structure of Billy Graham's revival machinery changed, so its marketing materials and advertising slogans also developed new levels of professionalism. The use of fifty thousand bumper stickers, neon signs, billboards, and posters during the 1952 Washington crusade were indications of the growing scale of Graham's marketing output: the decision in 1954 to boil down the slogan to "Hear Billy Graham" signaled increasing business savvy and confidence.[24] It was this brand of evangelicalism, centrally coordinated, fiercely marketed, and generously funded, that crossed the Atlantic with Graham in 1954 en route to Harringay.

Selling Revivalism Abroad

When the intensive planning period of the London crusade began in 1953, the United Kingdom was still suffering the economic aftermath of war; food rationing had yet to be lifted. This made preparations for the revival meetings significantly more complicated than in the prospering United States, with the proposed budget of £100,000 representing a serious financial commitment. Most of the money was earmarked for the rental of, decoration of, and insuring of the Harringay Arena (£33,000) and for publicity (£50,280). Other items in the budget covered transport, meals, and accommodation for the team. While it was assumed that £50,000 would be raised in the United Kingdom, the American team promised to fundraise the other £50,000 in the United States.[25]

It was clear from the outset that the crusade would not take place without funding from the United States. The bishop of Barking described the dire economic situation of the postwar United Kingdom in a personal letter to Billy Graham, in which he asked "for the financial help of American friends."[26] The London organizing committee was also well aware that American Christians were more generous with their donations to churches than their British counterparts,[27] in part down to greater economic prosperity but also due to a different philanthropic tradition.

Thus, Graham called his American brethren to action. He embedded his financial plea by pointing to a responsibility of American Christians toward the British churches that arose "out of the abundance with which God has so richly blessed them."[28] Graham's American supporters did not just give in their Sunday collections for the Greater London Crusade, but orchestrated a far-reaching fundraising campaign. Several of the businessmen who supported Graham's campaigns in the United States as well as political heavyweights such as the governor of Tennessee, Frank G. Clement, approached the Ford Foundation to raise funds for the London crusade. They assured the foundation that a combination of Graham's religious stance and his clear commitment to freedom and the free enterprise system made the Greater London Crusade extremely important for postwar Europe.[29] Similar words were used in invitations to ordinary Christians and ministers to donate to the campaign in England, "to stem the flood of Communism."[30] Graham's American donors did not just expect the spread of the gospel from Graham, but also believed they were building a commitment to the free market system in Europe. And the dollars did indeed roll in from the United States; by the end of 1953 $30,000, an equivalent of around £10,700, had been raised in America.[31]

In contrast, the British organizers found it significantly more difficult to hold up their part of the bargain, despite three experienced businessmen serving on the crusade executive committee: Alfred G. B. Owen of Rubery Owen, John Henderson, a conservative MP and also chairman of J. Henderson Ltd., and Lindsay Clegg, chairman of linoleum manufacturing companies in London. These men, like many of their American counterparts, provided the organizing committee with financial expertise, attracted public attention to the project, and launched a fundraising campaign that, in the best of all worlds, would "raise at least a similar amount to that contributed by Christians in the U.S.A."[32] But they could not build on the same close interplay between Christianity and business that saw Graham's revival work flourish in the United States.

Close links between businessmen and churches existed in the United Kingdom too, and were surprisingly complex.[33] But Christian businessmen in the United Kingdom were more concerned with mitigating the unattractive social and moral side-effects of rapid industrialization and capitalism than they were in supporting an American-style civil religious, national narrative centered on the God-given nature of capitalism. This distinctly different interplay between business and Christianity in the United Kingdom made fundraising and meeting the actual costs of the crusade in the United Kingdom significantly more difficult.

If business and faith were not instinctively accepted as compatible in the United Kingdom, Graham's crusade nevertheless provided a forum for British Christians to reconsider their attitude toward money. Rev. Godfrey C. Robinson summarized the situation for the *Baptist Times*: "Our American friends take seriously the teaching of God's Word about money and possession. They realize that Christian work cannot be carried on properly without proper resources and plan accordingly—and pay up. Why are we British Christians so hypersensitive about money . . . ?"[34]

British evangelicals indeed were reluctant fundraisers and certainly less creative than their American guests: when the editor of the *British Weekly* suggested that every contemporary British evangelist, given the same money, could do an even better job than Graham, one reader sharply disagreed. He pointed out that no one actively kept British evangelists from undertaking fundraising, but that "surely the organization and the money are part of Graham's genius which they don't possess."[35] It was an indication of the simmering debate in contemporary British churches about the financial future of faith and one that Graham catapulted into the headlines of secular and religious newspapers. However, fresh ideas about the interplay between business and faith did not take hold overnight, a factor that contributed, in part, to the failure of the British fundraising campaign for the Greater London Crusade, especially within the business community.

The fundraising effort for Harringay was launched a year before the crusade opened. The financial committee of the Greater London Crusade, formed in 1953 and chaired by crusade treasurer Alfred G. B. Owen,[36] commissioned ten thousand copies of an appeals brochure, entitled *Whither. . . ?*, completely different in design and content from material used in the United States. Five thousand were sent to members of the Federation of British Industries with an attached appeals letter signed by Owen. The letter echoed the language used by Graham's team in the United States, referring to the communist threat and the need for restored national spiritual strength.[37]

The response to Owen's appeal was little short of disastrous, with the British business community contributing a mere £1,367, a tiny drop in the ocean of corporate evangelicalism. The economic historian David J. Jeremy provides a detailed case study of the reasons for such an underwhelming outcome: none of the personal donations Jeremy was able to track down exceeded £100. Even large firms such as Rolls Royce and Associated Portland Cement Manufacturers only gave £10. The small manufacturing firms based in the British Midlands made small contributions, probably because of personal relationships and loyalty to Owen. Some of the letters Owen received from those who refused to donate illuminate the reasons for the failure of the campaign: it seemed clear that the strong anticommunist subtext of Owen's appeal did not resonate with British businessmen. Others expressed religious concerns about sponsoring a campaign in celebration of highly individualized American evangelicalism. As Jeremy observes, among the members of the Federation of British Industries "scepticism of evangelical Christianity evidently far outweighed their fears of communism."[38] Clearly, the American trinity of free enterprise, democracy, and Christianity was not as appealing to British businessmen as it was to their American counterparts.

But what did appeal to British Christians beyond expectations was the crusade's religious offer, but that only added to the financial pressures on the organizing committee. The growing nightly audiences at Harringay made further meetings, follow-up work, and relay services necessary that weighed heavily on the budget. In the end, the final cost of the campaign, £167,378, substantially exceeded the £100,000 budget.[39] Income during the crusade totaled £171,357, which mostly came from collections (£50,626), general donations (£48,435), sales of books and royalties, film broadcasts, and relay services. The appeal to British businessmen only contributed 1 percent of total income.[40]

While the local organizers clearly struggled with American expectations of fundraising, they readily embraced the need for modern marketing. The crusade publicity committee, chaired by Rev. F. T. Ellis, quickly adopted Graham's Madison Avenue rhetoric. In an article in the *London Crusade News*, Ellis explained why a new approach to Christian marketing was needed: "We are living in a day of big-scale advertising, and the same scientific principles apply when we are advertising motor-cars, furniture or ideas. We are in the biggest business in the world when we seek the salvation of souls."[41]

Therefore, just as in the United States, one of the largest items in the budget, £52,595, was set aside for marketing.[42] The London organizing committee also followed the American example in focusing the material on Graham's persona, without trying to explain the deeper meaning of mass evangelism or the faith behind Graham's mission. The organizers booked fifteen hundred billboards and displayed one thousand quad crown (i.e., thirty by forty inches) posters in Underground stations and on railway platforms. The crusade was advertised in religious journals and suburban weeklies, while the circulation of the *London Crusade News* reached 180,000 copies per month, helping to build awareness of the upcoming events.

Again as in the United States, the marketing of the crusade saw the evangelical organizers experiment with new advertising techniques. The key challenge was to take the message to every corner of a vast modern metropolis, so much of the advertising was booked with mobility in mind. Billy Graham advertisements appeared on the sides of 500 buses and 250 trolley buses; five million bus tickets sold in the Harringay area were printed with the message on the reverse, "Hear Billy Graham at Harringay." Billy Graham stickers could be seen in the back windows of cars all over the city.[43]

Marketing, fundraising, and the display of American lifestyle seamlessly blended in another marketing feature used by the organizers: the screening of the Christian movie *Oiltown U.S.A.* This also underlined the organizers' willingness to consider film as a new form of evangelism in a modern media age.[44] The film was produced by the BGEA's very own production company, World Wide Pictures, with the crusade committee holding the exclusive rights to organize public screenings in England.[45] It was shown in town and church halls from Lewisham to Reading, and Luton to Wimbledon in the Greater London area, but also in places such as Manchester, Bristol, and Liverpool.

The movie established a powerful visual link between business, consumption, and Christianity by telling the conversion story of the ruthless Texan oil magnate Lance Manning. It was clearly an endorsement of the free enterprise system and was promoted as such: every drilling scene seemed to highlight America's abundance in natural resources and its position as an economic world power.[46] *Oiltown U.S.A.* also shamelessly displayed, in glorious color, the prosperity and consumer lifestyle of early 1950s America. Shiny cars drove past abundantly stocked shop-windows; thick steaks sizzled on the grill; ketchup bottles and milkshakes decorated the dining tables. God obviously blessed those who he loved.[47]

Oiltown U.S.A. brought the smell of barbecued meat to austerity-ridden England, and the thousands of Britons who saw it gave donations to make Graham's crusade possible. It did not just prepare the audiences for Graham's revival mission, but also provided for an encounter with a new form of Christian faith. The movie, which featured Graham himself in one of the final scenes, replaced the image of the modest Christian disciple with images of the wealthy Christian businessman and Christian consumer who would soon populate the European religious landscapes. In *Oiltown U.S.A.* economic power and wealth were not presented in opposition to Christian faith, but as compatible with it.

Graham sanctioned the message of *Oiltown U.S.A.* in a sermon he preached on an American airbase in Britain during the crusade. Asking the audience, "You want more money, more glamour, more popularity?" he asserted that nothing was wrong with these ambitions as long as they were accompanied by a Christian attitude.[48] The next day *The Guardian* reported Graham's comments, presenting British audiences with this new kind of religiosity, one that added a sense of excitement to his mission.

Alongside this reverence for economic prosperity and money as part of revivalist Christianity, the Harringay crusade also projected a strong bond with American popular culture. In the United States it was a common feature of Graham's revival meetings for actors, sport stars, and war heroes to appear on stage to give their testimony, and many of them made the journey to the United Kingdom. Redd Harper, who starred in the Graham movies *Mister Texas* and *Oiltown U.S.A.*, and the actress Colleen Townsend, who had supported Graham during his Los Angeles crusade in 1949,[49] both gave public testimonies at Harringay, where they embodied the intertwined nature of evangelicalism, popular culture, and the American way of life. Because Harringay took place before Graham signed up well-known African American artists to travel with him, their appearance also demonstrated the whiteness of the American way of life that traveled with Graham.

Faith in Selling

While British evangelical organizers immediately embraced the efficient campaign style of the American team and enthusiastically bought into the business of revivalism, the collaboration between the American salesmen of faith and their German brethren was more fractious. This was due to a lack of traditional cooperation in the field of transatlantic revivalism, coupled with an underlying anti-Americanism in the German evangelical milieu and a distinct reluctance to prioritize what appeared to be secular over religious considerations. Nevertheless, the American guests came to teach, and the German hosts were willing to learn.

Because of its short duration—it was just two days long—the German campaign of 1954 carried a significantly lower financial risk and demanded less marketing effort than the Harringay crusade. However, it still created substantial tension between the American guests and their German hosts. The American budget had earmarked $50,000 for Graham's entire European tour, excluding London.[50] With Graham's team planning to pay for their own travel and accommodation, the Berlin organizing committee received only $5,800 in advance to pay for the marketing of the campaign. This sum was supposed to be paid back after the collection, but with only $4,600 taken in donations, the Graham team was forced to cover the difference, leading to a dispute about how this agreement was reached and if it was actually legally binding.[51] The working relationship between the German organizers and the Billy Graham team had clearly had a bumpy start. Even more importantly, the conflict around the Berlin deficit illustrated the fundamental inexperience of German evangelicals in dealing with large-scale financial projects.

If German evangelicals were inexperienced when it came to financing revivalism, they were even more so when it came to marketing it. The question of how to advertise Graham's revival meetings in Germany in 1954 immediately split the German evangelical family of faith: some German evangelicals, such as Wilhelm Brauer and Paul Deitenbeck, showed willingness to experiment with modern forms of marketing and advertising. Deitenbeck published a glowing report on Graham's revival work at Harringay in which he dedicated the first pages to a detailed exploration of the role of the marketing. He justified its use by explaining: "For those unfamiliar with the Christian faith, God and Jesus are not realities. They have no idea what to do with them. Aren't we then allowed to build a bridge for those who are used to visualizing things by putting something visual and real in front of them?"[52]

Walter Zilz, head of the German Evangelical Alliance, immediately criticized the publication, in which he saw menacing influences in the brash campaign style. In particular Deitenbeck's use of numbers and superlatives appeared to him too "American." The use of secular propaganda methods, Zilz warned, posed a serious danger to the future of evangelism in Germany.[53] The German organizers in the end settled for posters and handbills carrying Graham's image and the modest line, adopted from the English marketing slogan: "Billy Graham. Du mußt ihn hören" ("Billy Graham. You must hear him"). At least the organizers could state with relief that the advertisement campaign in Düsseldorf and Berlin appeared less American than in London.[54] The question of how to adapt the American marketing material to a German mentality was a recurring topic, even though the American organizers reassured the German side that the style of marketing was a decision for local organizers alone.[55]

These critical voices reflected the substantial anti-Americanism in the German evangelical community. In their arguments, the term "American" was transformed into a rhetorical placeholder for "secular." These reservations were fueled by substantial differences in approach: the American organizers of Graham's European tour did indeed seem to speak a different language and were clearly driven by many profane concerns during the planning of the crusades. For example, in the ongoing discussions about the location and length of Graham's next German crusade in 1955, German evangelicals favored long revival visits of a week or more in their pietist tradition, while Graham's team preferred the one-day, jet-in/jet-out visits to several cities, as had happened in 1954 with the Düsseldorf and Berlin events. While the German negotiators emphasized the spiritual importance of longer visits, the American side refused to risk a longer missionary endeavor in a country in which Graham was still relatively unknown. They wanted to keep an eye on money, numbers, and practicalities, while the German side agonized over the purity and tradition of pietist revival work. In the end, the American view prevailed: Graham's 1955 campaign consisted of five one-day visits to different cities.

As a result of the American financial concerns, Graham's European representative, Robert Evans, became known in Germany for his so-called stockbroker rhetoric.[56] At one planning meeting for the 1955 revival in Frankfurt, Evans clearly favored Graham preaching in the city's stadium rather than the festival hall, which was half its size. It would be impossible, he argued, to have only ten thousand people gathering in the small festival hall when every other city visited during the revival tour was capable of hosting at least twenty thousand. That would clearly affect the campaign's public image. When one of the German brethren challenged his point in biblical terms, declaring that numbers did not really matter, as every single sinner converted would be of joy to the Lord, Evans shot back: "That might be the case in heaven, but not on earth!"[57]

Graham himself did not make it any easier for the German evangelicals. When he addressed the three thousand ushers, ministers, and counselors who made up the ground crew for his Düsseldorf meeting in 1954, Graham openly compared his revivalism to the world of business. Elaborating on his experiences as a former salesman, he defined mass evangelism with the words: "We are salesmen of the most important treasure on earth." Referring to the use of modern marketing techniques, Graham insisted that "the best methods have to be used to fulfill our goals."[58] At the same meeting, Graham introduced his corporate evangelism by describing the functional division of labor he practiced within his evangelistic team and how it had made the Greater London Crusade possible.[59] Graham could not have been more emphatic: the Lord might rejoice in every single conversion, but behind the scenes more earthly and profane considerations had to be taken into account.

Surprisingly, the once-reluctant German evangelicals soon turned into confident businessmen of faith. In less than a year, they organized a revival campaign across five cities—Frankfurt, Mannheim, Stuttgart, Nuremberg, and Dortmund—adopting the catchy marketing and quantifiable goals that the Americans had championed. The German organizers substantially updated their marketing operation: Mannheim, for example, was plastered with six thousand posters and one hundred thousand handbills, while banners on trams, radio advertisements, and cinema spots were used to promote Graham's presence. The substantial collections taken at the revival meetings reflected a new financial determination: collected cash amounted to between DM 13,000 and DM 30,000 and allowed most local organizers to keep a surplus.

The final report on the 1955 German crusade, which lists the estimated number of participants and those who responded to Graham's altar call, is striking proof of a significant shift in the language and outlook of the German evangelical organizers. The report deployed the very same superlatives and exhibited the same exhaustive number crunching that Zilz had dismissed just a year earlier as being typically American.[60] This new focus on numbers and successes was evidence of the significant transformation the German evangelical milieu had undergone in developing a close partnership with the Anglo-American Graham team: overcoming reservations nourished by deep-seated pietist traditions, they joined the business of revivalism.

As Graham's evangelical celebrity in Europe increased, so did the ambition of his missions to Germany, again necessitating close cooperation and exchanges between local organizers and Graham's Anglo-American teams. In the late 1950s, when Graham's first three-week campaign in Germany was looming, the German organizers, led by the head of the German Evangelical Alliance, Paul Schmidt, relied heavily on the advice and support of their Western allies in faith.

In 1959, Charlie Riggs and Jerry Beavan met the local organizing committees and shared their experiences from the crusades in New York and the recent campaign in Sydney, Australia. Bevan emphasized the importance of prayer and personal evangelism, but also explained in detail the importance of structured teamwork. Bevan promised to produce a handout to pass on his organizational knowledge to the different local working groups.[61] The German organizers still felt that Harringay was the benchmark for modern metropolitan revivalism and invited English ministers to come to Germany during this period to share their experiences of the Greater London Crusade.[62]

Thus the planning for the 1960s Graham crusade in Essen, Hamburg, and Berlin mirrored the financial confidence, commitment to teamwork, division of labor, and willingness to take risks of the Anglo-American crusade organizers. The organizing committee proposed to host Graham for a full week in each of the cities. In a striking display of their growing ambition and their confidence in attracting new levels of attendance and fundraising, the committee rented a tent with a capacity of twenty thousand for each city costing DM 300,000. The campaign's overall estimated budget was DM 550,000, covering insurance and marketing in addition to the tent rental. Such was Graham's increased popularity in Germany that most funds were raised by local churches even before the campaign began. The German

Evangelical Alliance contributed DM 50,000, and host cities and individual citizens alike were generous with their money: in Essen, the city council paid for flowers to decorate the tent; the owner of a local printing company sponsored the campaign posters.[63]

The fact that the organizers now embraced big business also had an impact on the structure of the crusade organization. A central organizing committee was established to supervise three separate local committees, its increasing self-assurance communicated through the catchy new project title, which served as letterhead in all correspondence: "Großstadt-Evangelisationen mit Billy Graham der Deutschen Evangelischen Allianz." (City Revivals with Billy Graham of the German Evangelical Alliance.)

Each supervised local committee was composed of seven task forces specializing in management and organization, marketing and public relations, fire safety and transport, music, finances, the organization of prayer groups, and the education of spiritual guides. This structure was modeled on the London and New York planning processes, mirroring the typical workflows practiced during Graham's extended crusades around the world. Such a detailed approach to planning and fundraising was now essential, as the organizers were putting together events of a far greater size than earlier German crusades: 750,000 people participated in the three campaign meetings: 160,000 in Essen, 320,000 in Hamburg, and 270,000 in Berlin.[64]

The marketing campaign was common across the venues: the same poster with an image of Graham and the slogan "Komm und höre Billy Graham" ("Come and hear Billy Graham") was used in all three cities, where airtime was also bought for radio and television advertisements. A million copies of a special evangelical newspaper, Der Stachel, were distributed.[65] There was even a novel new form of aerial advertising: a helicopter hovered over the Ruhr area, promoting Graham's crusade in Essen by displaying the marketing slogan "Hear Billy Graham" on the bottom of its fuselage.[66]

However, despite the best intentions and even with the advice of experienced American organizers, the German campaign team still lacked real financial acumen. As a result, the charges for hiring tents and marketing were much higher than expected, and the campaign barely broke even, with the final budget of DM 816,231 delivering a small surplus of just DM 1,731. All the same, the experience of running a campaign of this scale offered a valuable learning curve for the organizers, whose attitude toward the business of evangelism, organizational efficiency, and financial rhetoric had clearly changed in the face of the challenges facing them. As Paul Deitenbeck remarked: "Wir haben den ersten Massenangriff gewagt ohne Vorerfahrung. Wir haben gelernt."[67] In these learning processes, the strong influence of Graham on the German evangelical milieu was particularly evident.

Recent studies on "the economic turn in religious history" have traced how the logic, methods, and language of business have shaped US evangelicalism specifically and religion more broadly.[68] Although a similar tradition is missing in Germany and the United Kingdom, it does not mean that those societies and their religious communities were unresponsive to Graham's business-flavored revivalism. While German evangelicals were unlikely to endorse fully the evangelical capitalism of their American brethren, their interaction with Graham and his team did help to shape a distinct German rhetoric of efficiency, organization, and financial risk. German scholars have already argued that German conservative Christians only adopted the term *evangelikal* from the mid-1960s to define themselves as a distinct community of faith; and they did so through their interaction with Graham, as observed by Friedhelm Jung.[69] However, a close reading of their newly adopted attitude toward business and its associated rhetoric highlights the fact that the transformation of the German evangelical milieu through their work with Graham ran significantly deeper than that. The German evangelical identity changed profoundly: conservative Christians did not just become *Evangelikale*; they too became salespeople of faith.

Rhetoric and Images of Business and Consumption

The close ties between revivalism and business were not just embedded in the way the crusades were funded and organized. Even more striking was the way in which Graham communicated those ties openly to give his free market gospel a face and a look with which his followers could identify. The narrative through which Graham disseminated his corporate evangelism consisted of two different layers: Graham's own rhetoric of business and consumption and his self-portrayal as *the* 1950s consumer. It built on the traditionally close relationship between evangelicalism and business culture, but through its increasing references to the world of consumption, it turned into a distinct 1950s version of this tradition.

Darren Grem and Sarah Hammond have demonstrated how Graham's rhetoric mirrored and endorsed the world of business and how he defined his own revival work in corporate terms.[70] Indeed, at the breakfast meeting to kick off his Los Angeles crusade in 1949, which several ministers attended, he summarized his mission in the words: "Our business is to introduce people to a personal relationship with God." In an article in *Look* in February 1956, Graham defended his corporate approach to ministry by saying: "In every other area of life, we take for granted publicity, bigness, modern techniques. Why should not the church employ some of these methods that are used by big business or labor unions to promote their products or causes, in order to win men for Christ?"[71]

But Graham's rhetoric had an additional register that specifically addressed the growing population of affluent 1950s consumers. His signature phrase, first published in *Time* magazine in 1954, was "I am selling . . . the greatest product in the world; why shouldn't it be promoted as well as soap?"[72] In the simplest of language, Graham highlighted his commitment to marketing and consumption as well as his role as the American salesman of religion. And he repeatedly deployed this technique, the integration of the metaphors of consumption, into his religious language. Asked once how he imagined heaven, Graham answered, "We are going to sit around the fireplace and have parties and the angels will wait on us and we'll drive down the golden streets in a yellow Cadillac convertible."[73] Graham's language spread images of suburban coziness and modern mobility under the protective umbrella of an evangelicalism that was perceived by many African Americans as genuinely white. When warning about Judgment Day, Graham offered a new, modern media version of the notion that God is always watching: "From the cradle to the grave God has had his television cameras on you."[74] It was the language of the American middle-class consumer, the very people who filled his revival tents. It was also the language that allowed Graham to build a rhetorical bridge between his corporate evangelism and the financial aspirations of his middle-class followers.

Graham combined this rhetoric with the traditional contractual business language of nineteenth-century evangelicalism when he promised "spiritual dividends"[75] and framed his call for conversion in the language of transaction: "Give your life to Christ tonight. Let him give you a new heart. Make you a new person. And give you the joy and peace you always longed for. Now it will cost you something. It doesn't come cheap. It cost Christ his blood, God his son, and it will cost you your sins."[76] You have to give up sin to get something in return, he explained. Salvation was an individual transaction in which God was the producer, Graham was his salesman, and each audience member was a consumer.

Hence Graham also put a rhetorical emphasis on "choice" that resonated well in a burgeoning advertising and marketing culture. Graham spoke of choice as a consumer decision, making it clear that his God did not just compete with other religious offers but also with the temptations of consumerism. As he reminded his audience during the New York Crusade: "New York has one thousand Gods and you must make a choice."[77] Contemporary observers saw in Graham's focus on an individual decision for Christ, a genuine Western commitment to individuality and nonconformity, in contrast to the mass character of totalitarianism.[78] Graham brought the same rhetoric of consumer choice to Europe, where participants in the crusades also commented on Graham's emphasis on "making a choice," which the preacher repeatedly used during his altar call.[79]

But Graham did not just address his followers as consumers to whom he was offering a commodity to acquire. He also legitimized their consumer lifestyle through his own identity and performance as a Christian consumer. The media coverage of Graham captured his "Hickey Freeman clothes," commented on the brand of car that drove him to the crusade meetings, and highlighted his passion for golf.[80] On stage Graham was happy to chat about his airmiles account or his favorite motels. Magazine and newspaper articles about Graham's fashionable wife, Ruth, were full of iconic artifacts of the 1950s suburban lifestyle, from the discussion of modern kitchen appliances to air travel. *Time* and *Life,* in particular, provided the media platform upon which Graham could orchestrate his version of a happy middle-class family life: playing golf, relaxing in front of the fireplace, and enjoying the company of his family at the table, with Ruth serving dinner.[81] It was a life projected as a billboard picture of middle-class domesticity and prosperity, images that clearly endorsed heteronormativity as well as the economic and cultural power of the new white middle class.[82]

The cohesiveness of Graham's middle-class performance was mirrored in those who attended his revival meetings. The media often reported on the shared class features of Graham's American audiences. Those who stepped forward in Los Angeles were described as doctors, lawyers, schoolteachers, and other members of the professional and business community.[83] Reports from other revivals, like those in Boston and New Orleans, indicate that the audience included a large number of white-collar employees, including salesmen, tellers, accountants, and managers, reflecting the rapid transformation of the American economy and society fueled by the growing service sector.

When the BGEA later collected and published the conversion stories of those who stepped forward, they also described the converts as predominantly white, middle-class citizens, "government workers, business men, and car dealers."[84] Kurt and Gladys Lang, two sociologists conducting a mass observation at the New York Crusade in 1957 described the "aura of middle-class respectability" at the crusade and declared the moment of stepping forward a "ritualistic middle-class performance."[85] They saw the typical convert as "the middle-class person, torn between the simpler, old-fashioned religious prescriptions and the need to accommodate to a mobile society, [who] is unsure of his identity."[86] Graham offered these audiences validation and legitimacy of, and security in, their lifestyle, helping them to find their place in America's rapidly evolving society. It is no surprise that observers across the United States confirmed that crusade participants from the suburbs were significantly overrepresented at the revivals.[87] And Graham did even more: by communicating his commitment to corporate America through the aspiring middle-class language of the traveling salesman, he allowed his followers to identify with economic circles and models still out of their financial reach. This, however, happened nearly exclusively along racial lines. The fact that the consumer images created around Graham were completely white may be a crucial factor in explaining why his early revival work did not attract African Americans to the same degree that it spoke to white Americans. Another significant factor, which explains the limited participation of African Americans in Graham's early crusades, were the specific social and economic living conditions of the vast majority of Graham's audiences: they traveled in from the white suburbs to which African Americans had no access in the 1950s.[88]

The American Gospel in Europe

Graham's complex performance of business and consumption through rhetoric and images traveled with him to Europe. It is through the eyes of European participants in the crusade meetings that we are able to fully assess the powerful imagery of modernity embedded in Graham's revival meetings, in which "every moment . . . was theorized, planned, tested, organized, assigned and managed"[89] and the ways in which their "details paralleled mass-market capitalism,"[90] in the words of Grant Wacker. Moreover, the unconcealed awe with which Europeans across political and denominational

boundaries responded to Graham's sales techniques reveals an untapped resource for a potential resistance to the inevitable process of secularization
in Germany and the United Kingdom. European Christians were clearly
looking for a more modern and consumer-friendly way of accessing faith.
The British and German responses to Graham's business of revivalism were
strikingly similar and saw its modernity become manifest in the technicalization of the pulpit, the division of labor in the campaign machinery, and the
counting and categorizing of believers.

Graham's crusade pulpits belonged to the tech-savvy and production-
focused world of modern industrialization. During the Los Angeles crusade, Graham's modern lapel microphone, which allowed him to pace the
platform while preaching, had become a symbol of the novelty and modernity of his revival work. Many observers in the religious and secular press
in Europe also tried to capture the modernity of Graham's revival campaign
through the materiality of his pulpit. Graham's pulpit at Harringay projected
technological progress: instead of a modest, wooden pulpit, the platform
featured multiple microphones connected to the latest high-tech amplifiers,
which carried Graham's voice through the eleven-thousand-seat arena. The
scene was dramatically illuminated by spotlights, with banks of newsreel
cameras operating in the space in front of the rostrum, next to the snapping
flashlights of press photographers.[91] German observers were impressed by
Graham's exciting use of light and sound, recognizing them as important
assets for the business and industry of faith.[92] In a strongly supportive article, the conservative newspaper *Frankfurter Allgemeine Zeitung* suggested
the microphones and the spotlights were symbols that connected Graham's
mass evangelism with the modern zeitgeist.[93] Based on a newsfeed from
the German press agency DPA (Deutsche Presse-Agentur), several regional
newspapers introduced Graham to their audiences under the headline
"Missionary under Neon Lights," highlighting the modern as well as urban
character of Graham's crusades.[94]

British and German observers admired how Graham's crusades ran with
the smoothness and speed of a spinning jenny. In an article on the Harringay
meeting, an observer for the *Baptist Times* remarked that "everything was
technically of the best, the items followed one another swiftly and easily."[95]
Aisle captains and illuminated signs to direct the audience around the arena
signified the organized efficiency of the revival space. The experience of a revival meeting as a smoothly operating production line was most evident in
the machine-like functionality of the altar call. Frank Colquhoun, a member

of the Greater London Crusade executive committee, observed that after the call "immediately a process, a machine, starts into motion."[96] Colquhoun referred to the hundreds of counselors who accompanied those who made a public decision for Christ into the prayer rooms, to pray with them, hand them a copy of the Gospel of John, and take down their details on a decision card. Equally, in the eyes of the German magazine *Kirche in Hamburg*, it was the presence and productivity of thousands of helping hands, who served as ushers, counselors, and choir members, and who recorded decision cards, handed out the paper baskets for the offerings, and cleared up the rubbish afterward, that let the crusade appear machine-like.[97] For the many volunteers, this was a labor of love; but in Graham's world of corporate evangelicalism, it was first and foremost labor.

In particular, the collection of the so-called decision cards was the most obvious symbol of the modern, corporate nature of Graham's revival work. The collection primarily fulfilled a practical purpose: those who had stepped forward to make a public decision for Christ stated their name on the card and the nature of their decision, and gave the details of a church they would like to be referred to. The local organizers collected the cards, followed up with reading materials, and established contact with a local minister. But the cards' meaning expanded beyond the practical: they provided the data to prove Graham's success in the most secular and scientific way. Secular newspapers and crusade publications distributed by the evangelical community transmitted and amplified the data: during the 1948 Los Angeles revival, 4,178 decision cards had been collected; at Harringay the figure was 36,431; and at Madison Square Garden in 1957, 61,148 cards were collected.[98] *The Times* of London published a summary of the Harringay events under the headline "Statistics of a Crusade."[99] In the eyes of Harringay participant Ruth Adams, the stocktaking embedded the crusade in the modern spirit of the decade: "They had taken a decision, and now they were going to sign a form recording it. This was most familiar and everyday. This belonged to 1954."[100] The system clearly highlighted the modernity of Graham's revival work through its commitment to data acquisition and statistics.

The collection of the cards at the end of the services was just one aspect of the rationalization of the evangelization process. Right after the collection, another example of modern missionary machinery whirred into action: the follow-up work. Crusade publications captured the rationalization of this process with images of the typewriters that volunteers used to document names and to write letters to the churches that the inquirer had identified as a potential spiritual home.[101] Converts were to be turned into believers with secular efficiency.

From the outset, the German and the UK press described Graham's religious mission in terms of production, marketing, and sales and they did so with clear admiration. Headlines above stories about Graham's first campaigns in London, Düsseldorf, and Berlin included words like "assembly line," "production," and "statistics"—all terms more typical of the world of industry and commerce. Even the left-leaning British newspaper *The Guardian* repeatedly commented on Graham's business style, but did so without being dismissive.[102] The *Church of England Newspaper* showed such a clear admiration for Graham's productive revival operation that it provoked a sharp response to the editor from one reader who was critical of Graham's supersalesman style and dismissed the idea that religion could be sold.[103] But for many, Graham's method of selling the gospel opened up new ways to imagine the growth of faith at a time of increasing secularization.

Graham wedded faith to the world of business but also to the world of consumption. Just as in America, it was hard to find an article published in Germany or the United Kingdom on Graham that did not highlight his good looks and fashionable appearance. The British press labeled him "the Hollywood version of John the Baptist."[104] Similarly, German newspapers and magazines carried headlines such as "Minister with the Looks of a Hollywood Star" and "Crusader in a Dashing Double-Breasted Suit."[105] Ruth embodied the female version of this new evangelism, with journalists describing her as fashionable and talented, cosmopolitan and articulate, efficient and faithful.[106] Religion had never looked this good, and unsurprisingly the religious press as well as secular publishing houses were keen to capture the essence of this stylish, modern, itinerant preacher.

Graham provided the images that melded faith, fashion, and a middle-class lifestyle in the dawning new age of postwar prosperity. And the European organizers of his crusades sensed that Graham's middle-class lifestyle formed an intrinsic part of his attraction. A small picture booklet, published under the auspices of Arthur H. Chapple, introduced Graham to the British public not just as an evangelist but also as a middle-class family man playing golf, going fishing, driving a car, and entertaining his children.[107] Another booklet, published by the *Sunday British Companion*, entitled *20 Lovely Pictures of a Happy Christian Family*, offered the images of family life that Graham's PR machine had already made so familiar to audiences in the United States: Ruth Graham in the role of the loving housewife, cooking, cleaning her husband's study, and enjoying her needle-work. The major symbols of 1950s middle-class consumer culture were pre-sent: Ruth was on the telephone, surrounded by modern kitchen appliances, while her husband was shown swinging a golf club or sitting behind the wheel of his car.[108] A special edition of the *Berliner Sonntagsblatt, die Kirche*, published by the Evangelical Church of Berlin in 1954, also introduced Graham as an American family man, highlighting his love for fishing and golf, and his passion for racing his car in his spare time.[109]

But the middle-class demographic that Graham represented and attracted to his crusade meetings in the United States did not yet exist in such great numbers in Europe: thus the economic and social background of those who attended Graham's European crusades was not as sharply defined along class lines as it was in the United States. Graham himself and the bishop of Barking assured the *Methodist Recorder* in a joint interview that people from all class backgrounds came to Harringay.[110] An article in *The Times* following the closing service at Wembley described those stepping forward as "being of all ages, of many social strata": "Here, an ill-dressed pensioner hobbled for-ward; there, a father, his face glowing with conviction, led out two very young and, apparently, puzzled children. They were soon lost to sight in a press of the smart and the dowdy, the schoolgirls and the matrons, the middle-aged men and the youth."[111] If those people attending American crusades were in search of affirmation of their new social status as middle-class citizens, then the crusades in Europe also offered their audiences an occasion and space to demonstrate their own social and economic aspirations through the interac-tion with a representative of the rising, consuming middle class in the United States.

One thing, however, the audiences in the United Kingdom and in Germany did have in common with the American ones was that they were to an even higher degree white. Of the entire coverage on the twelve-week Harringay crusade only one article mentioned a girl of color responding to Graham's altar call.[112] Of course, Germany and the United Kingdom at that time were ethnically more coherent than the United States and yet, espe-cially in London, the low participation of ethnic minorities in the crusade meetings reflected a deeper problem. In contrast to Germany, the United Kingdom had seen an increase in immigration of people of color since the arrival of the first Jamaican immigrants on the *Empire Windrush* in 1948. Those immigrants, however, felt often unwelcomed, patronized, or mis-understood in British churches.[113] Since it was exactly those churches that

Graham cooperated with and that paved the local ground for the events at Harringay, their local racial politics became visible and amplified during the Greater London Crusade. Those white members of the London working classes and aspiring lower middle classes who attended Harringay had no intension of sharing their economic hopes and dreams with the new arrivals. As in their neighborhoods, they preferred to stay among themselves, spiritually and economically.

Indeed, those who came to the crusades wanted to know how their own economic aspirations could be combined with their traditional faith. Hugh McLeod has compellingly shown how the rise of consumerism has played a distinct role in the process of secularization in Europe since the late 1950s. "Affluence," in his words, "had a wide-ranging influence on people's lives, and sometimes affected their ways of thinking, including their thinking about religion and their religious practices."[114] European evangelicals, churches, and secular observers, much as their American counterparts, used Graham as an example of a lived faith in an age of increasing prosperity. Graham's proud consumer lifestyle, combined with his genuine evangelical faith, allowed European Christians to think about themselves as Christian consumers, a concept with which they struggled significantly more than their American brethren.

Yet there was one theme of Graham's mission that proved hard, if not impossible, to transfer into the European public discourse: the close relationship between business, capitalism, and evangelical Christianity. Graham toned down his praise for capitalism when preaching in London and Berlin. The conversion story of the Minneapolis car dealer who ran his business for the Lord after his conversion was dutifully included in the German translation of one selection of conversion narratives under the flowery chapter title "Carry a Bible in the Glove Compartment."[115] But it is hard to imagine that German readers could really identify with it. The British publication "Harringay" featured one conversion story of a British businessman: a toy manufacturer who had found personal satisfaction through his conversion. But the typical line referring to how his business was blessed afterward does not appear in the published story.[116]

That Graham's view of the interplay between business and Christianity could lead to serious misunderstandings in the European context became clear when Graham was quoted in the German press as having called the economic miracle taking place in Germany in the 1950s a sign of God's grace. For him, the journey toward faith was identical with the journey toward peace and prosperity. Accordingly, he defined the German economic miracle as the reward for the strong faith of the German people.[117]

Many German Protestants who were bound to humility after the failing of their church during the Third Reich reacted with shock to Graham's words. Heinrich Sierig, Graham's most outspoken German critic, saw them as a clear indicator of the distortedness and boasting of Graham's gospel.[118] In his view it was too early to call the German nation blessed, only a decade after the liberation of the first concentration camp. In this context, it is not surprising that Graham's remark on the German economic miracle as a sign of God's grace stirred similar concerns in the United Kingdom. *The Guardian* felt compelled to provide Graham with a short history lesson on the German character: "German economic recovery is not a miracle, it is a result of the qualities and hard work of the German people, qualities which are also failings because in the past they have been as easily turned to the task of the efficient instigation and prosecution of aggressive war as they are now most admirably turned to economic recovery." The author warned against making Germany's economic recovery "a yard-stick by which to judge German moral recovery."[119] For local historical reasons, this example of Graham's American language of business and faith did not fall on fertile ground.

A Transatlantic Choir of Consumer Critics

Despite the vast audiences and the warm welcome Billy Graham received in Berlin, London, and New York, there was also a chorus of critical voices who spoke up against his corporate evangelism—what the German left-leaning magazine *Der Spiegel* famously called on its front cover "Religion for Mass Consumption."[120] These voices highlighted the fact that it was not the Atlantic Ocean that divided Graham's supporters and critics, but an understanding of what the future of Western faith should look like or, more precisely, what it should not look like. There were certainly some genuine European anti-American sentiments articulated in the context of the Graham crusades, such as when one journalist complained in a German conservative newspaper in 1955: "This mixture of blatant exaggeration, direct attack, and businesslike politeness is un-European and can only be explained on the basis of the American attitude to life."[121] But the core themes underlying critical statements on Graham's mission on both sides of the Atlantic show striking similarities, which mark them as part of a broader Western consumer critique with faith as its focus.

This criticism of Graham's missionary style centered around two core themes: the commodification of faith through the language of marketing and statistics, and the nature of Christian conversion. Rabbi Dr. Louis Gerstein of the Spanish-Portuguese synagogue of New York publicly stated in 1957 that he was "critical of the slick, smooth, high pressure salesmanship in selling religion in technique hardly different from the approach one might use in selling toothpaste or hair dressing."[122] In an article on Graham in *Der Spiegel* in 1954, Gerstein's words were echoed by a German journalist, who observed that Graham could also sell cars or washing machines instead of faith. On both sides of the Atlantic, the revivals were often perceived as smooth sales events by Graham's fans and critics alike. In 1955, one British observer asked in similar fashion: "Should there not be a 'commercial' for chlorophyll toothpaste inserted somewhere amid the spotlights, the rhythmic choir, the electric organ, and the soul washing?"[123] The fear that Graham's mission might advance the commodification of faith was obvious in the words of his most vocal critic, Reinhold Niebuhr, who famously called Graham's religious offer "a bargain."[124] Ironically, by doing so, he echoed and perpetuated his opponent's consumer-orientated language.

If Graham was indeed turning faith into a sellable commodity, then the altar call was his sales pitch and the conversion the transaction. This is at least how many of his critics around the world saw it. German journalist Barbara Klie, who covered Graham's German mission for the daily *Süeddeutsche Zeitung*, complained that his preaching transformed the relationship between God and the human being into a business relationship: "The doctrine of grace is turned into a business transaction: God says, 'I gave my son for you; now give up your sins and you'll be forgiven.'"[125] Yet it was not only Europeans who found this transformation of a holy moment distasteful. In a book review of Charles Templeton's *Evangelism for Tomorrow*, published in Graham's own magazine *Christianity Today*, the reviewer commented, in passing, on his tendency "to present conversion as transaction."[126] Graham's altar call reflected the bourgeoning 1950s consumer culture precisely in its emphasis on making a choice. But his critics saw this as a secularization of that moment: by selling conversion in such secular terms, Graham appeared to deplete it of its deeper religious meaning.

While many Christians invested their hopes in Graham's business of faith, many others worried. Their voices form a compelling transatlantic community of defendants of a traditional faith that was perceived as more authentic. But they are also part of a more comprehensive consumer critique, concerned about the shallowness of mass entertainment and the commodification of feelings and commitments. In airing their grievances about the close interplay between faith, business, and consumerism, or between the sacred and the secular in general, Graham's critics enlivened the public debate about the future of faith.

Conclusion

Graham's religious offer did not just blur the boundaries between economics, Cold War patriotism, and faith; it also successfully combined secular and sacred elements in its attempt to appear attractive and competitive in the modern culture of the 1950s. Through the technicalization of the pulpit, the documentation of those who had stepped forward, and the streamlined bureaucracy of the follow-up work, modern rationality, one of the cornerstones of secular culture, crossed over into the religious world of modern mass evangelism in the United Kingdom, Germany and the United States. Newspaper articles and pictures published as part of the crusade publicity and marketing projected this significant symbiosis beyond the immediate crusade communities, challenging generally held assumptions about the development of secular and religious life.[127]

Graham presented the British and German religious landscape with a different way of defining the relationship between religion and money via the embodiment of a new type of Christian businessmen and Christian consumer. He made an offer for a different kind of faith, more easily accessed and consumed, one that provided consumers and consumers-to-be with a Christian legitimization of their changing lifestyles. As much as this new faith briefly stimulated and energized the British and German religious landscapes, in the long term people of faith, European businessmen, and their churches seemed reluctant to reconsider their own attitudes toward the selling of religion, no matter how attractive they found Graham's religious offer in the early and mid-1950s. Too deep were the differences in the religious development of the old and the new continent, with a religious market and the Christian gospel of the economic free market existing only on one side of the Atlantic.

A significant transformation did not take place in the official churches, which had repercussions for the European religious landscape: in their un-willingness to embrace and address their members as consumers, the British and German churches might have too quickly given up on a new way to pro-mote Christian faith and to access new Christian audiences, paving the way for an even more rapid secularization of their respective countries. The large numbers of future Christian consumers who attended Graham's crusades in Germany and the United Kingdom highlight a change in their religious and socioeconomic identities that Graham was able to address; and he allowed them to make sense of this transformation.

It was only the evangelical organizers of the European crusades who fully embraced the business acumen and ambition of Graham's evangelism. Even today their descendents experiment with marketing materials and cultural products such as Christian rock, which easily combine secular and sacred elem-ents in a typical American style. Thus, their comparative success in Germany and the United Kingdom in defying the trends of secularization can be explained by their distinct openness to experimenting with marketing and fundraising.

Graham's religious offer was not comprehensively rejected as a cultural aberration in Europe; that mostly happened on the political and intellectual left. Instead Graham inspired British and German churches and people of faith to experiment with new forms of evangelism, to discuss new ways of protecting and spreading faith in an increasingly prosperous and secular world, and to rethink the boundaries between the secular worlds of business and consumption and the scared worlds of mission and faith. The fact that the majority of European churches in the end sided against Graham's corpo-rate evangelism does not diminish the significance of this specific transat-lantic transfer and opportunity that arose in the unique religious and cultural atmosphere of the 1950s.

The wide acceptance of Graham's consumerist campaigns during the 1950s in Britain and Germany was the result of his appeal to popular aspirations of prosperity, and an offer to bring together faith and the cultural and economic forces of transformation that people experienced around them. And it was legitimized by its success. The capacity of Graham to attract crowds and gen-erate carefully recorded conversions was not just noted by the press and a wider public: it also silenced many of those skeptical of his approaches among the local organizers in the United States, the United Kingdom, and Germany. Still, for Graham's consumerist appeal to enjoy the resonance that it did on both sides of the Atlantic, it required one further dimension: Graham's unswerving commitment to anticommunism.

When Graham stepped off the transatlantic cruise liner *United States* in Southampton, England, on February 23, 1954, he brought not only his fashionable wife and piles of luggage, but also his particular religious offer that combined elements of business, consumption, and American middle-class lifestyle. This offer took shape during his early American crusades, in which businessmen took active part through donations and the discursive power of their own conversion stories. It blended easily with the gospel of freedom and democracy that the United States spread to ideologically consolidate the imagined community of the Free World. The important role that the American evangelist, businessman, and consumer Graham played in the spiritual creation of this imagined Cold War community at home and abroad will be explored in the following chapter.

3

Politicizing Religion

Re-Christianization, Anticommunism, and the Making of the Spiritual Free World

In the summer of 1960, the local organizers of Graham's crusade in Berlin set up a modern revival tent in one of the most politically strategic and contested spaces in the divided city. In the words of Cecil Northcott, an American observer who captured the scene for the *Christian Century*: "On the west side of the Gate, right in front of the decaying Reichstag building, Billy Graham had his 22,000-seat tent pitched for a week of evangelism. Never before had he chosen such an emotionally strategic site. His amplified voice could be heard across the Iron Curtain, and every night busloads of East Berliners made an attempt to cross over and join the multitude in the tent."[1]

The location of the tent and the scale of his mission reinforced Graham's position as a cold warrior who had not just come to Europe to reenergize church life and to sell faith, but also to fight America's spiritual Cold War on foreign soil.[2] From the early days of his first campaign in Los Angeles in September 1949, Billy Graham had risen to prominence as a committed spiritual fighter against communism and a much-hoped-for restorer of the Christian identity of the United States. Through the fanfare and publicity surrounding his crusades Graham had been propelled into the center of discourses and actions involving political, societal, and cultural actors, creating a spiritual atmosphere that blurred the boundaries between civil religion, patriotism, and Christianity in the United States. As a result, Graham played an important role in what Jonathan Herzog has termed the "spiritual-industrial complex" "that represented the deliberate and managed use of societal resources to stimulate a religious revival in the late 1940s and 50s."[3]

The US re-Christianization discourse was mirrored in similar debates taking place in Germany and the United Kingdom at the same time. West Germany also embarked on a painful search for its new identity after the nationalistic project of the National Socialists had failed, at tremendous costs worldwide. Neither of the two leading churches, in particular the Evangelical

Altar Call in Europe. Uta A. Balbier, Oxford University Press. © Oxford University Press 2022.
DOI: 10.1093/oso/9780197502259.003.0004

Church, had done enough to counter the ideological project that had led to the Holocaust and a world war, and their moral leadership role in postwar Germany was questionable. Yet, in arguing that it was a broader societal secularization, the rise of materialism, technology, and sciences, that had caused the national catastrophe, Catholic and Protestant theologians and clergy pushed for a re-Christianization of postwar Germany in which they aimed to play a leading part. In the words of pastor and former Nazi prisoner Martin Niemöller in August 1945: "The times of ideas, ideals, and ideologies is over. All we have left is to rebuild our national culture on the foundations of Christianity."[4] Both established churches participated in this campaign to return to Christianity, and so did leading politicians such as Germany's first chancellor and chairman of the CDU, Konrad Adenauer, who built his party's election campaigns on a firm commitment to Christian values. In his first government declaration, Adenauer pledged to base the work of the first postwar German government on the "spirit of Christian-occidental culture."[5]

A similar discursive bond between Christianity and Western civilization had already been revived during World War II in Britain, when the nation's war efforts were often framed in spiritual language.[6] Winston Churchill himself declared famously in 1940: "Upon this battle depends the survival of Christian civilization." In the same year, Arnold Toynbee gave his famous lecture on *Christianity and Civilization* at the University of Oxford, providing the intellectual foundation for the political battle cry.[7] After the experience of war and destruction, and during the search of a new national identity at a time of the loss of India, the Christian foundation of Britain became a popular trope in British politics into the early 1950s. The Anglican Church, which according to Bishop George Bell was "the most venerable and the most influential of all the factors which have gone to the making of English history and English character,"[8] was able to lead the national discourse surrounding the re-Christianization of the country with significantly more confidence than its damaged German counterparts: in Britain, as in the United States, Christianity and patriotism could still work hand in hand. That was particularly obvious during the coronation of Queen Elizabeth in 1953, "which showed the world that the English were still at heart a kind of Christian nation."[9]

What all three countries had in common was, what McLaughlin called for the United States "a new interest in the Christian ethos which underlies American civilization" at a time of debates about emerging new national identities: the United States had to make sense of its new role as the leader of the Free World; West Germany had to learn to identify as a democratic part of a divided nation; and the United Kingdom had to redefine its historical role during the demise of its empire. In all three countries, an imagined Christian past became the focus of these searches for national identity. Graham's appearances tied these national discourses together across the Atlantic and amalgamated them in the transnational concept of the Christian West that would serve as the spiritual foundation of the Free World. His crusades made these debates accessible for ordinary citizens and allowed them to find their place in Cold War culture. Looking at Graham's role in the transnational re-Christianization project of the 1950s allows us to better understand the distinct revivalist atmosphere of the 1950s and to make the imagined community of the Free World more tangible.

Re-Christianization

During Graham's 1949 Los Angeles crusade the media, political institutions, and religious bodies had demonstrated a common cause by tying together religious commitment and patriotism. An editorial published in the Hearst-owned newspapers in Los Angeles in early November interpreted Graham's revival work within a framework of patriotic and democratic duty: "Let them attend and participate, to realize that the vast majority of true Americans understands and acknowledges that our entire moral and social law, and hence our peace and prosperity have their source and derive their being from the teaching of Christ."[10] Similarly, before Graham's first revival meeting, Los Angeles mayor Fletcher Bowron declared that personal Christian conversion could indeed benefit the city as a whole.[11] Both statements were deliberate attempts to turn faith into a resource for the public good and the effective functioning of democracies.

Graham reflected this belief in his own preaching in LA and elsewhere, revealing his vision for a Christian America that was spiritually, militarily, and economically strong and forcefully anticommunist. With refrains such as "If you would be a true patriot, then become a Christian" and "If you would be a loyal American, then become a loyal Christian,"[12] Graham echoed the anticommunist, revivalist battle cry of secular groups and leaders, and in doing so legitimized both the sentiment itself and those who propagated it. Religion was identified as the tool to restore the moral health of the nation. At a time of deeply felt societal anxiety, when people in the United States were still coming to terms with the aftermath of World War II, while simultaneously confronting the looming nuclear threat of the Cold War, Graham provided a message that promised to unify Americans around the restored Christian identity of the country. This was not just pure lip-service: Graham saw the early Cold War, as noted by Raymond Haberski, as "a moral crisis that demanded a return to religious fundamentals before it was too late to save the nation he loved."[13]

The fact that Graham preached at a time when religion was considered less a personal than a national affair became even more obvious during the preparation for Graham's revival tour through South Carolina in March 1950. Greenville's mayor, J. Kenneth Cass, urged businesses and factories to close early to allow their staff to attend the afternoon service at 3:30 p.m. Schools were also reminded to close on time so that teachers and pupils could get to the crusade.[14] When Governor Strom Thurmond opened the revival meeting by emphasizing the importance of Graham's work for America and calling him "a God-send,"[15] Graham's religious offer was effectively integrated into the national civil religious discourse.

Thus, it is not surprising that, less than two years later, Graham took this new alliance between evangelicalism and Cold War patriotism into the symbolic and political heart of the American nation. On January 13, 1952, Graham opened his first revival meeting in Washington, DC, a crusade that was scheduled to run until February 10 but was extended until February 17. As with his earlier campaigns, cottage prayer meetings and marketing—including pictures and neon signs, billboards and lamppost posters, and fifty thousand bumper stickers—prepared the city for Graham's arrival.[16] But this crusade had a distinct and new dimension: Graham had never before preached in an environment that allowed him to highlight the patriotic, civil religious, and political core of his mission to such an extent. Indeed, the spatial and performative arrangements for the Washington crusade were specifically designed to exploit the city's unique architectural, cultural, and monumental heritage.

For more than a month, Graham preached every evening at the National Guard Armory just to the east of the US Capitol, a large auditorium accommodating about eight thousand people that was decorated around the theme taken from Proverbs, "Righteousness exalteth a nation."[17] Typically his audience included leading political figures, including Democratic and Republican senators and representatives: Representative Wingate Lucas, a Democrat from Texas, served as an usher, as did his Republican colleague in the House, Orlando K. Armstrong. Senator Robert S. Kerr, a Democrat from Oklahoma, served as honorary chairman of the sponsoring Greater Washington Evangelistic Crusade, an organization composed of around 250 ministers and laymen. Former governor of New Hampshire and Republican senator Charles W. Tobey was among Graham's strongest supporters in the district.[18] Party affiliation, exactly like denominational affiliation, did not matter in the unified national Christian community that Graham intended to shape.

Graham's preaching in Washington built on his earlier sermons, focusing on the moral decline of the city, which he saw as emblematic for the entire nation, on corruption in government, and again and again on the communist threat. In his preaching, the boundaries between the personal and the national, and the political and religious, constantly blurred. Citizens who attended the meetings and later wrote to the editors of the *Washington Post* seemed to understand what was at stake. Their letters emphasized that they saw Graham as one of many Americans who still upheld ideals of "personal and civic morality" and acknowledged the current "hour of need for the individual and the nation."[19] In these letters, personal salvation sounded much like a civic duty.

While in the nation's capital, Graham made full use of the symbolism of the built environment of the city. When he toured the Mall one afternoon, press pictures captured the evangelist deep in thought outside the Lincoln and Jefferson Memorials. The *Washington Post* published these images alongside reflections by Graham on the nation's past and present, the legacies of former leaders, and the current need for a moral awakening.[20] On February 3 Graham held a large revival meeting on the steps of the Capitol, then followed it with an open-air meeting at the foot of the Washington Monument, within sight of the White House—two of the most symbolic spaces in Washington serving as his pulpit on a single day.

At the first of the two events, staged on the steps of the Capitol, about forty thousand gathered in drizzling rain along the Mall to listen to the young preacher's call for national revival. Speaking from a rostrum draped in the red, white, and blue of America, Graham was surrounded by senators, congressmen, and military personnel. With two sermons delivered in one hour, the whole event was transmitted coast to coast by ABC radio. The symbolism of its staging was not lost on the press, which made front page news of the fact that Graham spoke from the position where every four years presidents took their oath of office.[21] Indeed Graham's revival meeting echoed the civil religious performance of the presidential inaugurations. At the core of the orchestration lay a sermon that evoked the unity of the American nation and emphasized the importance of economic and military strength. Graham called for moral and spiritual regeneration: he saw communism as "a spiritual force [that] cannot be defeated on the field of battle alone."[22] As his call for action, he asked Congress to consider the establishment of a national day of prayer.

The Washington crusade embedded Graham's mission symbolically in the national civil religious consensus and spurred the new neo-evangelicals' reach for national and political power, whose ramifications can still be felt in US political culture today.[23] Prayer meetings that Graham held in Congress and at the Pentagon during the crusade added to this impression of evangelicalism as an emerging national political force. Never before had the close relationship between evangelicalism, patriotism, and civil religion been staged so persuasively. But despite its clear national focus, the Washington campaign had several transnational layers that pointed to Graham's future ambitions.

Creating the Spiritual Free World

Graham emphasized in his preaching in Washington, as he had also done in Los Angeles, that a spiritual awakening of the American nation would have a wider impact on the world.[24] But the international ambition of Graham's work extended beyond his preaching: press reports appeared during the final days of the crusade that announced that Graham was about to leave for an explorative visit to London to discuss the possibility of a crusade in the United Kingdom. Meanwhile, on the other side of the Atlantic, the Washington crusade was reported in detail in the British and German press, effectively introducing Graham to potential European audiences.[25] Graham's revival meeting in Washington attracted British visitors such as the Scottish Conservative MP John Henderson, who addressed a luncheon of businessmen on the question of "Religion and international Affairs."[26] Henderson and many others saw religion as a significant ingredient of the newly imagined special relationship between the United Kingdom and the United States.[27]

When Graham arrived in England to address an introductory meeting of six to seven hundred ministers and church leaders organized by the British Evangelical Alliance at the Assembly Hall of the Church House in

Westminster on March 20, 1952, he brought across the Atlantic his call for spiritual revival and re-Christianization. The chairman of the Evangelical Alliance, Lieutenant General Sir Arthur F. Smith, who presided over the meeting, was joined on the speaker's platform by the bishop of Barking, later a leading figure during the London crusade and prebendary Colin F. Kerr, who had also attended the Washington crusade.

Graham focused his remarks at the meeting primarily on the challenges and advantages that accompanied modern mass evangelism.[28] Yet behind the scenes the American organizing team emphasized the role of the crusade in the context of transatlantic Cold War culture. Willis Haymaker, Graham's central crusade manager, summarized the reasoning behind the planned London crusade in a memorandum that warned of the political implications for the future of the Cold War order of Britain's "leftist trends." Only a spiritual revival could "stem the tide of moral deterioration, spiritual negligence, and the Marxist philosophy" in the United Kingdom. He also stressed that after the economic and military commitment America had made to rebuilding postwar Europe, a comparable commitment was now needed for spiritual and moral education.[29] The memo demonstrated Haymaker's strong commitment to the spiritual dimensions of the special relationship and the vision of an ideal, Christian, anticommunist West.

Many American politicians shared Haymaker's convictions and understood the importance of extending the reach of Graham's ministry. Secretary of State John Foster Dulles met the bishop of Barking when he traveled to the United States to attend the Syracuse crusade in preparation for the London meetings. After his return to London, the bishop reported on Dulles's full support for the London crusade.[30] Dulles also endorsed the London crusade in a personal letter to Graham in which he stressed the religious bond between the United States and the United Kingdom. Referring to Arnold Toynbee, he declared that "the political institutions of our Western civilization become 'wasting assets' unless they are constantly fed by vigorous faith in the spiritual nature of man and in the supremacy of moral laws." The organizers took their commitment to the protection of Western civilization seriously, to such an extent that they toyed with the idea of President Eisenhower delegating Senator Frank Carlson as his official representative to the London crusade.[31]

The British side proved receptive to this American sense of mission. The literature published by the British Evangelical Alliance, introducing Graham to the British public, promoted an idea of him as a Cold War figure: a short booklet published by Arthur Chapple contained several images showing the young evangelist in conversation with President Eisenhower, addressing senators and governors, and preaching to the American troops on a Pentagon-sponsored trip to Korea.[32] A picture of Graham in conversation with President Eisenhower appeared on the front page of the first issue of the *London Crusade News* in October 1953.[33] In this issue, the chairman of the Executive Committee of the Billy Graham Greater London Crusade, Major General D. J. Wilson-Haffenden, and Graham did not just present their spiritual mission but also their civil religious and political mission. Wilson-Haffenden expressed his concern about the small number of truly born-again Christians in "a so-called Christian country," embedding the need for revival into a national framework. Wilson-Haffenden believed that the events surrounding the coronation of Queen Elizabeth II in 1953 proved that Britain's national culture was still essentially based on Christian principles, a situation that he was convinced Graham could build upon.[34] As in the United States, Graham did not invent the national re-Christianization project, but stepped into its midst, his Greater London Crusade providing a stage for the performance and experience of the strong underlying Christian "national culture" that, as the historian Callum Brown noted, was still a core feature of Britain's identity in the 1950s.[35]

In an era of Cold War global confrontation, these national projects no longer existed in isolation. In Graham's revival work, national Western re-Christianization narratives came together in a Christian vision for a unified Western world. Before the London crusade, Graham warned that the future of the Western world depended on a successful revival in Britain and the United States, two countries whose fate he saw as "inseparably linked."[36] Graham interpreted his mission abroad as a byproduct of the new global leadership role the United States had taken on after World War II, as a reflection of the new international awareness of the American people, and as a commitment to a world that was reaching out to the United States for leadership and guidance.[37] When Graham held his first official press conference during the London crusade, he accordingly made a reference to President Eisenhower and his vision for a spiritual awakening in the Western world.[38]

That the crusade was as much a confident staging of the US-UK special relationship as it was a religious event, was evident in the orchestration of the opening and closing services of the Greater London Crusade. When Graham climbed the rostrum of Harringay Arena on the first night of the Greater London Crusade on March 1, 1954, the arena was packed with eleven thousand people. He was accompanied on the platform by several church officials representing the different religious groups that had prepared and supported this first mission in Britain. Among the distinguished platform guests were several MPs and two American senators, Republican Styles Bridges and Democrat Stuart Symington, whom Graham introduced after the opening hymn. When Symington, the former secretary of the US Air Force, addressed the audience, he spoke of his pride in the fact that the United States was able to send a much-admired religious figure as "a messenger to the UK," and stressed Graham's close relationship with the US Congress, where the evangelist had recently attended a prayer meeting.[39] The participation of both senators highlighted the high-level political backing Graham received for his revival work, both in the United States and abroad.

How closely the British and American re-Christianization campaigns were intertwined in Graham's work became apparent during one of the open-air meetings held in Trafalgar Square on the afternoon of Saturday, April 3. On that occasion Graham repeated the call he had first made in Washington two years earlier, for a national day of prayer. This time, however, he put his proposal into a transnational framework by stating: "I think it is high time that the British and the American government called the entire world for a day of prayer. I would submit to the President of the United States and the Queen that our two nations take the lead in proclaiming a National and International day of prayer to save us."[40] Graham's ambitions were taking on an expansive international dimension.

At Graham's final London rally, on a cold and dull evening several weeks later at Wembley Stadium, an estimated 110,000 people witnessed another orchestration of Britain's Christian rebirth and staging of the special relationship with the United States. Beneath the Union flag and the Stars and Stripes, which flew side by side above the stadium, the meeting opened with the singing of the British and American national anthems. Seated alongside Graham on the platform was the archbishop of Canterbury, Geoffrey Fisher, representing the Church of England, while the Lord Mayor of London, Sir Noel Bowater, and his wife, several ministers, and MPs watched from the royal box. General Wilson-Haffenden spoke first, on behalf of the organizing committee, and in making a grateful reference to many prayer groups behind the Iron Curtain, embedded the final crusade meeting in the international Cold War context. Graham followed up in his opening remarks, expressing his hope that Harringay had helped to showcase "Anglo-American solidarity," a term of significant political importance in the first decade of the newly established special relationship.[41] After 2,184 people responded to the altar call, it was fitting that Archbishop Fisher, the head of the English state church, offered the final prayer and closed the service with the benediction.[42]

During his stay in London, Graham found his access to the seat of political power just as easy as it had been in the US Capitol. Often as the guest of his two strong supporters, the Conservative MPs Lancelot Joynson-Hicks and John Henderson, Graham made frequent visits to the Houses of Parliament, attending dinners and luncheons, and meeting members of both houses. It all added to the perception of him as an American ambassador. The day before Graham held his final meeting at White City and Wembley Stadium, five Conservative MPs, F. A. Burden, Nigel Fisher, Robert Jenkins, Gilbert Longden, and Thomas Moore addressed an open letter to the editor of *The Times*, expressing their deep admiration for Graham's campaign and declaring that they intended to participate in the last service to celebrate "the beginning of a great Christian awakening."[43]

By the end of the campaign Henderson estimated that 250 of his parliamentary colleagues had heard Graham speak, with the result, he hoped, that at least some of them had "laid a new emphasis on the spiritual and moral aspects of life" in their speeches.[44] Appropriately, Graham's first campaign in Great Britain ended with an audience at 10 Downing Street with Prime Minister Winston Churchill, who had coined the term "special relationship." The two men had a forty-minute conversation, in which Graham himself acknowledged the political significance of his first UK crusade by expressing his conviction that his work had enhanced the Anglo-American relationship. It was a statement well noted in the American press.[45]

Just as Graham in the United Kingdom had stepped into a vibrant discourse on the special relationship, so he also provided a focus for the simmering discussions about the ideal of a Christian Occident in German society, when, a few weeks after the London crusade, he traveled to Germany for his first crusade there. Both of Graham's strong supporters in official church circles in Germany, bishop of Hannover Hans Lilje and bishop of Berlin-Brandenburg Otto Dibelius, were committed to the ideal of the Christian Occident and the vision of a European community based on the principles of Christian traditions and Christian citizenship.[46] In the preface to his publication on Graham's 1954 and 1955 European campaigns, Wilhelm Brauer, the campaign's evangelical driving force, also proclaimed, "Kehre wieder, Abendland!" ("Come again, Occident!"),[47] a phrase that at that time was as much a religious as a political battle cry. As Catholic theologian Walter Dirks observed, the mass revivalism of Graham's campaigns in Germany seemed to be an inherent component of the reconstruction of Western political culture after World War II, in particular due to its strong anticommunist subtext.[48]

Indeed, Graham's revival meetings occurred during the lively debate in West Germany surrounding the concept of a "Christian Occident," the highly idealized vision of a premodern Christian Europe under which the continent could unite after 1945. A clear view of how the new Christian Occident should look did not exist. It was only clear that it provided a firm ideological bulwark against communism. Apart from that, Catholics and Protestants imagined the future Occident in many and often different ways: the term communicated a general pessimistic view of modern progress, a new orientation toward an integrated Europe, and it raised the difficult question if American mass society, liberalism, and culture did actually share the values of a Christian Europe with its stronger commitment to social policies.[49] The fact that Brauer used the term "Occident" so prominently in his publication shows that Graham was perceived as a possible bridge builder between a Christian Europe and a Christian America, thereby making his own small contribution to Germany's ideological and political alignment with the West.[50]

Considering the political prominence of the re-Christianization debates and "the hegemony of a Christian-conservative mentality"[51] in Germany at the time when Graham arrived, it is not surprising that Graham's mission in Germany, from the beginning, carried a strong political tone. This was, however, amplified by the unique circumstances in which he delivered his first sermon on German soil. Graham began his short visit with a service in the US Army's Christ Chapel in Frankfurt on June 23 in front of a predominantly American audience. Graham arrived in an army limousine, accompanied by the commander in chief, US Army Europe, General William M. Hoge and the commanding general of the Northern Area Command, Thomas W. Herren.[52] With his sermon being directly transmitted back to the United States for radio broadcast, Graham chose content and language familiar to his followers across the Atlantic. He did not just highlight the importance of a German spiritual awakening to defend the freedom of the Western world, but also explained that the journey to faith was identical with the journey toward peace and prosperity: the German economic miracle and the country's road to economic success were the reward for the strong faith of the German people.[53]

It was, however, another line of Graham's address that was repeated in most German national and regional newspapers the next morning: "Billy

Graham predigt Waffenbrüderschaft!" (Billy Graham preaches brothers-in-arms!) ran the headline in the widely circulated tabloid *Bild*.[54] Graham had addressed the special situation of Germans living under the Bolshevist threat and called for rearmament of the country, which he saw as a close American ally in defending the Free World. This statement fitted in with Graham's conviction that only a militarily strong West could prevent a third world war—an assumption he had emphasized during his Pentagon prayer meetings and on his visit to American troops in Korea. It was no surprise that his statement on rearmament was also picked up by *Time* magazine on the other side of the Atlantic.[55] But for some in the still fragile community of the Christian West, Graham's call for German rearmament was a step too far: in particular, the British press carried sharply critical comments about Graham, aware that the British people still viewed Germany as the former enemy, responsible for air raids and painful human losses.[56]

The German press seemed less disturbed by Graham's clear militaristic position and embedded his first German crusades in Düsseldorf and Berlin firmly in the ongoing discourse on the Cold War. Even though the organizing committees and the preacher himself constantly emphasized the religious core of his work, the German press welcomed Graham as an important political ally in the Cold War confrontation. On the day before his revival meeting at Berlin's Olympic Stadium, the tabloid *B.Z.* explained why Graham was coming to the city: "Because the heart of the world beats in Berlin, because it is here—more than anywhere else in the world—that people stand up against fear. That is why Billy Graham preaches in Berlin."[57] With these words, the paper placed the American preacher and his campaign in the middle of a political discourse that declared Berlin the center of the Free World. Despite his insistence that this was not a political mission to a Cold War city, Graham fueled this discourse when he spoke at the Stadtmissionskirche the day before the Olympic Stadium revival about the special situation of Berlin, which had turned it into a city prayed for by millions of Christians around the globe.[58]

The political importance of the Olympic Stadium revival meeting was underlined by the presence of leading figures from the city's political, religious, and cultural life, who took their seats next to Graham in the dignitary grandstand. The mayor of Berlin, Walther Schreiber, was present, as was the president of the Berlin police, Johannes Stumm. Federal minister Robert Tillmanns represented the government and the Protestant study group in the Christian Democratic Party, whose chairman he was. Bishop Dibelius represented the Evangelical Church, as Archbishop Fisher had done for the Anglican Church in the United Kingdom.[59]

The British and German public proved receptive to the civil religious subtext of Graham's revival work. Letters sent to newspaper editors during Graham's next crusade in Britain a year later showed that the seed of Graham's preaching had fallen on fertile ground. A reader of the *Manchester Guardian* expressed his conviction that only a religious revival could save the Western world.[60] This line of argument could also be found in higher church circles when the president of the British Methodist Conference, Dr. Leslie D. Weatherhead, stated in his presidential address in July 1955 that communism would not have any appeal in a country where the message of the gospel was alive. He clearly feared that effective communist propaganda could enhance secularization in Britain.[61] When Rev. F. Copland Simmons, moderator of the Free Church Federal Council, addressed the Baptist Union in London about evangelism, he compared the amount of churches he could mobilize to the number of current members of the Communist Party—a statement that echoed Graham's oratory while in London in 1954.[62]

Many German crusade participants also joined willingly in Graham's Cold War rhetoric when writing to their church magazines and their ministers, especially after the general secretary of the *Kirchentag*, Heinrich Giesen, published a harsh critique in which he complained about Graham's crusade rhetoric, his commitment to rearmament, and the ideal of a Christian West. Giesen interpreted Graham's campaigns as an uncomfortable echo of the politicized and nationalistic German Protestantism of the 1930s and 1940s, which contributed to Hitler's rise to power.[63] His readers, however, saw Graham's missions not as reflections of an often willingly forgotten German past but as defined by their importance in the context of the contemporary political atmosphere.

After the article appeared in the Protestant periodical *Kirche und Mann* in 1954, one reader wrote in fury that those in Giesen's camp were underestimating the Bolshevist threat.[64] Another reader responded to a dismissive article on Graham in 1960 by the minister Hartmut Sierig in *Kirche in Hamburg* with an elaborate statement on the American preacher's important role in the fight against communism. From the reader's perspective, the importance of Graham's revival meetings lay in the fact that they led ordinary Germans back to Christian values that would immunize them against communist infiltration.[65] By deploying this line of argument, many German Christians contributed to the discourse that framed the Cold War as a spiritual war on both sides of the Atlantic. Through the public controversy stirred by Graham, ordinary Christians were able to join discussions on democratization and re-armament in which the Protestants and Catholic churches in Germany participated with growing confidence after 1945. While the historiography of these debates has largely presented them as taking place between ministers, priests, and theologians, Graham, in fact, had opened them up to a much broader public.[66]

Established Cold Warrior

The European crusades significantly contributed to Graham's popularity in the United States, winning him increased political respect and consolidating his Cold Warrior image. When Graham returned from Europe in 1954, he met members of Congress and government officials to pass on his impressions of daily life close to the Iron Curtain.[67] Graham also profited from the election of Dwight Eisenhower, who shared his belief "that American democracy depended on religion, that Communism was at its heart a dangerous religious creed, and that successful nations balanced both material and spiritual strength."[68] Through President Eisenhower's support, neo-evangelicalism expanded its position in the civil religious realm and became a defining feature of the 1950s national and political landscape. Graham's acknowledged political know-how manifested itself during the orchestration of the New York Crusade of 1957—a several-month-long metropolitan crusade that even outstripped the political symbolism of the Washington crusade five years earlier.

Both Eisenhower and Vice President Richard Nixon publicly supported the New York campaign. In February 1957, Nixon had enthusiastically promoted the upcoming New York Crusade at the annual International Christian Leadership meeting at Washington's Mayflower Hotel, devoting nearly half of his remarks to the topic, addressing an audience that included senior government officials. That this episode was then again publicized in the *New York Crusade News* indicates how important government support was in the eyes of the neo-evangelical organizers.[69] Prior to the start of what Graham considered his most challenging revival campaign, he made a brief stop in Washington to see President Eisenhower. Their meeting was widely covered in the press and can be readily interpreted as the White House's endorsement of the New York Crusade.

Figure 3.1 Billy Graham preaching at Madison Square Garden, 1957 (copyrights: Granger Historical Picture Archive/ Alamy Stock Photo)

The crusade picked up on many themes established during earlier campaigns and in particular during the Washington crusade. Again the staging of the events, this time at Madison Square Garden (figure 3.1), underscored Graham's aim of national reaffirmation alongside religious conversion. The Garden was lavishly decorated with large American flags hanging from the roof; the hymn booklet contained "America the Beautiful" alongside traditional worship songs. Graham's sermons were again tailored to fit the setting. Beginning with his opening sermon on May 15, which was reproduced in full the next day in the *New York Times*, Graham put a strong focus on worldly affairs and the Cold War. Entitled "The Christian Answer to the World Dilemma," the sermon discussed the arms race, the upheavals in the Eastern Bloc, and the situation in the Middle East. It also touched on domestic problems such as juvenile delinquency and the unresolved racial tensions.[70]

In Graham's preaching, the personal decision for Christ was clearly contextualized in the political state of the nation. This was especially obvious in the last sermon Graham preached in New York City, at a final open-air service on Time Square, when he proclaimed:

> Tell the whole world tonight that we Americans believe in God. Let us tell the world tonight that our trust is not in our pile of atomic and hydrogen bombs but in Almighty God. . . . On this Labor Day weekend, here at the

Crossroad of America, let us tell the world that we are united and ready to march under the banner of Almighty God, taking as our slogan that which is stamped on our coins: "in God we trust."[71]

With these words, floating between the secular and the sacred, the political and the religious, Graham defined the two different cores of his mission, which were intertwined: one aiming for Christian conversions and one for national reconstruction.

This dual message allowed Vice President Nixon to blend seamlessly into the crusade performance, when he joined Graham on the platform during a special service at Yankee Stadium on July 20, attended by a crowd of one hundred thousand. Graham introduced Nixon as an "ambassador of good will, a young man with vision, integrity and courage"; the vice president returned the favor by delivering greetings from President Eisenhower, a "good friend" of Graham's.[72] The presence of Nixon conferred on the revival a sense of civic endorsement in the eyes of those who attended. In the words of one participant: the vice president surely wouldn't attend "some fanatical religious meeting."[73] The July 21 New York Times published an image of the preacher and the vice president with their heads bowed in prayer and the audience presumably praying with them, thus participating in this Cold War performance.[74] The audiences at Madison Square Garden, Yankee Stadium, and at home in front of television screens understood very well the message spread during the crusade. As a letter to the New York Mirror declared, "Billy Graham does more to emphasize the fact that America is a Christian nation in its character and substance, than all the other efforts put together since the founding of the Republic."[75] Graham brought the civil religious Cold War discourse alive for ordinary citizens.

But by then, Graham's mission was no longer limited to restoring the Christian identity of the American nation. Graham had committed himself to nothing less than creating and shaping a Christian Free World. His Cold War mission would peak again three years later when he returned to Berlin, as part of a three-week mission to Germany that also took place in Hamburg and Essen. The September 1960 Berlin crusade opened less than a year before the erection of the Berlin Wall, and with Cold War tensions close to boiling point at that time, Graham decided to pitch his revival tent in the most sensitive part of the city—right behind the Brandenburg Gate (figure 3.2).

Set in this atmosphere, Graham's crusade was from the beginning a political event, and, not surprisingly, different German political actors pledged

Figure 3.2 Billy Graham's revival tent in front of the Reichstag in Berlin, 1960 (copyrights: AP, Shutterstock)

their support. Graham met leading politicians including Vice Chancellor Ludwig Erhard, although Chancellor Konrad Adenauer kept his distance until 1963. Local politicians as well supported the crusade and by doing so highlighted the civil religious importance of the revival meetings. Following the example set in the United States, the CDU member and senator for education in West Berlin, Joachim Tiburtius, sent a request to universities, colleges, vocational schools, and high schools to excuse their students from classes to allow their participation in a special youth meeting held by Graham, which ended up attracting twenty-two thousand teenagers.[76]

The campaign also received substantial financial support from the Federal Ministry for Intra-German Affairs, which contributed DM 20,000 to the Berlin revival meetings. Some of the money went toward the cost of the revival tent, which was deliberately set up close to the East German border to allow East German visitors easy access: some was used to sponsor free hymn books for visitors from the eastern part of the city.[77] The revival tent fulfilled multiple political purposes: as the US press noted, it allowed Graham's preaching to be heard across the Iron Curtain, in the best tradition of the roll-back policies of the Cold War; from a German viewpoint, the federal government gave the event its own political spin by declaring it a unified German event in a divided city. The organizers shared this ambition to host a revival for audiences coming from both parts of the city: the refreshment stalls accepted the two different German currencies, and trombone players from the East contributed to the musical arrangements, until most of them lost their visitor's permits when returning to East Berlin and were not able to return.[78] During the closing outdoor service, Graham's often-used banner with the Bible verse "Jesus said: 'I am the way, the truth, and the life' " appeared under the inscription on the Reichstag's main facade, "Dem Deutschen Volke," a strong reminder of the unified German past, which blended with the spiritual call for a better future.[79]

The staging of the crusade as an all-German event was inevitably viewed as a provocation by the authorities in the communist part of the city, who launched their own propaganda offensive in response. In an internal memorandum, the East German secretary for church affairs lamented that the tent was an attempt to infect the East German population with "political clericalism."[80] The mayor of East Berlin, Waldemar Schmidt, officially asked his West Berlin counterpart, Willy Brandt, to remove the tent: the speaker of the Berlin Senate rejected the request as an interference in the internal affairs of West Berlin.[81] The West German press fueled the tense political atmosphere by reprinting excerpts from the propaganda articles published in the East German press. With both the West German and the international press gleefully ridiculing the communists' fear of the American preacher, Graham's credentials as a cold warrior increased even more. Meanwhile, American and British newspapers covered the political battle over the Berlin tent in detail, giving their readers a clear impression of the power and impact of religion in the divided city.[82] The eyes of the West lay on Billy Graham when he came to preach at the most important outpost of the Free World.

The Cold War discourse surrounding the event also held the evangelical organizers in a firm grip. When applying for funding from political bodies, the representatives of the organizing committee of the crusades, Paul Schmidt and Max Kludas, highlighted the importance of cross-border missionary efforts and the extraordinary situation of life in a divided city.[83] When the crusades were over, Peter Schneider, Graham's interpreter and general secretary of the organizing committee, sent out a press release in which he called the East German propaganda offensive an expression of the atheistic emptiness of the East. In addition, he implored Western political leaders to take the Christian faith seriously when addressing the prevailing problems of the world.[84] The culture of the Cold War had clearly penetrated the crusade Graham held in Berlin in September 1960, just as it had done in Washington, DC, New York, and London.

Shared Religious Anticommunism and Distinct Local Particularities

As much as Graham made a convincing discursive offer to British and German politicians, ministers, and ordinary Christians that confirmed their role in forming a spiritual Free World, he also encountered some cultural differences, most notably around his use of anticommunist rhetoric. Since the early days of his ministry, Graham's outspoken anticommunism had been an important political element of his campaign preaching. At a luncheon at the end of his Los Angeles crusade Graham said: "Guns are not enough to stop communism. . . . only God can hold it back."[85] For Graham, as for the early fundamentalist movement of the 1910s and 1920s, the fight against communism was not political lip service, but a serious spiritual concern, as he perceived communism as a religion in and of itself.[86] It was, according to Graham, a religion "directed by the Devil himself" already at play in the United States.

Repeatedly in his sermons Graham insisted that faith was in constant competition with the passion of the offer made by communism, a point he returned to again and again in his public speaking and in crusade publications. When, for example, Graham explained why it was important to present the gospel in evermore vigorous ways, he referred to the way in which communists spread their message: "I never saw a Communist orator standing up and giving a dispassionate little lecture."[87] During the New York Crusade, Graham called on the churches to catch fire, because communism was on fire, building on a quotation from the former president of Princeton Theological Seminary, Dr. John Mackay.[88] Through the repetition of such sentiments, Graham was expressing one of the core convictions of his international revival work: the Christian world was in constant competition with the materialistic, antireligious counteroffer made by the Eastern Bloc.

Furthermore, the framing of Graham's altar call with the political core of his message during the New York Crusade showed the degree to which Graham's anticommunism had become all-encompassing. Graham explained to those he called to step forward at Madison Square Garden that the decision he was asking them to make was not an easy one. However, he continued, "The appeal of Communism today is partially because it is a hard thing."[89] With this sentence, he rhetorically linked the appeal of communism with the offer he was making to the audience. Accepting Christ was transformed into a decision between communism on the one hand, and the ideals of the Free World on the other. The response to Graham's altar was not just a decision for Christ, but also allowed ordinary Christians to publicly show their commitment to the Free World.

It was this anticommunist battle cry that Graham brought with him to Europe. When one of the American sponsors of the Harringay campaign, Horace Hull, met with the London Executive Crusade Committee in April 1953, he explained that Graham believed that "he has the only answer not only to religious problems but to our social and economic problems. It is either Christianity or Communism."[90] When the local crusade treasurer, Alfred G. B. Owen, sent an appeals letter to the Federation of British Industries to raise funds for the London campaign, he also referred to the communist threat:

> We, in this country, are facing tremendous difficulties, not the least of these being the growth of Communism which is seeking to infiltrate the whole of our national life. The only answer to this is a militant Christianity. Dr Billy Graham brings such a message to the British people, and the coming Crusade is the result of his desire to present to our people the message which has had such a marked effect upon the American way of life.[91]

One year before Harringay Arena opened its doors for the Greater London Crusade, the American discourse on the political need for a spiritual revival had connected with a simmering anticommunism in the British evangelical community and beyond.[92]

The underlying anticommunism of the London crusade is reflected in the prominence of one conversion narrative that appeared in several published accounts of the meaning and impact of the London crusade: the story of the

"Communist Boss."[93] The short story captures the conversion of Charles W. Potter, the forty-two-year-old secretary of the Reading Communist Party who responded to the altar call at the White City meeting. The narrative depicted his complete turnaround in lifestyle by stressing that after joining Carey Baptist Church he gave a public testimony for Christ in the market square where he so "often preached Communism."[94] In his resignation letter to the party, written after his return from the White City service, he stated, "I feel belief in Jesus Christ to be incompatible with membership in the Communist Party."[95] Through narratives like this, the local campaign organizers added to the impression that the Greater London Crusade was a battlefield in the war between Christianity and communism.

At the same time, the creation of a binary between communism and Christianity was not uncontested in Europe: in Europe there existed a strong political Left, of which some parts showed sympathies for communism, while other parts were committed to the small but yet existing tradition of Christian Socialism.[96] Therefore, Christian critics of Graham's mission often picked up on his outspoken anticommunism. One Scottish minster wrote a long letter to *The Scotsman* criticizing Graham's campaign as "disguised political anti-communism."[97] Some unfortunately phrased marketing material circulated by the BGEA in Britain before the campaign had already aroused suspicions about the nature of Graham's brand of American anticommunism. The literature in question highlighted Britain's fall toward socialism after World War II as the reason why Graham's campaign in Britain was so important.[98] With the Labour Party until recently forming the government in the United Kingdom, the comment was understandably met with fury by many on the left. Unsurprisingly, the left-leaning paper *Herald* published the headline "Apologize, Billy—or Stay Away!" The Labour MP Geoffrey de Freitas considered proposing a debate about Graham's right to preach in the United Kingdom in Parliament.[99] Clearly, Graham's team still had a lot to learn about the particular local political and cultural circumstances of their first major campaign abroad.

The problem ran even deeper in Germany, where the evangelical organizers feared that Graham's very explicit anticommunism could alienate their brethren in the eastern part of the country and lead to a further divide of the evangelical community.[100] The West German Protestant and evangelical organizers saw themselves as representatives of all Christians living in divided Germany. Both the Evangelical and the Catholic Churches refused to accept the existence of the border running through their dioceses, with Otto

Dibelius, for instance, leading the Evangelical Church as bishop of Berlin and the surrounding area of Brandenburg. Dibelius's anticommunism notwithstanding, neither he nor other leaders could ignore the delicate political situation, in which the access of bishops to their divided dioceses was fragile. At the same time, these bishops had firsthand experience with the secularizing effect of communism, and the active initiatives undertaken by the socialist party in East Germany (SED) to impede religious practice. In this context, Graham's anticommunism had a particular resonance, but one that was unambiguous. The different reactions to Graham's anticommunism reflected the quarrels and fractures within German Protestantism over broader questions of alignment with the West, unification, and rearmament.[101] For every Protestant, such as Karl Barth, who publicly criticized Graham's political position there was another who shared the American preacher's ideal of the Christian Occident as a bulwark against secularization and the atheist communist bloc.

Two other aspects set Graham's mission in Germany apart from its evolution in the United Kingdom and the United States: the German past and the lack of bipartisan support. Graham and many evangelicals in the United States saw revival work in Germany not just as a battle against communism, but also as a belated assault on National Socialism. In their opinion, it was the rise of secularism and rationalism that had paved the way for Adolf Hitler's ascent. Graham now came to Germany to reverse that secular development. When Graham preached on the former Nazi rallying ground in Nuremberg in 1955, *United Evangelical Action* printed an image of the revival meeting, showing how the symbol of the cross had now replaced the swastika under the platform from which Graham gave his address.[102] The German organizers, such as Brauer, also lauded the fact that Graham preached at the Olympic Stadium in Berlin, in addition to Nuremberg, places where the anti-Christian ideology of National Socialism had been preached.[103]

This was, however, just one way of interpreting Graham's revival meetings. As much as the German past was a motivation for Graham to come to Germany in the first place, it also allowed some of his German critics to draw unpleasant comparisons. An article published by Heinrich Giesen in 1955 left no room for interpretation. Giesen referred to Goebbels's propaganda triumph in the wake of the German defeat at Stalingrad, and to the several thousand soldiers who had died in the World War I battle of Langemarck, whose deaths had been used as a propagandistic myth ever since: "We twice said yes with one voice—once in Langemarck and once [after Goebbels's speech] in the Sports Palace following Stalingrad. A people that has been as wounded as the Germans must not be subjected to the temptation of intoxication and must find time for its wounds to be healed."[104] German observers indeed feared that traditional peer pressure was at play at the revival meetings when scores of people stepped forward in response to Graham's altar call.[105]

Most importantly, as Giesen was strongly influenced by his engagement in the Confessing Church (Bekennende Kirche) during the Third Reich, Graham's mission reminded him of the worst possible relationship between the masses and their seducer, as well as the politicization of faith. Hartmut Sierig also criticized the mass character of Graham's events. Noting that the young American evangelist appeared to display admiration for the German nation, its poets, philosophers, and theologians, Sierig warned that Graham's events could easily be transformed into nationalistic celebrations. To Sierig, Graham had the potential to stir up the kind of nationalism that he hoped Germany had overcome.[106]

In Germany, Graham's style not only provoked opposition among Protestants, but failed to achieve the bipartisan success Graham had enjoyed in the United States and the United Kingdom. Reports about meetings with political leaders on the left or union representatives that took place in London are missing from the German press. This is striking in the context of Graham's revival meetings in Berlin in 1960. Despite the political dimensions of the crusade in the divided city, there are no images showing Graham with the Social Democratic governing mayor of Berlin, Willy Brandt. This is striking considering the political advantage the media-savvy Brandt extracted from the visit by John F. Kennedy three years later.

Graham's complicated civil rights record also intersected in different ways with his Cold War mission in the United Kingdom, Germany, and the United States. Since the beginning of his revival work, Graham was publicly criticized outside the Southern States for preaching in front of segregated audiences in the South, for instance when he toured in New England in 1950. In the southern states, during his Atlanta crusade in the same year, African American civil rights leaders and the *Atlanta Constitution* also raised their concerns.[107]

Graham had certainly tried hard to show commitment to the civil rights cause. For example, during his crusade in Chattanooga in 1953, he famously took down the ropes that separated the segregated seating areas for whites and African Americans.[108] And yet even after these actions Graham continued to accept segregated audiences, certainly in Dallas but most likely also in Asheville, North Carolina, in 1953.[109] His theology as well remained grounded in the idea that political change could only occur through personal conversion, not through social change.

Due to the increasing international reach of Graham's ministry, however, he feared that his position on segregation and civil rights might negatively impact his perception in Europe, as compellingly shown by Stephen P. Miller.[110] In July 1954, Graham wrote to a Southern Baptist minister with respect to the upcoming Nashville crusade, arguing: "The Nashville crusade will be written up quite extensively in the British press, and of course our work in England would suffer tremendously if they thought we were having a segregated meeting."[111]

This, however, did not quite accurately capture the way Graham's civil rights record had been discussed during the crusade at Harringay he had held earlier that year. There Graham's practice of preaching in front of segregated audiences in the American South was met with silence despite the fact that it was highly likely that Graham, before coming to London, had preached to segregated audiences at two crusades that were both covered in the *London Crusade News*.[112] Leading church magazines such as the *Methodist Recorder*, the *Baptist Times*, and the *Life of Faith*, which introduced Billy Graham in much detail to their readers, kept suspiciously quiet about Graham's position on racial issues.

It was the editor of the *British Weekly*, Shaun Herron, who stood out when actually asking Graham about the contradiction in his ministry of publicly condemning segregation and yet holding segregated meetings in the American South. Graham met the question with his standard reply that he had already taken ropes down, but that in other situations he felt bound to follow state law. He explained that "he did not think the particular Christian work he was called to do was prospered by defiance of even bad laws, when defiance created negative strife and bitterness."[113] In an article published a year later in the *Tribune*, Donald Soper criticized Graham for favoring personal salvation over legal and social challenges to segregation.[114] This indicates that there probably did exist a certain awareness regarding Graham's position on segregation and civil rights in British churches and among the Harringay organizers, and yet the topic was not discussed in public.

That quietness of the Anglican Church regarding the question of segregation during Graham's southern crusades was, however, not that surprising. The archbishop of Canterbury, Geoffrey Fisher, seemed to lack awareness of the growing racial tensions in his own country. In the sharp words of

Kenneth Leech, Fisher "was concerned about artificial insemination, premium bonds and homosexuality, but not apparently about race."[115] In 1954, British Anglican bishops seemed to fear interracial marriages more than they believed in the existence of structural racism in their country. As late as 1958 and despite an increasing number of signs outside British houses asking for "white tenants only," the Lambeth Conference refused to acknowledge that discrimination on racial grounds was a widespread problem in Britain.[116]

Thus it is possible that the conspicuous silence regarding Graham's commitment to civil rights among those in positions of power in white British churches originated from what historians Robin Kelley and Stephen Tuck have termed "the other special relationship" between the United States and the United Kingdom, "one rooted in histories of Empire, white supremacy, racial inequality, and neoliberal policies."[117] For those oblivious to their own racial prejudices and failing under the cover of past imperial glory, Graham's stance on the topic was just not an issue.

In Germany at the same time, not even the investigative, left-leaning journal *Der Spiegel*, which introduced Graham to its readers with a seven-page article, commented on the ambiguities of Graham's civil rights record. Remarkably, the magazine had published an article earlier in 1954 on racial segregation in schools in the American South. Along with the German weekly *Die Zeit*, the magazine followed the rising racial tensions in the United States closely. Maybe the German press just missed the fact that Graham's evangelism and the culture of segregation had intersected before. However, the absence of the topic also highlighted a general mood among West Germans after 1945, marked by a firm conviction that racism was only a feature of the German past.[118] Witnessing the practices of racial discrimination within the occupying US armed forces added to a new German sense of postracist innocence and even superiority.[119] This conviction was forcefully staged during Graham's revival meeting in Nuremberg in 1955, when again several thousand Germans gathered on the former Nazi Party rallying ground, reaffirming their return to Christian morality, with not a single German newspaper expressing concern about the unhealthy similarities with earlier events. This was only possible because Graham's Christianity itself was presented as fresh and unspoiled as the new German beginning.

It speaks for the cultural Cold War consensus that Graham's campaigns flourished on both sides of the Atlantic, despite these national peculiarities. Even though different interpretations of a possible relationship between socialism, Christianity, civil rights, and the national past existed, those seemed

to diminish under a shared fear of the communist threat. It was in this particular culture that Graham was able to transnationalize important debates
about the relationship between personal faith and public politics, between
Christianity and democracy. This transnational religious consensus, however, was short-lived and would be profoundly challenged by the Vietnam
War and the rise of an anti-American counterculture in the 1960s.

Conclusion

With Graham's first appearances in Berlin and London in 1954, close
interactions developed between American evangelism and the religious
and political landscapes of Germany and the United Kingdom, when dis-
crepancies in theology and methods of evangelism were obscured by a joint
commitment to re-Christianization and the overshadowing Cold War consensus. Graham did not invent the lively re-Christianization debates, which
took place in German, British, and American political, intellectual, and religious circles, but he stepped right into them, giving them focus and adding
to their momentum. His international revival meetings highlight the transnational interconnectedness of those national debates and discourses and
their joint contribution to the creation of the imagined community of the
Christian West.

Beyond his role of a transnational mediator in the shaping of the spiritual Free World, Graham played a distinct role in each national context: his Greater London Crusade provided powerful images and tropes to
nourish the special relationship between the United States and the United
Kingdom when the Union Jack and the Star Spangled Banner flew side by
side at Wembley Stadium, when American politicians took their seats on
the crusade platform, and when the young preacher visited the Houses of
Parliament. Graham's mission highlighted the shared Christian heritage of
both countries, which would become an important cultural ingredient of
this new special relationship, one that, however, was also built on the shared
white cultural and social identities of those in power in both countries.

Similarly, Graham's revival meetings allowed his German audiences to
negotiate their increasingly close political and cultural affiliation with the
United States. By propagating a version of the Christian West that broadened
beyond the traditional European cultural context and declared the United
States a cultural part of the Christian Occident, he made an ideological offer

to German Christians that allowed them to align themselves more closely with the United States. As in London and in the United States, his German crusades, particularly in Berlin, provided important forums for ordinary Christians and citizens to experience Cold War culture and to demonstrate their cultural and spiritual alliance with the United States and their belonging to the Free World.

Yet, in Germany, Graham also played an important role for Protestants trying to come to terms with their past. While, in the eyes of some, his revival meetings were a shocking reminder of former mass events, which had manipulated thousands of Germans into war and genocide, for others they represented the possibility of a fresh and innocent patriotic Protestantism cut loose from the memory of the Third Reich. By providing a focus for such different interpretations and discussions, Graham provided a space for German Protestants to negotiate their future place in the political culture of West Germany.

The millions of people who attended the crusade meetings in London, Berlin, New York, and Washington, the political honors that Graham received, and the prominence of his campaigns in the press highlight once more that a transnational religious revival took place in the mid-1950s. The Cold War provided the political and cultural framework in which this revival occurred, and anticommunist propaganda fueled the re-Christianization discourses of the decade. The imagined Free World provided those Christians who took part in the crusade meetings with yet another transnational concept to identify with. They had already identified with Graham's mission as revived Christians and prospering consumers; now they followed him as committed cold warriors. These newly emerging identities would allow them to increasingly define themselves as members of a transnational community of Graham's followers who shared a commitment to revivalism, consumerism, and the Free World. The following chapter will explore the practices through which Graham's followers would live and experience their new belonging.

4

Living Religion

Everyday Religious Life during
the Billy Graham Crusades

In his memoirs, *Life with Billy*, Maurice Rowlandson, a key figure in the
BGEA in Britain stated: "During those twelve weeks from March to May
1954, Harringay became a way of life."[1] Graham's crusades had indeed
entered the modern, urban households of tens of thousands of Britons,
through prayer, choir meetings, movie screenings, and the many preparatory
meetings for the revival. It was a way of life shared by the crowds heading
to and from Harringay on buses and trains, enthusiastically singing hymns
as they went, many making the journey more than once with friends and
relatives in tow. It was a way of life experienced by those who volunteered and
trained as counselors and stewards. It even penetrated the lives of those who
did not attend in person but heard about Graham in the multiple mentions
in radio broadcasts and in the conversations of daily life. Many who later
remembered Harringay highlighted the spontaneity and dynamism that
the revival meetings brought to their homes and churches. In Berlin and
New York as well, contemporary observers noted a new energy in religious
circles after Billy Graham had been to town.

For those running prayer groups in their homes and offices and for those
who organized and took part in joint travel to the crusades, the boundaries
between private religiosity and public mass evangelism blurred. Graham was
their focus and inspiration, but it was those ordinary Christians who turned
the crusades into a powerful force of renewal for churches and everyday religious life. While ministers, church leaders, businessmen, and politicians
had an interest in orchestrating the 1950s revival, it was the thousands of
Christians running the everyday preparation for the crusade who shaped the
revival from the bottom up, in close interplay with, but also beyond, existing
church structures. Despite the burgeoning historiography on Graham himself, we do not know much about these ordinary Christians. More generally,

Altar Call in Europe. Uta A. Balbier, Oxford University Press. © Oxford University Press 2022.
DOI: 10.1093/oso/9780197502259.003.0005

we know little about those who lived and prayed during the 1950s revival and by doing so carried it forward.

Graham played an important role in shaping their religious lives: his religious offer, as shown in Chapter 1, had already loosened concepts of belonging and obligation held by many Christians: this newfound freedom released new dynamics and sources of energy that became tangible in the different practices through which ordinary Christians prepared the spiritual ground for the crusade in their own local and private surroundings. This perspective offers important insights into the dynamics and mechanisms of the 1950s transatlantic revival. It also brings important national differences to light: while a clear revival took place in postwar Britain and the United States, as argued by Callum Brown and Robert Wuthnow, the German revival was more constrained and contested.

In the everyday practices of those attending the crusades, from collective prayer to joint pilgrimages, the boundaries between the profane and sacred were in constant flux. Their religiosity emerged from the uniquely modern, consumption-orientated, urban culture in which the crusades were embedded and that incorporated with ease profane practices, objects, and motivations. Graham's commitment to taking religion back into secular, urban spaces, with a message that was profane, politicized, business oriented, and deeply sacred at the same time, inspired his followers to similarly challenge and blur those categories. In this process, his followers joined an international family of faith through the way they imagined themselves as part of Graham's ministry and carved out their own role within the crusade machinery.

Pray for Billy Graham!

For future crusade participants, the revival meetings began months before the opening night and well before any publicity began appearing on billboards and in advertisements around the host cities. The spiritual journey began when they joined one of the many prayer groups whose task it was to prepare for Graham's arrival. Indeed in 1949 in Los Angeles, prayer was a lived reality for those involved in the spiritual support of the local crusade. The process started a year and a half in advance, with several prayer groups organizing all-day gatherings. Rev. Armin R. Gesswein vividly remembered the commitment and power of those he called, with affection, the many "old prayer warriors" who guaranteed that "prayer was very strong."[2] He saw those as the real makers of the Los Angeles crusade: "And God certainly answered prayer. I am sure that this Crusade came out of heaven."[3] The way Gesswein describes prayer highlights the quintessentially transcendent nature of the practice. It also shifts the explanation of the success of the Los Angeles campaign away from Graham himself and focuses instead on the thousands who individually and collectively prayed for him. As Graham remarked after the campaign: "Anyone could preach with that prayer support."[4]

The sacredness of prayer, however, did not mean that it could not be administered and delegated in a secular and businesslike manner. The organization of ever tighter prayer chains symbolized the early professionalization of Graham's revival work and demonstrates how easily religious practices blended with organizational skills and business rigor. "All evangelists ask for prayer and get it, but Billy works harder to get more prayer," recalled Gesswein.[5] The Atlanta revival of 1950 saw for the first time a highly sophisticated organization of cottage prayer meetings through the crusade's executive committee. The press reported that the organizers hoped to form one thousand cottage prayer meetings, with at least ten participants each, to pray for the crusade opening on October 29.[6] To meet the challenge, precise instructions were circulated stipulating the creation of prayer districts, the appointment of district lieutenants, the timing and procedure of the meetings, and the distribution of topic cards.[7] But the main incentive behind the formation of the prayer groups was to take religion back to the people and into their private homes.[8]

When Graham and his team crossed the Atlantic to prepare the ground for the Greater London Crusade they brought the American prayer chains with them. Thus, the London prayer organization developed as a mirror image of the American practice. The prayer subcommittee copied the formats used by the local campaign organizers in the United States, in particular the so-called cottage prayer meetings.[9] The prayer support for the Greater London Crusade was organized by the crusade's prayer subcommittee chaired by Rev. Geoffrey R. King. A quarter of a million so-called prayer cards were sent out one year before the start of the Harringay crusade. A detachable portion could be filled in and sent back to the crusade office to pledge personal prayer support and to indicate interest in receiving regular prayer letters. By June 1953, the first thirty-six hundred prayer partners had enrolled. Their number rose to sixty-five hundred in the following three months and up to an estimated twenty-five thousand at the time of the crusade.[10]

Not only was the scheme inspired by the American prayer meetings, but during the preparation of the Harringay crusade American voices were repeatedly printed in the prayer newsletters to stir and shape the program. In Prayer Newsletter Number 2, Jerry Beavan was quoted in support of the idea of forming prayer groups in neighborhoods, offices, and industrial plants.[11] Accordingly, London was divided into 120 areas, in which five hundred cottage prayer groups formed under the leadership of Ada Scarles. Prayer groups of all sizes, from only two or three to more than twenty participants, met usually once a week for about thirty to forty-five minutes. Local churches also kept the crusade on their agenda during weekly prayer meetings and nights of prayer that were held before the immediate opening of the crusade. Christians at Spurgeon's Tabernacle in working-class Elephant and Castle, St Mary Magdalene Community Hall in densely populated Holloway in North London, and at St Paul's Portman Square in upper-class, centrally located Marylebone prayed between 10:00 p.m. and 6:00 a.m. for the success of the crusade.[12] More prayer nights took place parallel to the events at Harringay, for example at Duke Baptist Church in Richmond, where prayers were held every Friday night from 6:00 p.m. to 6:00 a.m. the following morning.[13]

In May 1954, the secretary of the London organizing committee, Roy Cattell, sent out the organizing committee's first prayer newsletter to the prayer partners. Ten more would follow until April 1954, by which time the crusade was already well underway. The prayer newsletters showed the ambition to structure, organize, and regulate every aspect of the revival preparation. From the top, they provided "fuel for praise and prayer," in the words of prayer committee chairman Rev. Geoffrey R. King.[14] In great detail, the prayer committee asked for prayer for particular aspects of the crusade preparation, for certain team members, for special meetings, and for specific programs, such as the screenings of *Oiltown U.S.A.* These were also published in the *London Crusade News.* They recommended literature to be used in the prayer circles and encouraged, for example, the purchase of E. M. Bounds's *Power through Prayer* through the crusade office.[15]

Despite the high degree of regulation, the prayer groups empowered local Christians, giving them the feeling of actively taking part in the crusade preparation. Reports in the prayer newsletter assured those who prayed that they made a difference: the prayer committee publicly thanked those who prayed to secure the lease on the Harringay Arena.[16] Prayer was considered a productive, committed, and efficient way of supporting the organization of the crusade, as in the words of Reverend King: "Yes, real prayer is work and hard work at that."[17] Apart from the lease on Harringay, London prayer groups prayed for other practical requirements, such as choosing the right location for meetings and finding additional office space in the heart of London.[18] Through their prayers these profane concerns gained spiritual value in the minds of those who prayed.

Even though the German local organizers admired the liveliness of the British prayer groups during their explorative visits to Harringay, they found it hard to get a similarly structured scheme off the ground in their own country. The first German mission included only two one-day visits to Berlin and Düsseldorf, and although there was no pressing need for several weeks of prayer support, the German organizers still wanted a solid level of prayer for Graham's mission. Wilhelm Brauer took the initiative in setting up a prayer chain inspired by his London experiences.[19] But the endeavor was less professionalized: instead of the skillfully printed prayer newsletters seen in London, a woman by the name of Heide Meister circulated a very personal letter to enlist prayer partner support for the upcoming German visits.[20] The letter captured the awakening effect of Graham on the German Christian landscape. Observing the counselors, prayer partners, and choir members involved in the preparation, one of the organizers was quoted: "If we ever worked that hard, no Billy Graham would need to come!"[21] In the end, three thousand prayer partners enrolled into the chain to prepare Berlin for Graham's arrival. On the evening of June 26, the day before the revival meeting at the Olympic Stadium, the organizers invited those prayer partners to a joint prayer meeting at the Südsternkirche, conducted by Referent Golze and Dr. Fichtner, president of the Berlin City Mission.[22] German local organizers also felt empowered and legitimized through prayer: "We felt again and again that obstacles were removed through prayer and ways were cleared."[23]

Despite their commitment to and empowerment through prayer, the organization of the German prayer chain in 1954 revealed that the Berlin and Düsseldorf organizers still lagged behind London's professionalism. But the confidence instilled by Brauer and Deitenbeck did begin to pay off later, with organized prayer during future Graham campaigns reflecting a growing professionalization of evangelistic revival work in Germany. Just a year after his first visit to Germany, in April 1955 the German organizers proudly informed Graham of an existing prayer chain that had prayed for the follow-up work of his 1954 visit and for his return in 1955. The prayer chain included Christians in West and East Germany, highlighting how easily prayer crossed the Iron Curtain, creating a sense of unity in a divided country.[24] The prayer support for the 1955 German visit peaked in a prayer meeting at the Gustav-Adolf-Kirche in Nuremberg, which attracted a thousand people on the eve of Graham's revival meeting in the city.[25] Publications issued by the organizers also indicated an increasing awareness that their revival work was being supported through prayer across denominations in all parts of the world.[26]

In 1960, the German organizing committee finally adopted the practice of sending out a prayer newsletter every six to eight weeks, a clear sign that they had caught up with their counterparts in London and New York. The scope of their operation had become ambitious, creative, and highly professional: they distributed three hundred thousand prayer cards as supplements to religious newspapers such as the *Sonntagsblatt*;[27] some seven thousand men and women formed prayer circles to pray for the upcoming three-week campaign in Berlin, Hamburg, and Essen;[28] and the organizers in all three cities hosted prayer meetings in the revival tent ahead of the official services, attracting between two and three thousand people each day.[29]

For advice and inspiration the German brethren profited from ongoing meetings with Graham's team members Jerry Beavan and Charlie Riggs in which the topic of prayer featured prominently.[30] They did so for good reasons—the New York Crusade of 1957 had set the benchmark for the organization of prayer support. The first Prayer Planning Conference for the New York Crusade had been held in New York in November 1956, bringing together Willis Haymaker as prayer coordinator, Armin Gesswein, director of prayer commission for the NAE, and Tom Carruth, director of prayer fellowship of the Methodist Church.[31] In January 1957, Rev. Floyd George, pastor of the Hanson Place Methodist Church in Brooklyn, joined the team as chairman of the prayer committee.

The importance of prayer was highlighted by the fact that Haymaker, the brains behind the citywide prayer programs of past campaigns and the most experienced member of the Graham team, was put in charge of setting up the New York prayer program. Haymaker designed a three-tier prayer program to reach thousands of people at local, national, and international levels. The prayer program for New York was organized through prayer partner cards, and by December 1956, three thousand requests were arriving each day in the New York office.[32] This was on a completely different scale than the Harringay crusade. By April 1957, there were twenty-two hundred ladies' daily home prayer meetings, eight hundred men's industrial prayer meetings, and one hundred prayer groups in schools and higher-education institutions.

Prayer support at the local level was, as during all Graham crusades, organized along gender lines: the women's division of the prayer program established cottage prayer meetings, while the men's section was responsible for prayer support in the world of business, in industrial plants, stores, offices, and corporations.[33]

As the opening day of the New York Crusade approached, the starting date for the prayer program was set at Tuesday, April 2, 1957. As in London, the structure of the prayer program was top-down and hierarchical. The prayer chain was run by area directors and prayer group leaders. Literature including Graham's short pamphlet *Prayer* and a folder containing Bible references, prayer topics, and copies of the *New York Crusade News* was distributed through the executive committee's prayer subcommittee. By late April the executive committee reported that 105,992 prayer partners had enrolled in twenty-nine hundred prayer groups.[34] But these big numbers only fueled even greater ambition: neighborhoods already enrolled in prayer programs were instructed to use prayer cards to find new prayer partners.[35] The office in Minneapolis reportedly contacted one million people to ask for joint prayer. Finally, on May 14 and 15, as Billy Graham was preparing to take the platform at Madison Square Garden, all-night prayer meetings were scheduled right across America.[36]

Inside the Prayer Groups

Even though prayer group leaders were at liberty to run their meetings in their own style, many probably followed the choreography set out by the executive committee: meetings should open, the committee suggested, with the singing of a familiar hymn, followed by reading and discussion of the daily scripture passage and a deeply devotional prayer: "The prayers should not be too long, they should be specific, and audible so that all in the group can hear prayer being made."[37] Time was set aside for personal prayer requests and to share stories about prayers being answered, which gave every prayer partner the opportunity for individual, unregulated contributions. For all those participating, prayer was not just a way to connect to the transcendent, but a sociable act in which they as individuals and as members of the emerging Billy Graham community "ritualized their beliefs."[38] Prayers were made in front of others and heard by others, which turned them into an important instrument of a new evangelical style.

To help with this ritualization process, the prayer subcommittee advised prayer partners to empower participants by taking "the prayer meetings to the people," by rotating between different houses and apartments, and certainly not churches.[39] Emphasis was put on creating a relaxed atmosphere, highlighting the everyday character of cottage prayer meetings: "Keep your prayer meetings informal. They are not 'dress up affairs.'"[40] Participants were encouraged to bring their Bibles, but the meetings were established as spaces outside the churches. They also urged organizers to resist asking ministers to preside.[41] Furthermore, the committee advised, no meeting should have more than ten participants—any more than that and another prayer group should be formed.

An image of a prayer group meeting published in the *New York Crusade Newsletter* illustrates how the crusade entered the living rooms of ordinary New Yorkers. It shows nine women and a local minister, a breach of the regulations, sitting on loosely arranged chairs, sofas, and ottomans in a modern apartment. The women, some holding open Bibles, faced each other in a room tastefully decorated with table lamps and colorful curtains. A cup and saucer on a side table in the front-left corner of the image indicates coffee had been served before the meeting started.[42] The message that the image sent could not have been more powerful: the old-time revivalism of the crusade had entered ordinary, and highly modern, New York homes.

These sacred crusade spaces within urban and suburban homes were constructed with the materials that the Graham team offered to the prayer groups, including traditional prayer booklets and Bibles brought along by the prayer partners.[43] But the New York organizing team also showed its skill at blending the traditional materiality of prayer groups with the new marketing and consumer opportunities of the 1950s by distributing plastic inlays for telephones to remind Graham's followers to pray for the New York Crusade. The advertisements enticing followers to order this missionary gimmick show how new evangelical merchandising connected with the world of consumption in terms not just of discourse but also of practice: "Cleverly designed of clear plastic, exactly the right size to slip on the center of the dial of the standard telephone instrument," the advertisement read, "the reminders carry the message: Pray for Billy Graham New York Crusade— Madison Square Garden, Begins May 15, 1957."[44] The sales pitch was undoubtedly successful: the initial allotment quickly sold out and the organizing committee reported a backlog of seven thousand orders. The plastic telephone inlays transported the presence of the crusade into thousands of

American households, anchoring it solidly in the everyday life of American Christians. Dialing a number and calling a neighbor turned into a quasi-spiritual practice.

Another object that took center stage in many prayer group meetings in the United States was the household radio. Since the Minneapolis campaign in 1950, local radio broadcasts, running for fifteen minutes between Monday and Friday, had been used to provide a unifying focal point for cottage prayer groups.[45] In New York, the broadcast campaign followed a similar pattern. Themed "Noon time is prayer time," prayer groups were knitted together by a daily broadcast from 12:15 p.m. to 12:30 p.m. on WABC—the 50,000-watt "flagship" station of the American broadcasting company."[46] They began on April 1 and featured short devotional messages by team members and prayer requests, all framed by devotional music.[47] The prayer groups were encouraged to meet at the time of the broadcast and to listen to it together. This practice set the American prayer groups apart from their European counterparts. Even though religious broadcasts were popular in Britain before World War II, the restricted access to airtime due to the lack of private radio stations made it impossible in Germany or the United Kingdom to utilize radio for prayer groups. When, in 1965, the London organizers of the Earl's Court crusade proposed running prayer programs on local radio stations, they were informed that this would "hardly be possible through the BBC."[48]

The New York Crusade's organizers did not just take faith to modern urban and suburban households, but also reached out to the industrial world of labor, which posed a very different set of challenges. The formation of industrial prayer groups was considered especially important because they added a spiritual dimension to "a realm known mostly for profit-and-products materialism."[49] A short booklet with the flowery title *Sanctity on the Assembly Line* addressed some of the major concerns about the relationship between spiritual commitment and industrial productivity. In a circular to business owners, Haymaker himself assured them that, in his experience, prayer time was not a cost to businesses because employees, when given the opportunity of prayer during work hours, were keen to make up for lost time. Acknowledging the authority of management, Haymaker advised that groups should only be formed in close cooperation with the leadership of the plant, firm, or office. His suggestion to involve personnel directors and public relations managers in the discussions about the prayer groups embedded them firmly in US business culture.[50] Even so, Haymaker was not entirely convinced that appropriate spiritual leadership existed within the industrial realm: while he encouraged women to run their cottage prayer meetings without any church representative present, the organizers of industrial prayer meetings were asked to secure the support and leadership of local ministers, Salvation Army workers, or YMCA men.[51]

Meanwhile, the New York Crusade organizing committee asked the industrial prayer groups to report back to them on their activities. Joseph Overkamp, who ran an industrial prayer group at Federal Industries in Belleville, New Jersey, sent such a report on the activities of his small group, which worked across denominational lines, and which met three times per week. Overkamp diligently recorded the Bible texts his group had discussed and their prayer topics, which covered support for the organizing committee, the music ministry, and the crusade counselors. Again secular challenges were addressed with the same rigor as spiritual ones: a prayer for the new office assistant was listed, as was one for the "T.V. offer of Record 'How Great Thou Art.'"[52] Overkamp's group worked ecumenically across denominational lines and brought different faith traditions together in prayer. The groups also acted as fundraisers: in his final report to the crusade organizers Overkamp enclosed a donation of five dollars. At the group's last meeting, Overkamp presented each participant with a copy of the Billy Graham publication "The Secret of Happiness," which he had purchased during one of his own visits to Madison Square Garden.[53] In doing so, Overkamp demonstrated the creative and personal ways in which prayer group leaders ran their groups, connecting them to the crusade experience and turning them into a lasting memory.

Reports such as those by Overkamp offer a rare and invaluable insight into the atmosphere and forces at work within these prayer groups. Despite operating under a hierarchical structure that aimed to establish a unifying evangelical style of prayer support, the groups nevertheless developed their own dynamics and culture. And beyond these formal groups, there were undoubtedly many more spontaneously formed prayer gatherings that were not recorded in official accounts, such as the example from London of a "bed-ridden lady [who] arranged with some of her bedridden friends to pray for the crusade at a given time each week."[54]

A report submitted by Ada Scarles, who organized the cottage prayer groups in 1954 and the following year when Graham returned to London, gives some insight into the life of the prayer groups at the time of the Harringay crusade. The report was composed of statements from prayer groups' participants and leaders and highlighted their ecumenical and revivalist atmosphere. In one small village the chapel and church were said to have gathered for joint prayer for the first time "in living memory." Prayer groups organized at University College London sparked Christian fellowships among students. Girlfriends brought along their unconverted boyfriends and women their husbands. Small-scale revivals were noted, as well as broader testimonies to "a revival spirit of evangelistic zeal."[55] The report showed the important role that the prayer groups played in nurturing the revivalist atmosphere from below, taking the crusade to ordinary households and reaching out to the unchurched. The spiritual rigor and confidence created in the different prayer partners shines through the words of Thomas Livermore, who took part in a prayer meeting at St. Paul's, Portman Square: "We had some mighty times of prayer. They were wonderful times. And after about the second prayer meeting, I remember remarking one evening that we must change gear in our prayer because God is answering so wonderfully. We must ask at higher level."[56] All the reports, as limited as they were, indicated a significant transformative influence of the prayer meetings on the spiritual life of London: its increasingly ecumenical nature, the lively, on-the-ground revivalism, and the spiritual strengthening of individual participants.

Every night, prayer connected ordinary Christians in their own homes with the crusade itself. To establish this link as firmly as possible, the London partner newsletter encouraged a period of prayer every evening between 8:15 p.m. and 9:00 p.m., exactly the time at which the revival meetings took place at Harringay. It also reminded prayer partners to listen on the radio to Big Ben striking nine o'clock—the moment when Graham would be giving the invitation at the arena.[57] This enabled prayer partners to experience the spiritual and emotional climax of the event, and to envision themselves as supporters of Graham's work at Harringay through prayer.

Women's Prayers

Prayer meetings had yet another significant dimension and function: they empowered women within the crusade machinery.[58] Sources on women's roles in the crusade machinery are sparse, but considering their roles is important, not just at a time of increased interest into the gendered history of religion, but because Anne Braude's words still ring true: "Where women are present, religion flourishes, where they are absent, it does not."[59] Women constitute the majority of crusade participants and of converts, yet their voices are often lost in a narrative overshadowed by the all-male American evangelist. But numerous women pledged their support for Graham and worked in his shadow, most prominently Graham's wife Ruth, the First Lady of American evangelism.[60] Ruth never envied her husband's place in the public limelight and instead repeatedly spoke of the importance of the private home as "one of the greatest mission fields."[61] However, she took a special interest in the prayer groups and pulled strings in the background to influence their agendas. In February 1957, she suggested that prayer partners be asked to pledge prayer support for a specific team member and to write to that team member to assure him or her of this support, an idea enthusiastically endorsed by Grady Wilson.[62] This practice, which was encouraged during the New York Crusade, established a close emotional link between the prayer groups and the crusade team.

Ruth set the example, but many more local women discovered the prayer committee as their genuine home within the male-dominated crusade machinery. In doing so they chose the right vehicle to exert their influence: the central prayer committee was considered one of the most important, complex, "active and hard-working"[63] bodies within the local crusade organization. Being chairwoman of the women's prayer division involved much more than baking cookies and providing a warm meeting space, as became obvious in the description of the kind of woman the New York organizing committee hoped to appoint: "a deeply spiritual women with executive ability."[64] She would be supervising ten vice chairmen who were in charge of the ten different prayer districts (later twelve) set up in the Big Apple. The women's section of the New York Prayer Committee was formed under the leadership of Ruth Peale, wife of Norman Vincent Peale, the influential author of *The Power of Positive Thinking*. In Mount Joy, Pennsylvania, Mrs. Richard P. Sentz took out an advertisement in the local newspaper appealing for women to form an interdenominational prayer group, under the headline "Help Wanted Female."[65] Peale and Sentz were just two of the many women who demonstrated their own commitment and creativity in organizing thousands of cottage prayer groups.

And they all followed in the impressive footsteps of Ada Scarles, who led the Women's Prayer Committee in London 1954, organizing a prayer chain with an international dimension, and radiating confidence and professionalism when delivering her final report to the crusade committee. Scarles paved the way for the rise of influential British evangelical women within the crusade machinery. By the time Graham returned to the United Kingdom in 1966 for the Earl's Court crusade, women constituted almost 50 percent of the prayer committee, with Jean Rees, Ada Scarles, Mary Eggleton, and E. G. James all taking up positions.[66] Jean Rees, wife of evangelist Tom Rees, presided over the Women's Prayer Committee and enjoyed significantly more prominence in later crusade publications than her male counterpart leading the Men's Prayer Committee. She organized eight thousand prayer groups before the crusade, with publications describing her achievements approvingly through the profane and male terminology of planning and results: "Working through sub-chairmen and 'sub-sub-leaders,' she gradually created a multiplicity of prayer units such as no city had ever seen." Rees run a tight ship in her prayer groups and is quoted as saying: "You're here to pray. No nonsense now. Nobody backs out. If you can talk, you can pray."[67] The evangelist's wife was willing to demonstrate her very own leadership and organizational skills.

That the times were also changing in the evangelical world regarding gender roles manifested itself in the way Jean Rees articulated her own role and mission and the confident role she played within the executive committee organizing the Earl's Court crusade. Rees spoke openly about her belief in the spiritual superiority of women: "Their gift of being interested in others makes it easier for them to witness."[68] She expressed confidence in the future role that women would play in world evangelism and demonstrated her own leadership during the executive committee meetings: she was the one who proposed the time of the launch of Operation Andrew, an important strategic decision that was seconded by male member Rev. Kenneth Patterson.[69] She also took the lead on male activism in the field of prayer, suggesting in October 1965 that men's and mixed prayer meetings should be organized along lines similar to those in groups run by women. The committee took that suggestion so seriously that it "broke off for a time of prayer in order to ascertain who should be invited to lead this wider field."[70]

The increasing female power within the crusade machinery, however, led to conflicts behind the scenes that came to the fore during a visit to London by Ruth Graham in November 1965. On November 18, she addressed a prayer rally at City Temple in London with a thousand women in attendance. It is known that Jean Rees "gave a challenging and inspiring word" at the same occasion.[71] And indeed the aggressive rhetoric that Rees used at City Temple was remarkable. Basing her remarks on the opening chapter of the book of Nehemiah, Rees claimed that Graham "was not planning to conduct a spiritual picnic, but rather was inviting an aggressive warfare with the powers of darkness. Just as Nehemiah . . . could send up telegraphic prayers, so the women could launch 'prayer rockets' for their city."[72] Not many details are recorded, however, the contentious nature of Rees's words and style became obvious, when the idea took shape to invite Ruth Graham back to address a mass women's prayer rally to be held in St. Paul's Cathedral or at Westminster before the opening of the Earl's Court crusade. In early spring 1966, the prayer committee was informed "that other team members had expressed . . . the opinion that the proposed mass women's prayer meeting to be held in the week prior to the crusade, and addressed by Mrs. Graham, was unwise, owing to the distorted impression it could give the press of undue feminine interest."[73]

The subtext of this criticism was clear: women had found their voice within the crusade organization and were beginning to threaten the traditionally male leadership. And indeed, as Marie Griffith has marvelously shown in her study on the praying women in the charismatic fellowship Aglow, prayer is one practice that "provide[s] a means by which female submission may be subverted and transformed into a tool of authority."[74] The women who prayed for Billy Graham felt empowered: they made a significant contribution to the evangelistic endeavor; and they climbed the crusade hierarchy through the thousands of prayer groups they had successfully run. Women like Ada Scarles certainly did not turn into modern feminists, but they forcefully demonstrated leadership within a realm that was accessible to them because it was considered female and appropriate.

Global Prayer

Through prayer groups, the crusade entered the homes of ordinary Christians, blurring the boundaries between the public revival meeting and private spiritual practice as well as boundaries between the sacred practice of prayer and the secular setting of urban and suburban living rooms. Local congregations and individuals of faith felt as if they were taking an active part and making a significant contribution to Graham's ministry through prayer. Prayer was the practice that tied the local crusade supporters together. But even more so, prayer allowed Graham's followers around the world to imagine themselves as member of an international community of faith. Rev. Joe Blinco captured this dynamic when he spoke about the New York Crusade: "The shortest route to New York from any point of the world is not by the magnificent air lines that serve this fantastic age, but through the heart of God on the wings of prayer."[75] Armed with this thought, people could cross national boundaries and imagine themselves taking part in crusade meetings around the world through the practice of prayer. International prayer groups preparing for the New York Crusade pledged to "join hands across the seas in a great Band of Prayer."[76] However personal those individual moments of prayer might have been, they also fulfilled important "invisible institutional work" in the process of creating a global community of Billy Graham's followers.[77]

When the first prayer groups formed in support of the Harringay crusade, that chain itself was an American import. More importantly, the London prayer groups immediately plugged into an international network of prayer in support of Graham's ministry. Londoners did not just pray for the upcoming crusade at home, but also prayed and gave praise for successful crusades hosted by Graham across the world. In 1953, London prayer partners prayed for the crusades in Syracuse, Dallas, and Detroit. Brief reports on the US crusades printed in the prayer newsletters familiarized Graham's followers in Britain with the sort of everyday challenges encountered by those attending crusades in America—a bus strike in Syracuse or challenging weather conditions. But they also assured them that those could be overcome by the mighty power of prayer.[78]

Months before Harringay opened its doors, several international prayer groups formed in Europe, in the United States and Canada, Korea and India, as well as Australia and Africa with the help of missionary organizations such as the Church Missionary Society. Just as Londoners, encouraged and guided by prayer partner newsletters, had prayed since 1953 for the success of Graham's campaigns in the United States, so Americans too, prayed for the success of the London campaign. The audience present at Harringay Arena was well aware of this international spiritual backing. On the opening night, Cliff Barrows announced that Graham had received hundreds of telegrams and letters not just from the United States but from all over the world, including places such as Korea and New Zealand.[79]

These letters indicate the extent of the prayer support from America, in particular. With several newspapers covering the events in Harringay, messages were received from prestigious evangelical institutions such as Moody Church in Chicago and the influential First Baptist Church of Dallas, Texas. One member of First Baptist Church wrote to Graham about the joy he felt in supporting Graham's work in London as part of a local and national

Christian support community: "It is my pleasure to join with the thousands of Christians all over the United States and very especially with the several thousand in my own Church, the First Baptist, who intercede daily at the Throne of Grace for you and for the revival services you are conducting in that great City and Country."[80] Thousands of Christians all over the United States identified with Graham's work in England and imagined themselves as an intrinsic part of his mission abroad. Alice Simmons from First Baptist wrote to Graham enthusiastically, saying that she felt "that in my small way, through offerings and prayers, I am helping you in the Revival in England."[81]

Three years later, when Graham prepared for his New York Crusade, British Christians would return the favor. The *New York Crusade News* printed testimonies from prayer groups in England that enrolled in the crusade's prayer program. Three prayer groups at the Church of the Good Shepherd in Romford, Essex, explained the reasons for their commitment to the New York Crusade: "Our groups are part of the rich legacy from Harringay."[82] While some groups may have reassembled spontaneously, others followed the call sent by Willis Haymaker to the chairmen of the prayer committees of past crusade cities to revive their former prayer groups.[83] In 1956, Jerry Beavan telephoned Goodwin Hudson, a member of the Harringay organizing committee, to urge him to encourage prayer support not just in the United Kingdom, but also through the entire Commonwealth, making use of existing British missionary organizations.[84] With the increasing international dimension of Graham's ministry, these worldwide prayer chains linked together current and former crusade audiences. Prayer working alongside modern communication made the world appear much smaller.

Prayer for the New York Crusade was taking place in London, Basel, Mexico City, Havana, Hong Kong, and Tokyo, on a truly global scale. And it was also getting increasingly well organized. The prayer committee of the New York Crusade joined forces with the Prayer Life Movement, establishing a worldwide prayer chain. An extensive correspondence system was set up to link former crusade cities.[85] In April 1957, fifteen hundred international prayer groups gathered in forty-four countries. Five cities in India held all-night prayer meetings for the New York Crusade. Individuals now felt they were actively contributing to the worldwide evangelism of Billy Graham, transcending national boundaries through prayer. One Indian pastor made the point succinctly: "You have given us here in India a chance to take part in the New York Crusade, even from a distance, through the mighty medium of prayer."[86]

The figures were impressive: New York officials listed 8,731 world-wide prayer groups; the UK office reported 150,000 worldwide enrolled individual prayer partners, all praying in support of the New York Crusade.[87] Although Graham had only conducted very limited campaign work in Germany by 1957, the office in New York listed five prayer groups in Germany.[88] A bold initiative to reach out to Europe's ninety million German speakers was undertaken by a Swiss German-speaking congregation, which broadcast a prayer request in support of New York on the pan-European station Radio Luxembourg.[89] Despite the fact that the German prayer chains developed significantly more slowly than in the United States and the United Kingdom, only coming to full bloom before the 1960 crusade, the German evangelical organizers were becoming increasingly aware of the prayer support they were receiving from abroad. The special edition of the *Berliner Sonntagsblatt, die Kirche*, sold on the day of the Olympic Stadium crusade in 1954, assured the audience that tens of thousands around the world had put their hands together in prayer for the events in Berlin.[90] During one of the first organizing committee meetings for Graham's 1955 German mission, Wilhelm Brauer highlighted the importance of the fact that Christians outside the country were praying for Graham's return to Germany.[91] In London, Ada Scarles, who had successfully organized the cottage prayer meetings during the 1954 and 1955 Greater London crusades, now organized British prayer support for the European tour that would also bring Graham back to Germany for one week in 1955.[92] Representatives of the Graham team in Germany, including Jerry Beavan, assured the organizers that they would call on their worldwide networks to encourage millions of Christians to pray for the revival meetings in Germany just as they had prayed for revivals in other parts of the world,[93] Brauer, initially skeptical of Beavan's assurances, rejoiced after the 1960 revival meetings: "Our prayer at the local revival meeting united with those praying on all continents and who thought of our evangelist's work in this respective place."[94] The awareness of prayer support coming from abroad certainly contributed to the way in which German evangelicals increasingly imagined themselves as part of an international evangelical community of faith, and thus constitutes an important aspect of their internationalization.

Operation Andrew

One scheme that emerged from the London prayer groups exemplified the combination of commitment to revivalism and secular practicalities that characterized crusade organization in a modern metropolis. The brainchild of British evangelicals, the scheme saw churches and prayer groups chartering fleets of buses to transport their members and more importantly unchurched friends to the revival meetings. Operation Andrew, as it was called, was a direct response to the special challenges confronting the organizers of the first large-scale metropolitan crusade in Britain. Before the beginning of the crusade, Operation Andrew was introduced to the British audience in a prayer-partner newsletter.[95] The description of the program started with three quotations from the Bible referring to Andrew and how he had brought his brother to Jesus. The flyer, however, did not just make the scriptural case for Operation Andrew, it also described the modern phenomenon of urbanization as a significant factor in the creation of the new missionary tool that was simultaneously "scriptural, practical and effectual."[96] Operation Andrew embodied the modernization of missionary work, setting the template for the following decades. When Graham returned to London for his next large-scale metropolitan crusade in June 1966, the organizers again promoted Operation Andrew as "the application of 20th century methods to the 1st century Gospel message."[97]

The information page gave strict orders on how Operation Andrew should work: only church members plus one unchurched acquaintance each were permitted to travel on the chartered buses. The journey to and from the crusade should be used for praying, singing, and discussions about questions of faith, and that is what people did.[98] To provide serious spiritual counseling, Rev. Stephen Olford at Duke Street Baptist Church in Richmond in southwest London, for example, appointed six counselors, three male and three female, and a captain to serve on each of the twelve buses which left Richmond each night.[99] The London organizers defined Operation Andrew as the perfect space for individual evangelism.

At the crusade venue the travel companions would sit together in reserved sections. On their return home, some churches offered an open door, a welcoming tea or coffee, and an opportunity for further conversation and spiritual counseling, thereby establishing a close link between the revival meeting and the local churches.[100] The orchestration of Operation Andrew turned it into more than a bus ride. In the words of one Methodist coach trip organizer: riding on an Operation Andrew bus was "a pilgrimage to Harringay."[101]

Operation Andrew was perfectly designed for the pace and mobility of a modern city, and it is thus not surprising that it was exported as a concept to the United States for the New York Crusade. During an executive committee meeting in January 1957, which was discussing transport issues for the upcoming crusade, Charlie Riggs outlined the scheme that had been used so successfully in London.[102] The US Operation Andrew followed the UK model in such detail that the New York committee invited Reverend Olford, who had organized the fleets of buses from Richmond to Harringay, to publish his experiences in a small booklet entitled *Operation Andrew: Your Church's Most Vital Link to 20th Century Evangelism*. According to Olford, Operation Andrew reminded the churches of the responsibilities but also opportunities that came with evangelism. He stressed the importance of a systematic approach: each party's leader's responsibilities should include welcoming travelers onboard, observing their reaction during the crusade, and "organizing counselling on the return journey for those who required it."[103] Once back in Richmond, Olford said, he would invite his coach party to come to church next Sunday and give them a small souvenir, such as a booklet or a personal letter. Olford closed by pointing out how much the scheme had revitalized the London churches.

In the *New York Crusade News*, published in May 1957, Walter H. Smyth, director of the crusade's group reservations department, encouraged the use of Operation Andrew techniques, stating that "the effectiveness of this plan as a soul-winning effort cannot be over-emphasized."[104] In the American advertisements for Operation Andrew, sacred and secular reasoning blended as easily as it had on the other side of the Atlantic. The bus scheme was not just marketed as "a time of warm Christian fellowship"; it was also pointed out that it allowed participants to attend the crusade in probably the "most economical way," avoiding "traffic worries and parking problems."[105] Americans also took the advertisements for Operation Andrew into secular spaces. Bearing in mind the high number of female crusade participants, beauty parlors were identified as good marketing sites, as well as the traditional church bulletins and religious radio broadcasts.[106]

Stories that appeared in the local press about Operation Andrew confirm the vitality of this new missionary tool. A delegation traveling to New York from Virginia on a special train—a clear adaptation of Operation Andrew to American circumstances—arrived early in the morning with what they called a hymn-singing hangover. The party left Richmond the previous night on a train that included a chapel car. The railway company had created it by removing the tables from a diner and installing an electric organ. During the nine hours of the overnight trip, six Richmond pastors conducted services in rotation. Old-fashioned religious hymns were sung chain style.[107]

Christians promoted Operation Andrew in apartment blocks, businesses, and industrial plants, creating Christian fellowship in secular spaces exactly as the prayer groups did.

The American reports about the scheme, however, were different from those in the United Kingdom in one significant point: Operation Andrew blended seamlessly with the buzzing commercial atmosphere of 1950s New York City. For example, Operation Andrew participants were lured with the promise of dinner in New York City before the crusade meeting.[108] The "Crusade fare" for the chartered train from Virginia included a sightseeing cruise around Manhattan.[109] This was a heady mixture of big-city sightseeing and Christian commitment that could not be matched in London in 1954. Operation Andrew in New York City was not only important as a missionary practice, but as an iconographic link with US consumer culture—it became a symbol for the new mobility of evangelical faith in a secular world. The first crusade newsletter published after opening night exclaimed on page 1: "Police have named the 9th Ave. area where the buses are parked from 42nd Street to 57th Street, 'the longest bus stop in the world.'"[110] It was as if the media were attempting to capture the new dynamic in the world of faith, in the images of the thousands of cars, buses, and trains used to bring people to and from the crusades.

The bus rides were more than practical and symbolic; they also played an important part in the spiritual culture of the crusade and thus feature prominently in several conversion stories. Pete, a teenager finding Christ at the crusade, was reassured by the joint experience of leaving the crusade: "All the way home we sang Gospel songs and kids told what they had done that day. There were others saved in our bus load too, and that helped me a lot right to begin with."[111] One woman who traveled to Harringay on a charter hired by two nurses and their twenty-six girlfriends made her decision on the bus during a refreshment break while it was parked in a lot: "The nurse took her out to the bus and led her to the Lord."[112] Another young women, who arrived on one of the four hundred buses that drove nightly to the San

Francisco crusade in 1962, had stepped forward at the revival meeting, but
did not make it as far as the counseling room. She received her counseling on
the ride back.[113] These brief personal memories of Operation Andrew underline the scheme's importance as a space of lived religion in which participants
prayed, sang, conversed, listened in, and changed.

More significantly, Operation Andrew buses were ecumenical spaces in
which not just Christians and non-Christians met but which also brought
together Christians from different denominations.[114] Observers of the
Harringay crusade vouch for the presence of Jews and Catholics on the
Andrew buses.[115] Indeed, Operation Andrew helped to establish new
relationships between different churches. During the 1966 Earl's Court crusade, the Anglican church in Wigan, in northwest England, made contact
with the Baptist Chapel at Ampthill Bedford. Looking for a place to break
their two-hundred-mile journey to London, the Anglican congregation
was welcomed with open arms by the members of the Baptist congregation.
On the way to the crusade they stopped for tea and conversation, returning
after the Earl's Court service to spend the night at the houses of their Baptist
brethren. After a joint church service, at which both congregations wor-
shiped together, they enjoyed lunch before the Anglicans continued their
journey north. For many it had been a unique ecumenical encounter, its importance highlighted by the fact that it was reported in the *Baptist Times*.[116]
The participants in the Operation Andrew scheme lived the ecumenism that
Graham preached and that their ministers hoped to foster in the context of
the crusades.

As much as the scheme certainly contributed in a positive way to the
spiritual depth of the crusades, as damaging was its impact on the racial
composition of Graham's audiences in England and the United States. The un-
derrepresentation of racial and ethnic minorities at Harringay and Madison
Square Garden was often addressed in the press but rarely explained. When
looking closely at the organization of Operation Andrew, it becomes apparent that at a time when segregated housing districts were well established
in American cities and suburbs and landlords in the United Kingdom advertised for prospective tenants with signs reading "No Coloured, No Irish, No
Dogs,"[117] a transportation scheme that was mainly organized through personal relationships, churches, and neighborhoods reinforced the racial and
cultural homogeneity of Graham's crusades.

Yet the significant spiritual importance of Operation Andrew, as well as
the scheme's easy adaptability to modern, mobile, consumer culture, explains

its popularity in the United Kingdom and the United States in the 1950s. The planning of Graham's first extended three-city campaign in Germany in 1960, when he stayed for a week each in Essen, Hamburg, and Berlin, made the transfer of the scheme into the German context necessary. The racial and ethnic homogeneity of Germany in the decade before the arrival of large numbers of Turkish guest workers made conversation about which ethnic or racial groups the scheme might or might not include equally unnecessary. And the international spread of consumer culture made the adaptation process seamless.

At the beginning of December 1959, Jerry Beavan and Charlie Riggs, from Graham's team, personally briefed the German organizers, Paul Schmidt, Wilhelm Brauer, and Peter Schneider, on the past success of Operation Andrew and its importance for the upcoming crusade.[118] The three Germans were initially reluctant, insisting that Germany's famously efficient public transport system rendered it unnecessary. In the end, however, they were convinced by the "missionary opportunities" created through Operation Andrew.[119] They introduced the "Andreasplan," in a circular to all members of the central organizing committee in June 1960. Attached was a brochure that explained the goals and methods of the new missionary tool that was to be circulated among all participating congregations.[120] Mirroring the language of the British and American crusade organizers, the Andreasplan was couched in both religious and secular terms—advertised as an essential mode of transport to the crusade meetings and also as a missionary tool. The brochure promised: "many advantages, missionary and traffic-wise."[121]

As in the United States and the United Kingdom, thousands of German Christians made use of the organized bus transport. In 1960, 1,551 coaches ferried around eighty thousand people to and from the crusade meetings in the three host cities.[122] In Berlin, fifty buses brought four thousand participants to the revival meetings every evening. Individual congregations, particularly evangelical ones, created their own version of Operation Andrew by setting up carpools; those within walking distance organized joint marches to the revival tent.[123] Each initiative highlights how Graham's team inspired local participants to make their own unique contributions to the functioning of the crusade. With the backing of Graham's American advisers, spaces were created that local ordinary Christians filled with their personal understandings of mission, evangelism, and faith.

Moreover, just as in the United States and the United Kingdom, Operation Andrew became the icon of Billy Graham's modern pilgrimage (figure 4.1). Many German newspapers dedicated significant amounts of coverage to the description of the transport operation, capturing the new mobility in faith through images of the thousands of cars, buses, and trains that were used to bring people to and from the crusades. Against this background, the *Westfälische Allgemeine Zeitung* dedicated one of its crusade articles to Operation Andrew under the headline "Evangelisation beginnt im Bus," (evangelism begins on the bus) and many others at least mentioned the program.[124]

Even more attention was dedicated to the phenomenon in the church papers. Here the operation was discussed in the context of mission, the communication of faith, and the search for moments of community in the otherwise unfamiliar movement of mass revivalism. Hanns Lilje's *Sonntagsblatt* published an article on the preparations for Operation Andrew in Hamburg, which although cautious about its success, still

Figure 4.1 Visitors on their way to Billy Graham's closing rally in London, 1954 (copyrights: Johnson/ ANL/ Shutterstock)

expressed a deep belief that it could actually bring people in contact with Christianity who hadn't set a foot into a church for years. The article also pointed out that the scheme provided an important link between the individual and the mass experience.[125] That observation echoed the Evangelical Alliance's position that Operation Andrew was one of the most energetic connections between the revival event and local churches.[126] An article in the Hamburg church magazine *Die Kirche in Hamburg* opened with a picture of an Operation Andrew group getting back on their bus.

Operation Andrew made a lasting impression in Germany. The central church paper in Berlin covered Operation Andrew after the closing of the crusade and discussed it in the context of the need for more everyday missionary efforts. The author, Wilhelm Timmermann, asked if Christians should transform Operation Andrew into a daily task by communicating their faith to coworkers and neighbors and leading them to church.[127] In this context, Operation Andrew turned into a symbol for a more communicable faith. Operation Andrew was practiced again in Berlin in 1966 and during the Euro '70 campaign, when hundreds of buses brought audiences to each German city in which Graham held revivals. From its first use in 1960, Operation Andrew had become a permanent feature of the crusade experience in Germany.

Conclusion

The collected stories from inside the prayer groups and the Operation Andrew buses explain the dynamic impact that the crusades had on the local religious landscapes they took place in. Those practices and experiences often proved more lasting than Graham's preaching or the individual memories of the evenings at the crusade. In Jerry Beavan's words: "Often the local pastors have said that even if the Crusade had never been held, it was worth all the work just for the blessing of the united prayer meetings in the homes, offices, stores, etc."[128] Through organizing bus rides and prayer groups, local churches significantly contributed to the running of the crusade and were in return energized and rejuvenated.

"Despite the millions attending, Graham's work did nothing to arrest the imminent commencement of rapid secularisation," states Callum Brown in his history of religion in twentieth-century Britain.[129] And he is right;

church membership fell rapidly after the mid-1950s. But a close reading of the initiatives taken by local churches in preparation for Graham's crusades and during their running permits a different interpretation, one that captures a liveliness in religious circles that perhaps allowed them to resist secularization just a little bit longer. Graham strengthened those who were already churched; that is an assessment many contemporaries agreed on. Albert Neibacher from the St Luke's Lutheran Church in New York City noted: "We feel he [Graham] has done more for the churched than for the unchurched."[130] Through the personal contributions by the churched and some of the unchurched, Graham's crusades were able to make a lasting impact on local religious scenes. While Graham's crusades inevitably moved on, those who had chartered buses and organized prayer groups remained in their communities, continuing some of their practices, discarding others, but certainly keeping his memory alive.

The religious identities of those who joined prayer groups and rode on the Operation Andrew buses changed through their participation. Women found their voice and extended their power within the crusade machinery; and local organizers, such as Stephen Olford, grew from coordinators in Graham's name into spiritual leaders in their own right. And every single participant who prayed and rode on Operation Andrew buses took part in a fresh evangelical lifestyle. Those evangelicals imagined themselves and acted as a significant force within the crusade machinery and as members and makers of Graham's international family of faith. Graham never formed a church or a denomination, but through the religious practices that traveled with him and were encouraged and implemented by his team, he allowed his followers to imagine and express themselves as part of one international community of faith.

The prayer groups and bus rides show how easily participants combined their traditional religious practices with their changing modern and urban lifestyles. Modern mobility, marketing, and radio programs blended seamlessly with the traditional practice of pilgrimage and prayer. For those participants, " 'religion' cannot be neatly separated from the other practices of everyday life. . . . Nor can 'religion' be separated from the material circumstances in which specific instances of religious imagination and behavior arise and to which they respond,"[131] as Robert Orsi once noted. Those bending their heads in prayer for Billy Graham have not yet found entry in the religious histories of Germany, the United Kingdom, and the United States, even though they are important practitioners of a unique faith shaped in the interplay between the international, the urban, and the everyday.

There were significant local differences. The number of prayer groups that formed during the New York Crusade indicates that the revivalism taking place in the United States was not matched in the United Kingdom and even less so in Germany. Germany, in particular, lagged behind in terms of the professionalization of its revivalism—a factor explained by the distinct development of German evangelicalism, which never gained the numbers or cultural influence achieved in the United States or Britain. That is also precisely why its close work with and support of the Graham crusades would be so essential to the prosperity of the German evangelical milieu. Despite those differences, though, Graham's revival work was able to connect three different religious landscapes through the practice of prayer, precipitating the rise of an international community of Western evangelicals. This community formed at the revival meetings themselves and lived on in a shared memory of participation—two aspects that will be explored in the next chapter.

5

Experiencing Religion

Communities and Conversions at the Billy Graham Crusades

Whether in London, Berlin, or New York, most of the elements of a Billy Graham crusade never changed. There was the structured formal event that invariably ran like clockwork—the choirs and announcements; the joint singing with the congregation and the prayers with heads bowed; Graham's sermon delivered in his characteristic southern accent; and finally the call to step forward to accept Christ. There were also the informal experiences that were an important part of the occasion: the journeys of thousands of people to and from the venues by bus, train, tram, or car, with their noisy excitement and choruses of community singing. And once people were inside the arenas, there was the assault on the senses experienced by the crusade-goers, embracing the mundane and the uplifting: the aroma of sizzling sausages and the brush of shoulders with one's neighbor in the tightly packed seating; the glaring spotlights illuminating the stage and the soaring sound of thousands of voices. Alongside Graham's spiritual message and the commitment to Christ, these were the countless experiences—sights, sounds, smells, tastes, and touches, the sacred and the profane—which ingrained themselves in the memories of all those who attended. This immersive practices and performances of a Graham crusade were colorfully captured in a report on the Madison Square Garden revival in 1957 in the *Jamaica Press* of New York:

> Seldom has such sound been heard over Broadway. It's the spine-tingling vibrancy of thousands of voices blending in lyric gospel hymns. . . . Familiar rhythmic old hymns are chosen for the massed singing—instead of formal church music—and strains of "Trust and Obey" and "What a Friend We Have in Jesus" make the rafters throb. Song leader Cliff Barrows slices and slams the air, his body stretching, as he leads the white-shirted, 1,500 voices choir. The whole congregation frequently joins in. . . . But whatever spell

Altar Call in Europe. Uta A. Balbier, Oxford University Press. © Oxford University Press 2022.
DOI: 10.1093/oso/9780197502259.003.0006

the music weaves, Graham adds to it a persuasive finale after he steps to the microphone.[1]

At the heart of every revival meeting was a process of transformation from the secular to the sacred—an emotional transformation experienced by many of those in the audience and a physical transformation of the revival arena itself. The process began from the moment a visitor entered the crusade hall, often hours before Graham appeared. There was the noise—the scraping of chairs across the floor, the clink of coins dropped into offering tins, singing among the crowd, quiet prayers and murmurs of anticipation. There was the presence of the media—film cameras whirred and photographers snapped and flashed their pictures. But as soon as Graham stepped to the podium this hubbub ceased and thousands fell silent. On the opening night at Harringay in 1954, Graham emphasized this transformation of the space. Before beginning his sermon he asked the press photographers to put down their cameras, with the words: "This is a holy moment, a sacred moment for which we have long prayed."[2]

Indeed it was a long-awaited moment for the many thousands involved in staging the events: the culmination of months of preparation by prayer groups; by those running the buses that brought in the visitors; and by the ministers, marketeers, and fundraisers who had devoted their time and energy to making Graham's mission a success. And for many of those who were present, it was the moment when they would experience for the first time a fresh and "modern faith" as Christian consumers, connecting themselves through prayer and song with Graham's worldwide evangelical community.

Many had been motivated to help behind the scenes because they believed Graham's American-style religious offer presented them with an opportunity to imagine themselves and their faith in new ways. Attending the crusade in person now allowed their imaginations to become real.[3] Participants experienced the revival through all their senses: they smelled and tasted the food on sale in the arenas; they listened to the music and the sermon; their eyes took the revival space in; they felt the breath and touch of those around them.[4] In these ways, Graham's revival meetings were the enactment of abstract notions of a more modern faith that had been so widely debated in Europe in the 1950s—an orchestrated blend of the sacred and the profane. This modern faith, observed by the sociologists Ole Rjis and Linda Woodhead, was "dominated not by the consecrations of higher authority, but by the promptings of personal experience and conviction."[5] But even though crusade participants encountered a new religious offer and spiritual opportunity, they often experienced and narrated the transcendent nature of the events in very traditional ways.

On the face of it there would seem to be few similarities between the "quite messy mix of religion, entertainment and politics"[6] on show in Graham's mid-twentieth-century revival meetings, and the revivals of previous centuries. But in many important respects parallels with earlier revivals can be drawn. The cultural historian Christoph Ribbat has highlighted the presence of tearful, fainting girls during the nineteenth-century revival of the so-called Schwärmer, evangelical, apostolic, and Pentecostal revival groups in Germany.[7] David Bebbington in his transnational study of Victorian religious revivals also records the "unashamed tears" of those answering the altar call.[8] Both interpret these nineteenth-century displays of emotion as expressions of underlying class conflicts, struggles over religious authority, and responses to political change and challenges. Similarly, I argue, the tears shed at Graham's revival meetings reflected Cold War anxieties and economic aspirations, demonstrating an individual commitment to a new form of faith—an emotional dynamic that has been largely overlooked by religious historians of twentieth-century Europe. Therefore, Graham's revival meetings in London, Berlin, and New York stand in the long tradition of earlier revival meetings as a powerful religious response to social and cultural change, even though they took place in what was seen by many as an increasingly disenchanted world.

In this final chapter we will accompany Graham's audiences into the very arenas where his revival meetings were held, observing how they encountered and experienced a modern faith through their negotiation of a new relationship between the sacred and the secular. Building on studies of earlier revivals that see audiences at revival meetings functioning as fluid religious communities in their own right, I will also demonstrate how different religious communities formed and overlapped at Graham's crusade meetings.[9] They were important forums for those in search of a modern faith who had hitherto been reluctant to step forward, and they functioned as a lived religious community in which relationships formed and emotions were shared, challenging the widely held perceptions of the anonymity of mass evangelism. And, of course, each of Graham's successful revival meetings saw a step taken along a path toward a transnational community of Graham's followers that spanned the globe. The communities that emerged from the Graham crusades embodied hopes, emotions, and ambitions that fueled the transatlantic revival and embraced a new form of faith shaped by a rapidly modernizing world.

A Modern Community of Faith

In the eyes of his many European critics, Graham took faith where it did not belong. Those who arrived on the hundreds of chartered buses, emerged from their parked cars, or poured out of the nearby subway stations in London, Berlin, and New York found themselves entering secular event spaces. Tainted with memories of a dark German past in the case of the Olympic Stadium in Berlin, bathed in the consumerist glamour of Madison Square Garden, or cherished as the locus of the London sporting scene such as Harringay Arena, all these venues had one thing in common—they were, and were perceived as being, quintessentially secular.

The arriving crowds would have already been familiar with the output of Graham's immense advertising campaigns—billboards, placards, and flyers had been part of their everyday lives for weeks across their home towns and cities. Now as they queued to enter the venue, they were confronted with more marketing. Above the southwest entrance to Harringay Arena the giant billboard read, "Hear Billy Graham. 7.30. All seats free. 1000 voice choir." Outside Madison Square Garden the illuminated signs boasted: "Nightly at 7.30 pm Billy Graham New York Crusade. Air-conditioned. All seats free." In Berlin, the crowds making their way to the Olympic Stadium walked past the blue placards with the invitation: "Jung, modern, Christ—Man muß ihn hören" ("Young, modern, Christian—you must hear him").[10]

Outside the stadia, those waiting to get in could catch up with the latest Cold War headlines by buying an evening newspaper; or they could purchase chocolate snacks to munch on during the long wait for proceedings to begin. At Wembley Stadium, where the London crusade closed, those who sought a moment of prayer and reflection while queuing for admission were likely to be interrupted by vendors shouting, "Buy a souvenir of Billy Graham, only penny 'apenny.'"[11] Inside there was no escape from the world of consumption—Coca-Cola, sweets, and hot dogs were all on sale.[12] The *London Crusade News* as well highlighted the catering arrangements for Harringay, informing readers that several snack bars at the arena would be open before and after the event. For those interested in a more formal sit-down dinner, the main restaurant would serve meals from 6:00 p.m.

onward.[13] These new Christian consumers were as well looked after as they would be on a night out at any popular entertainment event.

The organizers contributed to this culture of consumption by selling their own wares, especially books and Bibles, within the revival spaces. A new German translation of Graham's *Peace with God* was on sale at the Olympic Stadium, alongside reprints of the New Testament for ten Pfennig each.[14] *The Greater London Crusade Song Book*, compiled by Cliff Barrows, was sold at Harringay, raising £3,000.[15] At Madison Square Garden, sales of Graham's books, gospel recordings, and Bibles outstripped those of Coca-Cola and frankfurters.[16] When Graham returned to Germany in 1960 for a three-week crusade, his books again proved to be bestsellers. The German translation of *Peace with God* sold 9,164 copies; *Billy Graham Talks to Teenagers* 9,250 copies, and *The Secret of Happiness* 4,975 copies.[17] By 1966 Graham's merchandising had reached another dimension, with stalls at the London crusade at Earl's Court selling records and the "Billy Graham Verse-a-Day Scripture Key Chain."[18]

While modern consumer culture established a foothold in many revival spaces, religious culture also reclaimed parts of the secular arenas. Venues that were more accustomed to hosting boxing, football, or ice hockey were reconfigured to make them suitable for the revival meetings. At Harringay, a rostrum that had been built for the pulpit was flanked by a Hammond organ, a grand piano, and seating for honorary guests and the platform party. The scene was illuminated by powerful spotlights. Ten thousand seats were laid out on the floor and a further 1,500 installed behind the rostrum for the choir.[19] Madison Square Garden made some less obvious but equally significant adjustments: hot-dog stands were banned from selling cigarettes, and beer signs were covered with strips of cardboard.[20] Little else was changed: the crusade organizers simply took full advantage of a ready-made, high-tech, air-conditioned auditorium with 18,500 seats and newly installed escalators.[21]

Just as the venues embraced consumer culture in a religious setting, so did the audiences. As people took their seats, they posed for souvenir pictures, snacked on their purchases, and chatted with those around them.[22] At the Olympic Stadium in Berlin, teenagers were seen smoking, and toddlers crawled about in the audience.[23] The minister of the Fifth Avenue Presbyterian Church of New York, Dr. John Sutherland Bonnell, blamed the atmosphere of Madison Square Garden for conspiring "to create a spectator mood for the first 15 minutes."[24]

But gradually the atmosphere in these spaces changed as the evening got underway, with audiences becoming increasingly aware that they were surrounded by religious content and texts. At Harringay a massive cube was suspended above Graham's pulpit with each side showing the verse from John 14:6: "Jesus said: I am the way, the truth, and the life."[25] At Wembley in 1955, the same verse was displayed in front of the scoreboard, with Graham's call for the audience to join together to read it aloud contributing to a powerful religious presence inside the stadium.[26] The same quotation appeared at Madison Square Garden, positioned just above the platform and the two thousand choir stalls. As one convert recalled: "I can never forget the sudden feeling of hope I received through the clear message of that banner."[27] In 1954, the Berlin organizers opted instead to put Matthew 11:28 on the scoreboard: "Come to me, all you who are weary and burdened, and I will give you rest." The use of that part of stadium architecture for religious signage was a clear transformation of its function and meaning as a space of popular sports culture.[28]

For the press, this blurred line between entertainment culture and religion, which was inherent in the choice of venues, was a great opportunity for creative and engaging copy. With Harringay a regular venue for boxing, the columnist Cassandra wrote in the *Daily Mirror* about Graham's first London crusade, under the headline: "Billy Graham versus the Devil": "I must say that it was a thundering good contest with the Rev. Billy Graham (height 6 ft. 2 in., weight 11 st., reach 74 in.) beating the Prince of Darkness on points."[29] German and American journalists amused their readers with similar popular narratives and sports metaphors.[30] The *Journal-American* published a cartoon of a disheveled looking Devil beaten by the well-toned prizefighter Billy Graham.[31] While on the face of it much of this content was lighthearted, it actually documented a religiosity that was confidently reestablishing itself in the marketplace of popular culture.[32]

Thanks largely to the enthusiastic singing and praying of the audience, the transformation of the secular event spaces into sacred settings took place long before Graham stepped to the pulpit for his sermons. Cliff Barrows noted this at the Los Angeles revival in 1949, when "some of the best singing was that which took place before the service actually began, as the people sat together thinking and praying. They just naturally burst into songs of praise and thanksgiving to God, such songs as "Shall We Gather at the River" and "There's a Land that Is Fairer Than Day."[33]

Barrows built on this transformational power of music with his mass choirs, which at some Graham crusades brought together up to two thousand voices. On the evening of the first crusade at Harringay, Barrows's choir opened with "Praise to the Lord, the Almighty" set to a German tune, creating a "devotional atmosphere" from the start."[34] Ninety days later, when the crusade ended at Wembley Stadium, 110,000 voices again joined in this German traditional hymn, turning the home of England's national football team into a cathedral. Bonnell described a similar transformation at the opening night at Madison Square Garden. He observed that during the first fifteen minutes, the audience was wrapped up in the spectacle but not yet caught by the spirit of worship. "It was not until the 1,500-voice choir began to sing the Lord's Prayer that a hush descended on the audience and slowly this great sports arena became a cathedral."[35]

The community singing of thousands of people was itself a highly emotional experience for those taking part. Morag Allardice, who reported on the opening night at Harringay for the *British Weekly*, describe the "thrill" of hearing the congregation sing "Guide Me, O Thou great Jehovah" to the tune of "Cwm Rhondda."[36] When Barrows encouraged the New York audience to join in with the choir toward the finale of "The Lord's Prayer," many were moved to tears.[37] Not surprisingly, the importance of the music is often recalled in the accounts of those who answered Graham's altar call.[38] Singing allowed every member of the audience to contribute to the creation of a spiritual atmosphere, a feeling that peaked in the moment when Graham made his altar call. The audience was not just participating in the spectacle, but also creating it, just as many had done for months during their prayer meetings, choir practices, and counselor-training sessions.

While the crusade venues ensured that individuals entered a space unlike any they had experienced before, the hymns often tied their experiences to their personal religious traditions and local contexts. British Methodists were pleased to see that thirty of the hymns in the crusade songbook at Harringay were also part of their Sunday hymn books: the chorus of one of their favorites, "Blessed Assurance" by Fanny Crosby, was sung every night,[39] and as a result would gain newfound popularity in British and American churches.[40] The sound of Cwm Rhondda transported the audience at Harringay to the hinterland of Welsh Methodism, while "Let the Lower Lights Be Burning" introduced traditional American revival tunes.[41] At Madison Square Garden many familiar American gospel hymns, including "This Is My Story, This Is My Song" and "Amazing Grace" were sung. German audiences sang their traditional hymns in Berlin in 1954, including the Lutheran classic "Ein feste Burg ist unser Gott," which had also appeared in English translation in the Harringay crusade songbook. Other songs gained worldwide popularity through the Graham crusades, such as "I'd Rather Have Jesus Than Silver and Gold," composed and performed by Beverly Shea, who traveled with the Graham team to London, Berlin, and New York. The hymns strengthened the crusades' roots in different denominational settings and local traditions, but also constructed a specific transnational context as popular hymns from one crusade were integrated into another. "How Great Thou Art" and "Just as I Am" proved especially popular and became a strong component of the crusade memory for thousands, so shaping the musical vocabulary of evangelicals around the world.[42]

But the main purpose of the music was to prime the audience for the moment Graham stepped to the podium to deliver his sermon. An important role in this task was played by Shea, who delivered his last solo immediately before Graham left his seat. In the words of Edith Blumhofer: "Graham found that Shea's singing prepared his heart to preach, while others noticed that it also quieted the audience and disposed them to listen."[43] Graham then moved into the spotlights flooding the rostrum, a moment recalled by the sociologists Kurt and Gladys Lang, who attended the New York Crusade: "Once there, Graham dominated the Garden. All that had taken place before his entry was but a prelude to his appearance, and all that the evangelist would do and say after the beginning of the sermon would be but a prelude to the final appeal, the call for the decisions for Christ."[44]

Graham's preaching focused mainly on traditional themes such as the existence of God, the meaning of the cross and resurrection, and sin and forgiveness. He built on the conviction that men had to be reborn in order to live a fulfilled Christian life. And he tied his biblical explanations to current political issues such as the political instability of the Middle East and the Cold War. When preaching on the opening night at Harringay, Graham focused his remarks on John 3:16, while also elaborating on God's role in the international crises in Korea and Indo-China.[45] In New York three years later, he made reference to the Hungarian uprising of 1956 and the arms race.[46] The threat to humankind posed by the hydrogen bomb, which was tested in the Pacific for the first time on the day Graham opened his London crusade, was a constant feature of his preaching: the specter of annihilation presented by "the bomb" allowed Graham to highlight the urgency of his call for spiritual renewal. It was a call that irritated critics like Ralph Lord Roy, who accused

Graham of "scaring people into salvation" when he warned New Yorkers in 1957 that one hydrogen bomb could wipe out the entire city.[47] But Graham's references to the Cold War were more than just a warning: they drew the political discourses that invariably swirled around Graham during the buildup to his crusades into the actual experience of the event. These debates were as much a part of a Graham revival meeting as were discussions about the future Christian consumer that were initiated by the sale of hot dogs and Coca-Cola alongside Bibles.

Graham's rhetoric of resurrection, the Cold War, and postwar prosperity shifted seamlessly between the scared and the profane, as did the entire orchestration of his revival meetings. When preaching, Graham did not hide behind theological jargon; instead he repeatedly chose examples taken from the here and now. On the opening night in both London and New York, Graham compared the feeling of alienation from God to a plane circling over the Rocky Mountains and losing radio contact with ground control.[48] This narrative of anxiety and deadly threat, with the pilots desperately trying to re-establish contact, allowed Graham to frame the existential search for guidance and security in the most profane way. One journalist attending the Berlin revival meeting in 1954 later recalled that Graham's examples from everyday life were so "trivial" that at some points during the sermon his interpreter seemed to be genuinely shocked.[49] But Graham's performance turned the profane into the sacred: with the open Bible in his hands, he urged his audience to accept Jesus as a chance for a new, protected, fulfilled life.[50] This kind of simple rhetoric, drawing on secular experiences and using everyday language, connected him to his audiences: "As Reverend Graham spoke, it was like he was speaking to me."[51] Added to that was the urgency of his preaching that drew an equally urgent response: some of those who answered his altar call reported that they literally "ran" from the balcony of Madison Square Garden to the front where Graham was waiting.[52]

A close reading of the atmosphere at the revival meetings highlights the ease with which Graham's team, the local organizers, and the audience shifted between and intermingled the scared and the profane. In their religious worlds, buying souvenirs and eating snacks on the one hand, and spontaneous singing and praying on the other, were not mutually exclusive. The multifaceted experiences of Graham's meetings required all these ingredients to allow participants to live a religiosity that they perceived as simultaneously both traditional and modern. If religious life in Britain, Germany, and the United States indeed underwent a transmutation during the 1950s transatlantic revival then the need for a more modern and easier consumable faith became tangible at Harringay, Madison Square Garden, and the Olympic Stadium. Those present were thrilled by the quality of the music and enjoyed the all-round entertainment, without the meetings' religious substance being diminished. That religious essence manifested itself in the practices and emotions of those who were spiritually moved by the event, and of whom many expressed that experience through their act of stepping forward in response to Graham's altar call.

A Lived Community of Faith

With Graham's altar call the event reached its spiritual climax. Months of praying, walking past billboards, and choir lessons had prepared large parts of the audience for this moment. Graham's invitation was straightforward: the words sometimes varied, but the content and the simplicity of his offer did not change. "I am going to ask you to come forward. Up there—down there—I want you to come. You come right now—quickly, if you are with friends or relatives, they will wait for you."[53] At this point, the choir softly intoned the traditional revival hymn "Just as I Am without One Plea." Written by Charlotte Elliott in the nineteenth century, it was popular both in the Anglo-Saxon revivalist world and in Germany, where it was sung in translation: "So wie ich bin." Some 38,447 people answered Graham's call at Harringay Arena, 178 on the opening night. This number rose to 500 toward the end of the mission, with visitors appearing to be increasingly aware of what was expected of them. Across the entire Harringay crusade an average of 400 per night stepped up.[54] During Graham's five revival meetings in Germany in 1955, 10,153 people out of 256,000 participants responded to his altar call: between 2,500 (Dortmund) and 4,000 (Stuttgart) per evening.[55] At Madison Square Garden in 1957 about 53,626 left their seats in the course of the sixteen weeks long revival, between 500 and 700 each night, starting with 485 on the opening night.[56]

Graham's audiences in Germany, however, did not share the historical tradition of revivalism of their Anglo-American brethren. Several German publications addressed this by explaining what would be expected of those answering the altar call. A special edition of the *Berliner Sonntagsblatt, die Kirche* sold outside the Olympic Stadium contained a German minister's eyewitness account of the altar call at Harringay.[57] Erich Sauer, who also witnessed Harringay, published a detailed description, including references to music, the altar call prayer, and even the earnestness etched into the faces of the respondents.[58] Publications such as the translation of Charles T. Cook's *Billy Graham* introduced the world of American revivalism into the German religious landscape. And Graham himself, in a sermon delivered in Berlin in 1960, addressed the Germans' unfamiliarity with the act of stepping forward. Graham reminded his audience that Jesus himself had called and healed his disciples and followers in public, so directly addressing the reluctance on the part of many Germans to take part in public religious expressions.[59]

Graham often spoke of those who stepped forward as coming from all parts of life, yet the official statistics indicate that certain demographics were especially attracted to his religious offer. Women, in particular, were significantly overrepresented. At Harringay 65 percent of those who stepped forward were women and young girls.[60] At Madison Square Garden, women also outnumbered men two to one.[61] Of the eighteen thousand who signed up for the follow-up work in Berlin, Hamburg, and Essen in 1960, 69 percent were women.[62] These figures also probably reflected the significant role women played in crusade preparations: for example, there had been a strong female participation in the cottage prayer groups ahead of the Greater London Crusade in 1954. When audiences are broken down by age group, it is clear that the young were also disproportionately represented among those who stepped forward: 52 percent at Harringay were aged between twelve and eighteen;[63] twenty-two thousand in New York were under twenty-one; and in Germany 28 percent of the converts of the 1960 crusade were under twenty.[64] This preponderance of young people mirrored the generational appeal of many revivals of the previous century.[65] But it also highlighted the very modern appeal of Graham's religious offer: the revival celebrated a religiosity tailored to the future, not the past.

Newspapers and magazines, which saw Graham's missions as sources of colorful and uplifting stories for their readers, often carried detailed descriptions of those responding. *Life* magazine captured images of those who stepped forward in New York in a seven-page photo story.[66] Elsewhere, words were used to paint intimate portraits. The *British Weekly* described those approaching the platform in Harringay: "A shabbily-dressed boy of about 12 was the first to make a decision. A man and wife followed. Teenagers came—some of them looked like leaning-on-the-lamppost youths and the girls from Piccadilly. More teenagers came and more. Some 'churchy' middle-aged people—men and wives came forward, more hesitantly than others."[67] The *New York Times* reported in similar vein from Madison Square Garden: "There was a teen-age boy in sport shirt and slacks, black motorcycle jacket over one arm, walking next to a woman of about 30 who wore a black cocktail sheath and mink stole. A Puerto Rican lad in jeans and T-shirt was followed by a white-haired gentleman in a gray silk suit. There were girls in party dresses and innumerable housewives, clerks, and young executives. A few were Negroes."[68] The selection of characters could hardly have been more random, and an observer of the altar call in Stuttgart in 1955 came to a similar conclusion: "Women holding their children's hands, men of every age, the elderly, people as one encounters them every Saturday in the streets, just less elegantly dressed compared to the weekend moviegoers."[69]

It is impossible to know, or to measure, what exactly made these apparently arbitrary groups get up from their seats. But contemporary observers, such as the British Methodist leader Dr. Leslie Weatherhead, were clear about what they thought did not: there was no "emotional pressure or unpleasant tricks."[70] Academic and popular accounts of Graham's meetings have tended to highlight a striking absence of emotionalism, especially from Graham himself. Indeed, the Graham team orchestrated the crusades in order to minimize emotional outbursts: before the official beginning of the service, Barrows stepped forward and "laid the crusade policy politely, but firmly on the line."[71] Applause was forbidden and so was shouting out for joy. However, these calls for restraint were not reflected in many of the accounts of those who stepped forward and who went through strong emotions while doing so. Their experiences were captured in firsthand reports by journalists, in letters to ministers, and in interviews organized by the BGEA. Their stories reveal strong bodily responses: the feeling of being torn between the emotional and the rational, and the bonding with others while making their decision. Like Ribbat's German *Schwärmer* of the nineteenth century, Graham's audiences constituted religious communities in flux, composed of all those present, of those who left their seats, and of those who watched.[72]

Those who stepped forward responded with all their senses. Their hearts pounded, their knees trembled, and their eyes filled with tears.[73] As one convert described: "I began to feel hot. My heart beat so loud that I thought sure the lady next to me could hear it. My body trembled, my hands shook."[74] Another reported that it felt as "if someone were tugging at me from inside";[75] and another convert felt "as if pulled by some strange power."[76] Some heard their names called or experienced a unique lightness; others began to sweat.[77] One person reported: "My heart groaned and I felt a strong pull upon me, as if from a great magnet, which almost lifted me out of my seat."[78] Others wept uncontrollably.[79] Bible quotations during the sermon were described as arrows entering one's heart: "I could almost feel them strike."[80]

These intense bodily reactions reveal the all-encompassing nature of the converts' decisions. And bystanders also witnessed and recalled the depth of the emotions on display. A report on the revival meeting in Mannheim in 1955 noted: "It was for many an overwhelming experience to see the deeply moved crowd in front of the platform which was seeking Salvation, yearning for repentance, and ready to give witness. Young and old men had tears streaming down their faces, and honest decisions and conversions took place under the unambiguous doing of the Holy Spirit."[81] These stories highlight the transcendental dimensions of the experience. They not only articulate what actually took place, but they also communicate the elements that those stepping forward considered important in their religious lives.

That moment when people left their seats in response to the altar call was the experiential climax of the meeting. It was a decision that was often far from straightforward and one born out of deep agonizing. Many describe their attempt to reason and rationalize while simultaneously being overwhelmed with emotion. Methodist Rev. James R. Course later recalled how "my mind and my soul were in a riot of conflict."[82] A young woman from New York, whose conversion narrative was later published, felt herself responding to the spiritual vibrancy of the moment first, "as if her body were aware of something not clear to her mind."[83] Another described how she tried to control and explain her strong physical reaction: "How silly I was, I tried to rationalize. Who am I that God should give me special attention?"[84] A reporter, recalling his decision not to step forward, remembered: "I felt the compulsion of the call. It was as if some superhuman power had hold of me. I didn't go, for there was a conflict with my responsibility as a reporter."[85] These narratives show how Graham's altar call challenged both established forms of religious service and expression and the secular, rational authority of a quintessentially modern decade.

Many in attendance experienced the meeting as a rite of passage in which they were first irritated, then disturbed by the experience, before finally embracing it: After attending the Harringay meeting, a Methodist minister described how, at first, he deeply resented the traditionalism of Graham's preaching. But his perception changed, and when Graham made the altar call he rejoiced: "For us, heaven's doors as well opened and the vast space was insufficient to receive the number seeking our Lord and his salvation. Here was the house of God and the gate of heaven for hundreds."[86] Maria Redemaker, who attended the meeting in Stuttgart in 1955, was also initially appalled by the unfamiliar secular atmosphere of the space, the ice cream sellers and the discarded Coca-Cola bottles. Later, however, she remembered: "What stirred us so internally during the event, and opened one's heart against every intention, could only have been God's Holy Spirit."[87]

Clearly, for some who stepped forward a significant transformation was taking place, an experience they later recalled through traditional narratives of the sacred and the transcendent: The Holy Spirit appeared, Heaven's doors opened. In the words of Mary, who attended the New York Crusade: "It was the Holy Spirit who spoke while Graham preached."[88] This highlights both a very traditional religious core within Graham's revival work and also his ability to work hand in hand with religious authority: his revival meetings enabled a new, personal, spiritual experience to take place, but the organizational and interpretative frameworks were provided by the established churches. Thus, his religious offer was often not perceived as radically new but, to a degree at least, comfortably familiar.

Many eyewitness accounts highlight the quintessentially religious nature of Graham's revival meetings, despite their political underpinnings and their consumer-friendly appearance. Participants also seemed to experience the revival as significantly more social and personal than many contemporary critics of modern mass evangelism suggest. Instead of feeling lost in the crowd of people, some participants formed individual emotional and spiritual bonds of comfort, support, and encouragement within the mass audience. Not only the official ushers but also ordinary participants acted as spiritual guides for other crusade-goers, thereby building bridges among the thousands attending.

The decision to step forward was often described as an individual act, but it was made easier by the presence and support of others. This is clear in the following account: "On June 2nd, I heard the message with my heart as that of a little child. When Billy gave the invitation I trembled and wept. A young woman sitting behind me touched me, and when I stood to go forward she came with me."[89] Another woman, a member of the choir, was supported in her decision to step forward by the singer sitting next to her, Alice, whom she had just met that evening. Alice later told her, "I didn't think you were saved when you came tonight. I've been praying for you all through Mr. Graham's sermon." The woman who finally stepped forward continued: "I left my place in the choir and found my way down where all the people were standing, who had come to Jesus that night. I went down, not knowing the joy I could find. All I can say is that Alice certainly knew how to pray."[90] A young teenage girl was torn over whether or not to get up from her seat. Eventually, the support of another girl made her step forward: "She must have seen the trouble I was having. I was trying so hard not to shed any tears. . . . When she offered to go with me, I got up right away, and together we went down, and I found God."[91] Press reports sometimes focused on the relationships that were forming within the crusade audience. Husbands glanced at their wives before stepping forward, children looked up to their mothers, and complete strangers provided individual support: "A uniformed woman Salvation Army officer passed by, gripping a weeping girl by the arm and whispering urgently."[92]

Support for an individual's decision to step forward also came from another important group—the people who attended Graham's crusade more than once. Graham's show of hands from those who were first-timers, which he conducted at the beginning of his services, also indicated the presence of many in the audience who returned regularly.[93] These returnees were first observed by the sociologists Kurt and Gladys Lang, who studied the audiences at Madison Square Garden in 1957: through the act of watching, they not only "derive[d] a vicarious pleasure from the decision-making of others" but also came to demonstrate their support for Graham's mission.[94] One group, consisting of "mostly women wearing hats," had no intention of stepping forward themselves but kept returning night after night to affirm their own faith through watching others. Other reasons for repeated visits included the need to build up the courage to step forward, or to affirm, demonstrate, and celebrate their own previous decision.[95] These crusade regulars—and published reports indicate that their numbers should not be underestimated—demonstrate the importance of watching and witnessing in the making of the revivalist atmosphere.[96]

Not every experience at the crusade was entirely positive, with many converts confessing to having mixed emotions about their decision to step forward. Several accounts highlight the shame felt about one's own decision when taken under the critical eyes of others present. A report of a sixteen-year-old girl published in a German newspaper the day after the crusade meeting in Essen told of her hesitation in stepping forward, fearing a negative reaction from her peers:

Billy Graham stands at the front praying. He does not say, "Come to me." He says, "Come to God!" I felt the strong beat of my heart as I got up in

front of them [her peers]. I avoided their eyes, full of shame. But then
I went forward, and many came with me, many more. It was not that hard
anymore.[97]

George, who would answer the altar call in New York, struggled with
the conflicting pulls of pride and shame: "I knew I should make a decision
but didn't know what the people of the church would say."[98] He was already
regarded by them as a Christian and feared the unknown consequences of
answering Graham's call. Many future converts acknowledged that they had
to overcome their pride first.[99]

Clearly, a dynamic lived religious community developed within
Graham's revival meetings bound by different emotions, shared
experiences, and interpersonal gestures. The orchestration of the revival meeting provided the framework in which this community took
shape. Despite the modern surroundings, the religious community that
formed in front of Graham's platform was strikingly traditional in its
expressions and in the narratives its members later used to communicate
their experiences. The modern faith they sought was not fundamentally
new: Graham was not perceived as a radical reformer but as an enabler
of a new and more emotive faith that was entirely compatible with the
Christianity with which they were familiar.

After people had stepped forward, Graham prayed with those lining up
in front of him, inviting them to confess and repent. The inquirers were
then taken to counseling rooms where they discussed their decision with
volunteers, recruited in their thousands from local churches. There the
inquirers were given the booklet *Beginning with Christ* and a copy of the
Gospel of St. John.[100] Their details were taken on decision cards: from then
onward their spiritual future would lie in the hands of the local churches.
Those relationships would be built over weeks and months, but descriptions
of the scenes immediately after the revival services indicate how the events at
Harringay, Madison Square Garden, and the Olympic Stadium empowered
individual people of faith (figure 5.1). Many left the stadia singing, taking
their religion back into the profane world of urban space. It was not orchestrated or scripted, and yet "all the way down the Piccadilly Line there were
train loads of happy people singing 'This is my story, this is my song.'"[101]
It was the same in Los Angeles, New York, and Berlin.[102] Thousands had
prepared the revival in their living rooms, and now they were taking it
back home.

Figure 5.1 Billy Graham preaching to the masses at Harringay Arena in London, 1954.
Original Publication: Picture Post—7081—Billy Graham—pub. 1954 (Photo by Haywood Magee/Picture Post/Hulton Archive/Getty Images)

A Transnational Community of Faith

Bebbington has described how local Victorian religious revivals, which took place in locations scattered around the globe, "displayed a common evangelicalism that transcended national boundaries."[103] Likewise, Graham's crusades created a transnational community of Christians yearning for a more modern faith and a more consumer-oriented religious experience. On the day of the Berlin revival in 1954 a special edition of the Protestant weekly *Berliner Sonntagsblatt, die Kirche* stated: "German Christians now belong to a community of the tens of thousands who heard Graham in Chicago, St. Louis, Albuquerque, Houston, London, Stockholm, Copenhagen, and Düsseldorf."[104] London newspaper coverage also highlighted the international character of the events at Harringay. International prayer chains, as previously shown, contributed significantly to the forming of the international Graham family of faith. In Berlin, London, and New York, foreign visitors were embedded in the structure of Graham's events, turning them into genuine transnational forums in which the international was part of the revival experience.

The international reach of Graham's ministry was evident in the long list of international visitors who traveled with him, who took their seats next to him on the platform, or who simply found a place in the audience. Given that travel was an essential part of Graham's own modern persona, the jet-set lifestyle of those around him blended neatly with the international image of his ministry. Wilhelm Brauer, who brought Graham to Germany in 1954, attended the Greater London Crusade at Harringay, as did other German clergy, such as the Lutheran minister H. Katterfeld from Munich.[105] One of the most prominent German visitors to a later Graham crusade was the theologian Helmut Thielicke. An outspoken critic of Graham's revival work, Thielicke joined Graham on the platform in Los Angeles in 1963, an experience that turned him into a supporter.[106] In New York in 1957, the Indian evangelist Dr. Abdul Akbar joined the crusade team, while the published accounts of the 1954 London crusade indicate the appearance of several international visitors, including the bishop of Singapore and the kabaka of Uganda.[107] Contemporary observers, such as the Methodist Rev. James R. Course, commented favorably on the fact that two Hollywood stars had crossed the Atlantic in order to give testimony of their conversion on the platform at Harringay,[108] among them Colleen Townsend, who played the lead in *Oiltown U.S.A.*

The meetings at Harringay and New York were closely tied thanks to the administrative links between Graham's two first major metropolitan crusades. Rev. Joe Blinco and Rev. Stephen Olford from the United Kingdom, both key figures at Harringay, joined the New York Crusade team, participating as scripture readers in the crusade meetings, taking on speaking engagements across the city, and sitting next to Graham on stage. Rev. John Scott, a thirty-five-year-old Anglican clergyman, was featured as a New York Crusade team member in the *New York Crusade News*, as was Irene Hicks, a Harrods employee who accepted Christ at Harringay, who was on a business trip to New York in the summer of 1957 and gave a public testimony at the crusade.[109] Also at Madison Square Garden was Charles, a London businessman who had also stepped forward at Harringay. When asked to draw a comparison between the two meetings, he replied: "This is just another Harringay. It's just like going back four years and living it over again."[110] His words capture the extent to which Graham's crusades had turned into a global product to be experienced and consumed anywhere. Charles was not

an exception—some of those interviewed for published collections of conversion narratives recalled that they had heard Graham in different locations,
often in Europe first and then again in New York.[111]

The presence of guest preachers and foreign visitors reflected the genuine transnational character of Graham's revival work, marked by a constant flow and exchange of people, practices, and ideas. Their visibility
through preaching and witnessing turned each crusade into a microcosm
of Billy Graham's transnational community. The international was present in many forms: even the counseling rooms were small cosmopolitan
spaces. Counselors looking after the inquirers at Harringay spoke several
languages, including German, French, and Russian.[112] In New York, twenty-
five languages were spoken by 295 multilingual counsellors: the follow-up
material was prepared in twenty-seven different languages.[113] At Madison
Square Garden, the international dimension was not just visible but audible, with Olford's preaching with a "slight British accent" being a source of
comment.[114]

News about the activities of international prayer groups was also weaved
into the crusade meetings to become an integral part of the event. On
opening night at Harringay, Barrows spoke about the cables and telegrams
received from all over the world from people praying for the success of the
campaign. Barrows said he knew of thirty-five thousand in India alone.[115]
Two weeks later, he again reminded the audience of the thousands of people
in India praying for the events in London.[116] In Berlin, Graham assured his
audience that thousands of Christians all around the world were supporting
them in their decision to answer his altar call.[117] The *New York Crusade News*
published images of worldwide prayer groups and reprinted their telegrams
of support.

Yet prayers were not the only narratives that traveled between Graham's
different crusade audiences. A significant contribution to the internationalization of the Graham ministry was made through the publication of conversion narratives. Conversion narratives have traditionally played a significant
role in the history of religious dissent. They are not just important acts of
self-fashioning, but also make a significant contribution to the creation of
religious communities and their underlying political meaning.[118] The conversion narratives, published by the BGEA, under the editorial leadership
of Robert O. Ferm and Curtis Mitchell, certainly helped in constructing
the imagined community of Graham's worldwide followers. Ferm edited
Persuaded to Live: Conversion Stories from the Billy Graham Crusades in

1958.[119] He was also responsible for *They Met God at the New York Crusade*, published in the aftermath of Madison Square Garden. In 1966, Mitchell published a collection of conversion stories under the title *Those Who Came Forward*; the Christian publishing house J.G. Oncken printed ten thousand copies in German translation.[120] Graham did not start his own church, yet he created an international community of those who attended his revival meetings and who afterward felt bound together through a shared experience and memory. The published conversion narratives framed and cemented the identity and memory of this new, fluid religious community. They also installed signposts for those who were not yet part of the community but who wished one day to belong: some of these signals were socioeconomic, while others related to lifestyle and personal well-being.

The distinct, white, middle-class religiosity that Graham shaped and which became manifest in the socioeconomic composition of those who attended his revival meetings in the United States, and added to his allure in Europe, is also reflected in the economic background and social status of those portrayed in the collections of conversion narratives. Young executives and women office workers have a particularly strong presence, but there are many recollections from businessmen, Wall Street brokers, Madison Avenue creatives, estate agents, and salesmen. Some converts belonged to the world of entertainment that Graham had warmly embraced since his breakthrough crusade in Los Angeles. Ferm describes the converts as clean-cut men and beautiful women. In Ferm's edited collection, and in Michell's later publications, the future converts live in houses equipped with washing machines and television sets: they drive shiny cars and hold memberships in golf and country clubs.[121] This highlights the political dimension of Graham's revival work that went beyond simple anticommunism: it was an attractive blend of aspirational class status and evangelicalism. Thus, it is not surprising that the narratives of converts of color are largely absent.

Indeed, these depictions of white, middle-class lives were straight out of 1950s television shows. Tensions, frictions, and conflicts in the lifestyles of those who are economically well-off lay at the core of the conversion narratives: financially solid homes were still haunted by emptiness and loneliness that led to infidelity and alcoholism. The prominence of the theme of an emptiness waiting to be filled by faith tied Graham's revival work to the emotional history of American Christianity, which partly evolved around a rhetoric and practices surrounding "emptiness."[122] Some references were made to broken homes and juvenile delinquency. These narratives resonated with the themes of Graham's preaching and thus extended and amplified it through their publication. Interestingly, the underlying causes that led to the feeling of emptiness—urban living and money-focused consumerism—were not generally critiqued or condemned. In fact they were endorsed with the additional value and meaning that came through faith—a strategy already noted in the public statements from businessmen who spoke up in support of Graham.

The conversion narratives contributed significantly to the shaping of the international community of Graham's followers, capturing their socio-economic identity and influencing how they expressed themselves. Edited and published conversion narratives provided a blueprint for British and German Christians who wished to step forward. They helped to make sense of their unique personal experiences and to communicate those experiences through an internationally recognized and respected narrative. They were also an integral part of the internationalization of Graham's mission: the edition *Persuaded to Live* tied different crusade audiences together by publishing narratives of converts who had stepped forward in different locations. Narratives of Harringay conversions played a particularly important role: future converts first became aware of Graham's revival work through reports about the London crusade. The later collection edited by Mitchell also prominently featured Harringay converts.[123]

The lasting impact of these narratives is reflected in the way in which future generations of converts told their stories. By 1966, when Graham returned to London and Berlin, a recognizable style had been established to describe feelings about the moment of stepping forward. A fourteen-year-old from Brixton recalled, "I felt hot and sweaty. Something inside me said, 'Stand up and go.' Before long, I was walking with others down the aisle. I felt very sure—it was as though God himself were telling me what to do."[124] An eighteen-year-old Londoner spoke of "the most difficult thing I have ever done" and the experience of God speaking directly to him: "I could hear God calling—my heart beat like it had never beat before, and my hands were shaking, I was really sweating."[125] This conformity in the descriptions of emotions was part of a shared language that Graham created among his worldwide following. It was a significant factor in establishing the imagined community of those who shared the experience of attending the crusades, even if they returned to local churches with different denominational affiliations. In this way, Graham established "a common evangelicalism that transcended national boundaries." Yet this vast and diverse community of

Christians also extended beyond the evangelical community in each country. Graham offered the experience of transnational belonging to those who may not have self-identified as future evangelicals, but as Christian consumers, Christian anticommunists, or just as modern people of faith.

Conclusion

The moment when Graham called his audiences in the United States, Great Britain, and Germany to step forward to accept Christ as their savior was the culmination of months of preparation. The experience began for many participants long before they walked through the doors of the meeting spaces. The crusades had entered their households, their churches, and their everyday lives through prayer meetings, flyers, and marketing gimmicks, and through the organization of and participation in the joint transport arrangements. All these different religious practices and spiritual experiences prepared the ground for the actual participation in the revival meeting, the climax of which was the altar call.

The raw numbers of those who attended Graham's meetings, figures that were widely reported in contemporary press accounts and appear in much of the academic literature, point to the occurrence of a very real religious revival in England and the United States in the 1950s. However, the experiences and emotions behind those numbers have received considerably less attention. The tears and trembling knees of those who converted have too often been dismissed as the vestiges of a long-lost, more religious world. Yet they were the powerful signifier of those in search of a more modern faith. A close reading of Graham's revival meetings offers a better understanding of the different expectations attached to the abstract notion of a more modern form of faith taking shape in a dynamic interplay between the traditional and the new, the sacred and the profane. It was at the revival meetings that the imagined communities of those Christians in search of a more modern faith, Christian consumers and Christian Cold War warriors on both sides of the Atlantic, became tangible.

Those anxious about the Cold War and their place in the Free World were addressed directly during Graham's sermons. Those who had grown into Christian consumers were presented with a religious event that featured not only the sale of Bibles and hymn books but also snacks and soft drinks. And those in search of a modern faith marked by "personal experience and conviction"[126] found it through the emotions, tears, and the struggles over their decisions in response to the altar call. This mixture of politics, the everyday, and the sacred was Graham's signature. It built on traditional forms of revivalism witnessed in earlier centuries, but it did not profoundly challenge the authority of the established churches. Instead it offered something new that was in addition to, and sat alongside, established forms of Protestant faith. Accordingly, Graham left it to the churches to work with this new form of religiosity and to foster and cultivate those who had come to his meetings.

The narratives of those who attended Graham's revivals across the world make it clear that these meetings were bound together by a similar style that made them consumable in different local contexts. And yet local differences remained, often expressed through preferences for particular songs and music. Different historical traditions of revivalism and different political settings also shaped Graham's transnational revival work: when Graham preached in Berlin, he was significantly closer to the Iron Curtain than he was in London, and his political message was adapted accordingly. His missions responded to these different circumstances with flexibility and ease. In Grant Wacker's words: "From first to last, Graham displayed an uncanny ability to adopt trends in the wider culture and then use them for his evangelistic and moral reform purposes."[127]

When comparing Graham's revival meetings with their nineteenth-century predecessors, one is struck by the degree to which they shared traditional core elements: misty eyes, the altar call, and the feeling that heaven's gates just opened. And yet Graham made full use of what the 1950s had to offer in terms of technology and speed. Earlier transnational religious communities had evolved around the exchange of preachers and the circulation of sermons, conversion narratives, and hymns. All those activities also featured in Graham's missions, but now messages of support and prayers were sent by cable and reproduced in glossy publications like the *New York Crusade News*. Modern air travel allowed Graham to appear in different places in a shorter time span and to cover more missionary ground than his predecessors. It also offered his followers the opportunity to travel: the numbers of those who heard him preach several times in different localities, sometimes on both sides of the Atlantic, is remarkable and inspired by Graham's own globetrotting example. In the second half of the twentieth century, the world had become a smaller place, allowing the transnational community of those who had heard Billy Graham to become even more closely knit.

Giving a face, a first name, and a voice to those who stepped forward at the Graham crusades provides them with a place in the religious histories of the United States, Great Britain, and Germany in the 1950s. Their narratives reveal that they formed a genuine religious community within the anonymous mass of the meeting; they show that their search for faith was marked by emotion and personal decision; and they illuminate a dynamic interplay between the traditional and the modern, the profane and the sacred, the local and the transnational, all of which shaped those individuals' spiritual experiences. The revival meetings provided them with important spaces to interrogate their identity and status as Christians, as consumers, and as citizens of the Free World. Thus, Billy Graham's crusades deserve a place in the histories of the Cold War, of consumerism, and of the transatlantic revival of the 1950s. They also deserve their place in the very personal spiritual histories of those who answered the altar call. In the words of Mary, who did exactly that in New York in 1957: "That night I found the Savior and gave my heart to Him."[128]

Epilogue

The Secular Crusades: Graham's Return in 1966

When Billy Graham's train pulled into Waterloo Station in London on May 24, 1966, it seemed history was about to repeat itself (figure E.1). Although the reception was smaller than in 1954, there was still a substantial crowd of between fifteen hundred and two thousand to welcome the American preacher and his wife. Just as they had done twelve years earlier, the waiting audience sang religious songs. Strains of "This Is My Story" could be heard, and the singing of Harringay hits such as "Cwm Rhondda" bore testament to the importance, in the imagination of the audience, of the memory of Graham's breakthrough crusade.[1] A woman threw a bunch of flowers into Graham's car with a card saying, "Thanks from a Harringay convert."[2] Yet the crusade that was about to open at the Earl's Court Arena was not a second Harringay. It differed from the 1954 event in important ways. And Graham's return to Berlin a few weeks later would also indicate that his revival work was changing, as were the religious, political, and cultural landscapes of which it was a part.

Before his return to the United Kingdom, Graham's ministry in the United States had gone from strength to strength. The story of Graham's American crusades in the early sixties was one of enormous and expanding success: seventy thousand prayer partners were enrolled before the Chicago crusade in 1962; in just over two weeks, around 705,000 people attended.[3] The organizers of the LA crusade in 1963 recorded one and a half million homes visits by twenty thousand volunteers; more than nine hundred thousand attended the four-week-long revival meeting. *Decision* magazine did not hold back with its superlatives: "Nothing in the annals of Christianity can quite compare with it."[4]

Therefore there were good reasons for the organizers of the 1966 crusades in London and Berlin to feel a good deal more confident than their counterparts who had organized Graham's first visits to both countries in 1954. The scale of ambition was evident in London with the selection of an

Altar Call in Europe. Uta A. Balbier, Oxford University Press. © Oxford University Press 2022.
DOI: 10.1093/oso/9780197502259.003.0007

Figure E.1 Billy Graham's arrival at Waterloo Station in 1966
(copyrights: Shaw/ANL/Shutterstock)

impressive venue: the Earl's Court Arena had 18,087 seats in three tiers and overflow halls equipped with closed-circuit TV and seating for another 6,678. Despite this large capacity, the arena was filled by Graham for the entire four-week revival.[5] Around a million people heard him preach (including closed-circuit relays) and forty thousand stepped forward, four thousand more than at Harringay. In Berlin, renting the Deutschlandhalle for a religious event was an equally bold move. Partitions limited the capacity to around twelve thousand, and it too was almost full each evening. In total some ninety thousand attended, of whom around two thousand answered Graham's altar call.[6] By German standards, these were impressive numbers.

More important than the difference in audience sizes at the London and Berlin crusades were the similarities in the cultural and political contexts within which they were embedded. Both countries had rapidly secularized since the mid-1950s (albeit from different starting points). On both sides of the North Sea the discourse surrounding the Christian identity of each nation was dead; the diplomatic relationship with the United States was overshadowed by events in Vietnam; and the debates surrounding the existence of God and the interpretation of the historical realities of the New Testament were marked by a new fervor. All the important trends that shaped the "Religious Crisis of the 1960s," according to Hugh McLeod's compelling analysis—the loss of national Christian identity, diminishing religious knowledge and education, a new spiritual plurality, and the deepening religious conflict lines within denominations—were brought into sharp focus during the 1966 crusades.[7] And yet a close reading of these events also highlights slightly different secularization speeds in Germany and the United Kingdom, while the transnational context of the US crusades shows which secularization trends were shared on both sides of the Atlantic and which were not.

This book has analyzed the religious revival of the 1950s that was common to the United States, the United Kingdom and Germany and the sacralization of the Cold War order that was integral to it. This concluding chapter discusses the different trajectories the three countries embarked upon when this revival came to an end. It traces how Graham's crusades responded to, and were shaped by, new secular realities and how the crusades, particularly in London and Berlin, indicated that a desacralization of the Cold War order had taken place. Graham still drew record numbers in the United States and Europe in the 1960s, and yet the religious worlds—and the secular context within which they were embedded—had clearly changed.

Secular Crusades

When Billy Graham returned to Britain and Germany in 1966, secularization was in full swing, with the number of baptisms, confirmations, and ordinations dropping significantly in both countries.[8] These obvious signs that religious engagement had declined since 1954 were not lost on Graham's team: "Throughout London, at deanery meetings and minsters' fraternals, they detected a sense of failure, a loss of initiative to the secularists, even an infection of doubt that the classic doctrines of Christianity had relevance, power or validity for twentieth-century men."[9] To be sure, the take-up of training sessions for counselors, with twenty-five thousand enrolled members, was still impressively high. So were the eight thousand prayer groups, which compared favorably to the five hundred that had formed before Harringay. But Graham's backing from churches was not as solid, even within the evangelical community. Indeed, some churches, such as Duke Street Baptist Church, a spiritual and organizational powerhouse in 1954, were markedly less enthusiastic about the revival this time around.[10] In sharp contrast to 1954, some churches found it challenging to organize their

Operation Andrew fleets because of a lack of genuinely devoted members.[11] Likewise in Berlin, there was only limited trust in the commitment of the local congregations. Not wanting to risk embarrassment, the organizers ran Operation Andrew centrally through their committee rather than through local partners—a first in the history of Graham's crusades.[12]

In Germany, the successful recruitment of fifteen hundred counselors for the crusade exposed another secular reality: although the volunteers came in equal parts from the Evangelical Church and the Free Churches, an overwhelming 95 percent of those from the Free Churches were under thirty years old, while the vast majority from the official Protestant churches were over fifty.[13] This reflected the growing inability of the Evangelical Church to make an attractive religious offer to the young—a spiritual vacuum that Free Churches were more than happy to fill.

Graham's success had always relied on the power and passion of local churches. As secularization gradually quashed this source of spiritual passion, Graham's revival work became significantly more challenging. As one commentator mused in the *Methodist Recorder*: "Someone told me that the opening night at Earl's Court lacked fire. Could it be that the churches here at home are not supplying the right kind of fuel to feed the flames?"[14] Similar remarks were heard in the United States, when Bishop Gerald Kennedy of the Methodist Church in Los Angeles blamed his church for "inadequate spiritual preparation" of its own evangelistic efforts.[15] But in the United States, Graham was able to rely on an increasingly powerful and patriotic neo-evangelical community that dwarfed the evangelical communities of Germany and Britain.[16] As *Time* observed in 1963, this conservative wing of evangelicalism proved especially successful in defying secularization trends.[17] The seed planted by Graham and his team of an inclusive civil religious neo-evangelicalism during the 1950s came to bloom in the 1960s, providing a strong backbone for his revival work in the United States, while in Europe the number of supporting hands declined in comparison.

Secularization, however, did not just manifest itself in weakening religious commitment and energy—it was also apparent in a changing theological climate on both sides of the Atlantic. The Anglican Church reacted to the challenges of secularization with new popular and liberal theological trends, which appeared in publications such as John Robinson's *Honest to God* in 1963. In Germany, the theological controversy launched by Rudolph Bultmann in 1951 surrounding the demythologization of the New Testament reached its second peak at around the same time.[18] Both Bultmann and

Robinson featured prominently in the *Time* article of April 1966 that accompanied one of the most provocative magazine covers of the decade, asking in red letters: "Is God Dead?"

The article, about the future of faith in an increasingly secular world, discussed the fierce theological debates engulfing the divinity schools in the United States and featured Graham, in opposition to Robinson, Bultmann, and American theologians such as Harvey Cox, who had written the *Secular City*. The author declared that "for uncounted millions, faith remains as rock-solid as Gibraltar. Evangelist Billy Graham is one of them."[19] It was not just Graham's faith that was perceived as rock solid; he himself was also defined as a religious rock in the stormy waters of secularization, seemingly above public criticism. This became obvious during a panel discussion, "Evangelism and the Intellectual," organized by the Harvard Law Forum in March 1962: the panel of Harvard Divinity School professors, Krister Stendahl, Richard R. Niebuhr, and James Luther Adams, all treated Graham with the utmost respect. As Niebuhr remarked: "How does one make a comment about Billy Graham? How do you comment about the American flag, or any other institution that we all accept?"[20]

Encouraged by such endorsements, the British edition of Graham's *Decision* magazine asked provocatively on its front cover in the days before the opening of the Earl's Court crusade: "Is God then Dead?"[21] And Graham, although not known for his theological rigor, now confronted British theology head-on. At his first press conference, Graham outlined what he considered to be Britain's secular diseases, listing not only the rebellion of the young generation, the moral breakdown of the country, and declining church membership, but also the ongoing theological debates in church and society.[22] At the opening night at Earl's Court he spoke of "'so-called theologians' who were 'jumping up and down on God's grave.'"[23] And in his sermon on the first Friday of the crusade, he warned of the theological opposition to his revival work calling it "more intelligent, sophisticated, sharper and far more cynical."[24]

In Britain, however, Graham was not as untouchable as he was in the United States, which became obvious in the Anglican Church's response. When the archbishop of Canterbury, Geoffrey Fisher, had spoken the benediction at Wembley Stadium in 1954, he had symbolized a national consensus, that Graham had come to strengthen the core of a Christian country. In 1966, his successor, Archbishop Michael Ramsey, denied Graham this favor. In the *Canterbury Diocesan News* he gave Graham only lukewarm support, highlighting instead the fact that neither the Church of England nor the dioceses in the London area had been involved in inviting Graham back.[25] Three diocesan bishops of the Greater London area took their seats on the platform at Earl's Court, as did the bishop of Coventry and the archbishop of York.[26] Archbishop Ramsey, however, did not attend. On a trip to Vancouver in October1966, Ramsey went even further, declaring Graham's evangelism as inadequate to meet the challenges of an increasingly secular age. He was quoted saying: "We need an intellectual thoughtful approach, not bursts of emotionalism."[27] His remarks upset those Anglicans who supported Graham's Earl's Court crusade, and Ramsey later said he had been misquoted. However, in a clarifying statement, Ramsey did not make any significant retreat: "I think that these times need an evangelism which gives more place to the social content of Christianity and gives more help to intellectual difficulties."[28]

If Graham had been perceived as fundamentalist and theologically old-fashioned by some back in 1954, he now looked even more out of step with Robinson's and Bultmann's followers. This was not just a concern of the Anglican Church. The former president of the Methodist conference, Lord Donald Soper, thundered: "Ultimately the one certain effect of a presentation of Christianity which side-steps the intellectual issue is disillusion, and no catalogue of converts, however long, is a sufficient answer to this indictment."[29] German theologians also found it harder to relate to Graham's faith. Bishop Heinrich Meyer of the Protestant-Lutheran Church of Lübeck explained this reluctance in the context of a transformed theological climate: "German theologians have been confronted with the problem of history and God's revelation in history by Bultmann and his disciples in such a way that the easy solution of American fundamentalism does not solve his problem."[30] German theologians now criticized Graham more fiercely: his latest book, *World in Flames*, was reviewed in leading Protestant journals under headlines accusing him of "intellectual crouching"—"Geistig in der Hocke."[31]

Apparently learning from his experience in London, Graham toned down his language on critical theology while in Berlin, even though the concurrent issue of his magazine, *Decision*, still warned that Bultmann's theology had infiltrated several state church pastors and 150 pastors of the Free Churches of the city.[32] Graham also benefited from the backing he received from the recently retired bishop of Berlin, Otto Dibelius, and his successor, Kurt Scharf. Both openly acknowledged the theological problems with Graham's religious offer but accepted that there might still be a demand for such a faith among ordinary Christians. While Dibelius, like Ramsey, viewed Graham's "fundamentalism" as outdated and "hard to bear," especially for theologians, he nevertheless argued that the majority of ordinary Christians in the pews needed a message that provided them with clarity and answers, not with soaring flights of intellect.[33] Scharf struck the same note on the opening night at the Deutschlandhalle, when he welcomed Graham as a mediator between the evangelical Free Churches and the mainline Protestants. Because Graham avoided theological battles and relentlessly focused on the Bible, he returned to the essentials upon which both camps could agree.[34] While Ramsey was certain in his belief that his Anglican Church did not need Graham, Dibelius and Scharf were more inclined to think that their churches actually did.

These small but significant differences in the way Graham was received in London and Berlin were evident not only in the attitudes in the established churches, but also in the output of the news media, which reflected a contrasting relationship between religion, media, and the public in the two countries. Shortly before Graham's return to the United Kingdom, the director general of the BBC, Hugh Carleton Greene, had declared that the broadcaster would not shy away from "religious controversy"; by the mid-1960s it had become possible to mock religion on TV, and indeed programs were regularly made that did exactly that.[35] Shortly before the opening of the Earl's Court crusade, Greene's expectations of religious controversy were met when Graham appeared on the BBC television program *Twenty-Four Hours*, facing two of his most outspoken British critics, psychiatrist James Mitchell and novelist George W. Target. Both men questioned Graham's marketing style, the psychological impact he had on his followers, and, more generally, his credibility. The criticism had a distinctly agnostic subtext: at one point Graham's message was labeled "sanctified lies."[36] It was clear that the tone in the media about Graham's mission had changed substantially since 1954, when even the left-leaning *Guardian* had been guarded in its criticism out of a respect for religion. Twelve years later guests on the British national broadcaster displayed no such restraint.

The response in the evangelical milieu was just as forthright, with *The Christian* calling George Target "Judas Iscariot."[37] Indeed, Graham's visit highlighted the deepening demarcation lines in a secular society between those with faith and those without. Even before the opening of Earl's Court, the debate on faith had evolved: while in 1954 the press seemed to be most concerned about what kind of faith was appropriate for the day and age, now the benefits of faith itself were being questioned, its presence in society presented as a potential psychological pitfall. Interestingly, the German press still treated Graham with more respect and gave a generally positive impression of events at the Deutschlandhalle.[38] This was partly thanks to some fortunate timing for Graham: the article in *Der Spiegel* titled "What Do Germans Believe?," which had a significant impact on how faith and the churches' role in modern society were discussed, appeared a year later, in 1967.[39]

Graham's 1966 crusades took place in an increasingly secular climate in Europe. Yet there was an additional question about the interplay between secularization and revivalism arising from the ever more secular nature of Graham's revival work itself: to many observers it seemed as if the rapid professionalization of his mission threatened to compromise its spiritual energy and authenticity, with his revival events, as well as other parts of his ministry, becoming more and more glittering and grandiose.

When Graham returned to Los Angles in August 1963, fourteen years after his global ministry began in a comparatively modest tent at the corner of Washington and Hill Streets, the venue he chose demonstrated the scale of the transformation. Graham now rented the LA Coliseum, the nation's largest stadium, which made New York's Madison Square Garden look small in comparison. There, he drew crowds of between thirty thousand and sixty thousand each evening for three and a half weeks; 134,254 attended the closing service.[40] Another indicator was Graham's decision to launch a glossier and more accessible magazine alongside *Christianity Today*. In November 1960, the first issue of *Decision*, under the editorial leadership of Sherwood Wirt, was distributed to 253,000 households, a number which would rise to 5 million only five years later.[41] In contrast to *Christianity Today*'s dry theological content, *Decision* carried lively images and journalistic reports of Graham's crusade work around the world. Graham's film ministry took off around the same time.[42]

The increasing professionalization of Graham's revival work inevitably impacted the way his team engaged with local hosts. It had already led to criticism from potential host cities in the United States. As early as 1958, the Protestant Church Federation of Greater Chicago aired concerns about "the high-powered bureaucratic approach Graham's team imposed on churches in a crusade city."[43] When evangelical circles in northern England considered inviting Graham back in the mid-1970s, they wanted "him to come without his organization."[44]

Throughout the 1950s and early 1960s, European Christians held the organization of Graham's American spectacles in awe and admiration. And in 1966 it was clear that his crusade operation was even more efficient than it had been in 1954. "You just push a button and the whole machinery comes into operation," said Harold Parks, a minister of Christ Church in North Finchley, describing his own church's preparation.[45] But this increasingly businesslike approach raised the question of whether it had unavoidably led to a secularization of Graham's revival work. As one Methodist observer lamented after spending an evening at Earl's Court: "There are moments when one senses that Billy Graham is becoming over-burdened and over-organized by the crusade machine, that he needs to be liberated for true evangelism."[46] Henry Hole, chief steward at Earl's Court, remembered Harringay as "more personal" and praised its "informal atmosphere."[47] One of the former organizers of the Greater London Crusade, Oliver Stott, framed the changing atmosphere of the crusades within the secularization paradigm: "I think after Harringay we began to depend very much more on organization than on the Holy Spirit."[48] Even the BGEA acknowledged that Earl's Court was never filled with a "cathedral-like atmosphere."[49] While Graham had once come to Europe to fight secularization, now, in the eyes of many, he had fallen victim to the secularization of his very own revival work.

Perceptions of the Earl's Court crusade as a more secular event were fueled by the youthful crowd it attracted. Back at the London and Berlin crusades of 1954 young people had formed the majority of his audience. Building on this experience, Graham now specifically catered to the younger generation by holding two youth nights each week and designating the Earl's Court revival as "a youth crusade."[50] The Earl's Court statistics show that those in their teens and twenties far outnumbered other age groups, with official figures confirming that 74 percent of those who stepped forward to fill in a decision card were between twelve and twenty-nine years old.[51] At the Deutschlandhalle a similar age group responded enthusiastically to Graham's religious offer. Even though most of the audience was described as "middle-aged," 50 percent of those stepping forward were under twenty-five.[52] But Graham's special attraction to the young made his crusades in London and Berlin appear to be more secular because of their attitude and demeanor. While in 1954 those attending had dressed up as if for church, teenagers now wore leather jackets and skirts so short that they would have raised an eyebrow at any Sunday morning service. "Young girls wore false eyelashes, wigs, and mascara, stripe shirts, stretch pants and cloth shoes; boys wore leather jackets, black and red raincoats, their hair matted or stringy, and their feet in cloth shoes."[53] Contemporary reports gave the impression that many were not familiar with the behaviors associated with churchgoing: it was noted that "one man kept his hat on; another smoked a cigarette."[54] Girls talked through the entirety of Graham's sermons; others unwrapped and noisily sucked on sweets.[55] At the Deutschlandhalle babies shrieked and were fed and had their nappies changed in open sight.[56] It seemed that those who attended in London and Berlin were no longer grounded in basic religious custom: they embodied, in this small regard, what Callum Brown saw as the end of the churches' "moral regime."[57]

Indeed, the Earl's Court statistics confirm that while in 1954 90 percent of those who stepped forward had indicated at least some kind of church connection, however loosely, in 1966 only 76 percent reported a connection to a certain church.[58] Counselors commented on the fact that they were dealing with inquirers "who had no previous idea of Christianity."[59] The apparent religious illiteracy of many of those attending raised the question of whether they were actually looking for a genuine religious offer. An observer from the *British Weekly* suggested that "for many young Londoners it was 'fab' and 'gear' to go to Earl's Court in June 1966."[60] That was certainly the case the night the British pop singer Cliff Richard took to the stage to speak of the relevance of being Christian, before singing "It is No Secret What God Can Do." Richard attracted an audience of 30,000 inside the arena, while 5,000 waited outside; 1,370 responded to Graham's altar call.[61] In a cultural climate that appeared to focus on the individual's quest for a meaning to life and which consequently attracted millions of young people to Marxism and consumerism, peace and women's movements, LSD trips and party raves, Billy Graham seemed to offer just another route to personal fulfillment.

Yet many of the secular characteristics of Graham's Earl's Court events were a function of the specific cultural landscape of 1960s London. Indeed, the way the Earl's Court crusade was perceived differed hugely from the way Graham's crusades appeared in the United States or in Berlin just weeks later. What happened at the Deutschlandhalle was not a youth gathering, despite the many teenagers who stepped forward, and it was not a party. It was a conservative church service that attracted what one contemporary observer described as the "ecclesiastical Middle Ages" ("innerkirchliches Mittelalter").[62] This highlights how strongly Graham's revival work depended on, and was shaped by, local religious and cultural circumstances: the way the organizers marketed the event, the venue itself, and the different secularization speeds. In terms of secularization, London in 1966 was ahead of Berlin and many of the American cities in which Graham could still draw massive, religious, conservative crowds.

The Secularization of the Cold War Order

As the process of secularization impacted the running of Graham's European crusades and the way they were discussed, so it also shook the sacred underpinnings of the Cold War order. In the 1950s, Germans and Britons had shared Graham's commitment to the re-Christianization of their countries and supported his religious campaigns against communism and for democracy, allowing them to overlook some of the complexities and contradictions within his revival work. These included his questionable social justice record, his spiritual support for military operations, and his unabashed commitment to consumer culture. Reservations on these issues were swept under the carpet of a joint commitment to the spiritual Cold War. Yet when that framework became fractured because of events in Vietnam, Europeans showed a declining appetite for discussing their political health and future within a religious framework. As a result, Graham's mission was seen through new eyes.

Graham's commitments to social justice and his relationship to the civil rights movement were the first to come under public scrutiny. The Anglican priest and Christian socialist Kenneth Leech spoke up forcefully against Graham in an article published in the *Church of England Newspaper*, a publication with a large evangelical readership. Under the headline "degutted and individualized," Leech pointed out that Graham "has no genuine social theology. Rather does he see renewal of the social order as something which will gradually follow from the conversion of individuals."[63] This critique echoed the arguments made by Graham's critics in the United States, such as Reinhold Niebuhr. It gained new momentum as public sentiment in the United States, United Kingdom, and Germany slowly shifted toward demanding social change, with churches redefining their role as agents of social justice in an increasingly secular world. Thus, it is not surprising that Graham's weak social justice record now featured prominently in debates across the Christian landscapes: his positions on racism and the Vietnam War in particular ended up in the spotlight.

In 1954 only one public voice, the editor of the *British Weekly*, challenged Graham on his stance toward the civil rights movement, even though he had preached in front of a segregated audience just weeks before opening at Harringay.[64] This reflected the Anglican Church's general "deafening silence" on the simmering racial tensions in Britain at that time.[65] In 1954, German organizers had been equally disinterested in Graham's civil rights record. But now, ahead of the crusade at the Deutschlandhalle, they sought assurances about Graham's position on race and civil rights from his American team.[66] This indicates an increasing sensitivity among German evangelicals to the political debates surrounding Graham at home, although these concerns were rarely articulated in Germany in public. In a society as white as Germany in 1966, racism could be easily defined as a problem of the past.

But this was impossible in an increasingly multicultural society like Britain, where highly contested immigration laws both reflected and ignited public expressions of racism. In this explosive atmosphere, Graham's position on race was inevitably catapulted into the public eye when his African American associate evangelist, Howard Jones, was asked to leave his rented flat in London on the basis of his race. Graham's support for Jones was not only reported in Christian periodicals but also in *The Times*.[67] Indeed Graham's personal stance against racism had never been doubted. He had left his mark on the American civil rights scene when he preached to an integrated audience of thirty thousand in Birmingham, Alabama, after the Ku Klux Klan bombing of the Sixteenth Street Baptist Church in September 1963, which cost four young girls their lives. However, it was his unwillingness to acknowledge that certain injustices needed structural change rather than just personal conversion that was now seen as problematic at home as in Europe.[68]

This issue overshadowed Graham's otherwise successful outing to St. Matthew Church in Brixton, one of London's predominantly black neighborhoods during his Earl's Court crusade. Ministers of white and black local churches had organized the service, and the audience was diverse, indicating that Graham's civil rights' credentials were sound enough to attract a multiracial congregation. However, as Graham's otherwise sympathetic biographer, John Pollock, pointed out, Graham failed to preach on racism at this occasion.[69] His only reference to race came in his opening remarks, when he said that if Americans truly believed in God (a recent poll suggested 97 percent of Americans did), it would inevitably mean the end of racial violence.[70] This was also the line he took in Berlin, where racism featured in his opening sermon at the Deutschlandhalle.[71] On both occasions, Graham fell into the theological trap that stirred such strong criticism among American civil rights leaders: he favored personal conversion over structural changes in overcoming racial injustice. His German critics pressed home the point, observing that Graham had been absent when the white mob threw stones at Martin Luther King and arguing that his gospel "did not seriously lead people to take responsibility in the world as Christians."[72] British critics struck a similar note when reminding Graham that ultimately Christianity was also "about shift work, housing policies, inter-racial understanding, peace in Vietnam and justice in Rhodesia."[73]

Indeed it was the controversy surrounding America's war in Vietnam that overshadowed Graham's return to London and Berlin more than anything else and that heralded the end of the spiritual Cold War order. When the general secretary of the World Council of Churches, W. Visser 't Hooft, sent a telegram to President Johnson "expressing serious concern about the intensification of bombing in Vietnam," when the archbishop of Canterbury conveyed "deep sorrow over the continued and increasing suffering of the people in Vietnam," and when the Methodist Conference publicly condemned the US conduct in Vietnam, Graham remained silent.[74] Despite his refusal to comment publicly on the Vietnam War, Graham's statements going back to his earliest crusade in Los Angeles left little room for doubt: Graham was a fervent opponent of communism and a supporter of US military intervention abroad.

Graham's backing for the US government was clear for all to see in November 1965 when he invited President Johnson and his wife, Lady Bird, to attend the closing service of his Houston crusade: Graham reportedly asked the audience to express loyalty toward America and to pray to God to continue blessing the president with wisdom, strength, and courage. He also made a dismissive comment about the growing number of antiwar protesters.[75] This did not go unnoticed in the American or the German press.[76] Furthermore, Graham's outspoken British critic George Target tracked down a report in the *Rocky Mountain News* that quoted Graham as saying: "I have no sympathy for those clergymen who urge the U.S. to get out of Vietnam."[77] Not surprisingly, the question of Graham's position on Vietnam came up during a press conference at the Waldorf Hotel ahead of the Earl's Court crusade when journalists pushed him to address the war as a "moral issue."[78] Even though Graham repeatedly insisted that he would not comment on Vietnam, many British Christians, such as Rev. Ronald Lewis, were convinced that the American preacher was not among "those who consider the indiscriminate burning of women and children with napalm to be sufficient cause for protest."[79] Bearing in mind Graham's role in establishing the moral and spiritual stability of the Cold War world order, the critical voices who now lined up against him were challenging not only the man himself but the entire Cold War consensus. European perceptions of Graham, dating back to 1954, as both a religious and a political figure now backfired on him. While in America Graham was just one of many religious figures who supported the Vietnam War (which explains the absence of protests at the US crusades), in Europe he was *the* American preacher who refused to speak up against the war.

As a result, Graham encountered political protests at his revival meetings. The weekend before his opening at Earl's Court, Graham returned to preach at St. Aldates in Oxford, where he was met by student demonstrators. During the Earl's Court crusade itself, on the evening of June 28, a group of antiwar protesters disrupted the altar call with chants of "Pray for the souls in Vietnam," while some of their fellow demonstrators dropped antiwar leaflets "through ventilation holes in the ceiling."[80] Protests at Graham's events in the United States would come later, at the university campus in Berkeley, California, in 1967,[81] and more significantly at a crusade in Knoxville, Tennessee, in 1970 when Nixon and Graham appeared together just ten days after the Kent State shooting. It was the first time that a sitting president did not just pray at a crusade but actually spoke. Inside and outside the stadium antiwar protestors could be heard yelling, "Stop that crap and end the war!"[82] Similar protests followed in Chicago in July 1971 and Oakland a month later.[83]

In 1966, the German press noticed the shifting political tide surrounding Graham's mission in the United Kingdom: a journalist with the left-leaning *Frankfurter Rundschau* suggested that Graham's crusade in London had proven less successful due his problematic position on the Vietnam War.[84] Even though it is debatable if Earl's Court was really less successful, the Vietnam issue followed Graham to Germany. When Rolf Zundel of the German weekly *Die Zeit* discussed the deepening tensions over Vietnam in the American Christian landscape, he mentioned a statement signed by twenty-two American minsters in response to Johnson's proclamation of a national day of prayer for the troops. The ministers had accused the president of turning the atrocities in Vietnam into a holy war. But, as Zundel pointed out, Graham's signature was missing.[85] Ahead of his return to Germany, Graham's proximity to the Johnson administration and his support for the US military Cold War strategy clearly raised concerns in some religious communities. And the emotions stirred by Vietnam were even more pointed because the American organizers remained steadfastly committed to a Cold War discourse in which Berlin was a "city clinging stubbornly to its political freedom, but urgently in need of the liberating Gospel."[86]

The *Berliner Unterwegskreis*, with its roots in the Confessing Church, was especially sensitive to questions of war and nationalism and expressed its concern that hosting a revival meeting with Graham came close to an acceptance of his Christian nationalism. Gustav Roth of the *Unterwegskreis* warned that in the twentieth century, German Christians in particular had had bad experiences of this perverted ideology.[87] His comments mirrored the concerns aired in German Protestant circles during the crusades of the 1950s about the militaristic core of Graham's mission. Now, and with significantly more conviction than in 1954, the Evangelical Church, took these worries seriously. As early as 1965, General Superintendent Hans-Martin Helbich invited all members of the Protestant church in West Berlin and members of the German Free Churches to express any unease they felt about Graham's political activities.[88] With Vietnam in mind, Helbich aimed to create a democratic forum within the Protestant churches in which Graham's upcoming campaign could be discussed openly. In the best Protestant tradition, he declared the question of participation in, or withdrawal from, Graham's revival meetings a question of individual conscience. However, he also made an appeal for tolerance within the Christian community toward differing political, economic, or theological systems and opinions.[89] The German evangelical organizers went further and publicly defended Graham's civil right to have a personal opinion on the Vietnam War, an issue, they argued, on which neither the Bible nor the Christian family had a clear position.[90] Much of the public criticism of Graham, and indeed some of the support for him, was still framed within a Cold War discourse: Eckard Spoo, writing for the *Frankfurter Rundschau*, described Graham's revival at the Deutschlandhalle in military terms: run with "military precision," it was where "God's machine gun" (Graham's old nickname) "fires on Berlin."[91] In doing so, he rhetorically presented Graham as just another exponent of US military power abroad. The evangelical editor Sherwood Wirt titled his article about the twenty-four hundred people who had stepped forward at the Deutschlandhalle "Stand Fast in Freedom,"[92] making much less critical connections between Graham's mission and the Cold War world.

This fierce debate in 1966 about Graham and Vietnam, which spanned the public arena and religious communities in the United Kingdom and

Germany, revealed that the Cold War consensus had fractured. For the thousands who attended his revival meetings in the 1950s, Graham had provided the spaces in which participants could locate themselves in a Cold War culture, which combined anticommunism, Christianity, and a commitment to the Free World. By 1966 this holy trinity did not exist anymore. In the crusade's preparatory materials and in publicity content, like *Decision* magazine, which had been published in Britain since 1963, there were hardly any references to the Christian identity of the country or the quasi-sacred special relationship between the United States and the United Kingdom. Both these tropes had dominated the discourse surrounding Harringay. The same was true for the German crusade organizers, who resisted references to the Cold War or the Christian Occident. These imagined communities had fallen victim to the rapid secularization processes in both countries, reflecting a deep and increasing wariness about the close interplay between politics and religion in Europe. The United States, in one important aspect, embarked on a different secularization path with its entanglement of religious and political discourse—an intimate relationship that gained momentum with the election of Richard Nixon, and which remains an important element of America's religious landscape today. Reporting on Graham's New York Crusade of 1969, the *Washington Post* journalist Nicholas von Hoffman observed icily that those assembled to listen to Graham "looked like the Republican Party at prayer."[93]

The European and American secularization paths also diverged in another important respect: the incompatibility of mainline Christianity and consumerism in Europe. In the 1950s, Graham's middle-class consumer lifestyle had been an important part of his attraction, alongside the perceived modernity of his religious offer. But attitudes toward American-style consumerism, which had taken such a firm hold in Germany and the United Kingdom after the crusades of 1954, were changing. So too was the place of consumerism in the Western Cold War consensus. In the end, European Christians did not side with Graham on the compatibility of consumerism and Christianity. The *British Weekly*, in its first issue in the year of Graham's return, identified commercialism as a key challenge to the Christian conscience and bemoaned the state of a society dedicated only to "specks on a graph" and "the next 'trend.'"[94] In a climate increasingly critical of consumer culture, Graham's ever more extensive merchandising, so much part of his success in the United States, came under scrutiny. The Billy Graham Verse-a-Day Scripture Key Chain, marketed as a "practical unique gift of spiritual value" at Earl's Court, became the symbol of a highly commercialized revivalism.[95] A survey of sixty-eight clergy and 211 laypeople conducted by the *Church of England Newspaper* indicated that the commercialization at Earl's Court was a major concern. The fact that refreshments were sold during the sermon was excoriated, while the appeal for collection was criticized for being an "American style" experience and out of place.[96] Similarly in Berlin, the plea for offerings made by Heinrich Giesen became the focus for German press criticisms of commercialization. Willi Kieninger echoed his British colleagues, when he spoke disapprovingly of a "fair of evangelism," referring to the stalls in the Deutschlandhalle that offered books, LPs, and Bibles with flashy modern covers.[97] Cecil Northcott, editor of the mainline *Christian Century*, captured the consumerist atmosphere of Graham's mission when he called the performance at Earl's Court "a package deal wrapped with all the proper labels."[98] These debates drew a line under the conversations of the 1950s about a possible fruitful interplay between consumerism and faith, and again the paths of US and European religious history diverged.

The reason for an intensifying critique of Graham's corporate evangelism was not only the increasing professionalization of the BGEA, but also Europe's changing intellectual and political climate. Under the shadow of Vietnam, Graham's gospel was tied to broader debates about what was perceived as US military, cultural, and economic imperialism. Thus, his critics focused less on the commodification of faith and its possible implications for the future of religion. Instead, they openly questioned and attacked Graham's belief that capitalism formed a kind of God-given order. Kenneth Leech ranted: "Perhaps the most significant and frightening fact is that throughout all Billy Graham's writing and preaching there is not one single doubt that American capitalism and imperialism are fundamentally righteous. . . . For Billy the American way of life, imperialism and capitalism are inseparable from Christian civilization."[99] The Cologne-based minister and member of the Deutsche Friedensunion Heinrich Werner, echoed Leech's word when he called Graham's message "the religious trimming of an un-Christian anticommunism and the inflation of the American way of life to a model of Christian life."[100] When the American way of life came under renewed intellectual and political scrutiny amid the rising 1960s counterculture, so did the faith that Graham proclaimed.

Maybe God was not quite dead in 1966, but the transatlantic Cold War revival certainly was. In the 1950s Graham had bound together the revivals in the United States, Germany, and the United Kingdom with his ability to mobilize untapped spiritual resources and to address unanswered religious questions on both sides of the Atlantic. He provided imaginative frameworks, such as the spiritual Cold War and the Christian consumer, that allowed Christians and non-Christians to reflect on the future of Christian communities, identities, and tasks in a rapidly modernizing and globalizing world. Millions of ambitious and creative local organizers across the world grappled with these frameworks, giving them life and meaning. But from the beginning these concepts were caught up in the riptides of American political, economic, and cultural power abroad; and thus, by the mid-1960s, they fell apart under the pressure of new world-political circumstances. With the decline in religious affiliation and commitment resulting from secularization draining European and, to a certain degree, American churches of their spiritual energy, Graham's revival work became increasingly challenging. Therefore it is no surprise that the focus of his mission would shift from Europe in the 1950s to the global South in the 1970s. In the United States, where he could live off a quasi-civil religious reputation and count on the support of increasingly powerful religious pressure groups, Graham would remain committed to his revival work, continuing to thrill a loyal and large evangelical community of followers.

Despite the diverging paths between Europe and the United States, the events at the Deutschlandhalle still prompted a German commentator to identify "a global congregation [which] moved its international star into the headlights."[101] In fact, Graham never aimed to form his own denomination: every inquirer was supposed to be sent to a church of his or her choice. And yet, Graham *did* form a transnational community of evangelical Christians, one that is still tied together by a similar worshiping style and musical taste, evangelical merchandising and media products, and most importantly through prayer and the memory of having attended one of Graham's vast revival meetings or answering his altar call. These "communities of affect"[102] proved stronger than the political and economic divergencies and the secularization processes that were apparent in London and Berlin in 1966. This book has explored the story of this evolving community, the professionalization and politicization of the British and German evangelical milieus, their forceful battle against secularization—a process that shaped them as much as it shaped Graham's crusades—and the songs and prayers that tied them together across national boundaries.

Acknowledgments

I vaguely remember the day when I was on one of my first research trips to the Billy Graham Centre Archives all those years ago. I wanted to write a book on American evangelicalism as a German historian, and that was how far I had come. One day Mark Noll invited me to have a cup of coffee at his office at Wheaton College, and we talked about the history of a movement he knew so well. We discussed my home country he was so fond of and the many academic, religious, and political connections between Germany and the United States. At the end of our conversation, he encouraged me, as he had encouraged so many other researchers before me, to pursue my ideas. Later that day, back at the archives, Bob Shuster, with his intimate knowledge of all of Graham's files and his movements, put a folder onto my desk asking: "You know that he went to Germany?" The folder contained the schedule for Billy Graham's first European tour in 1954, and that very moment the idea for this book was born.

What followed were years of transnational research that matched my own career trajectory. Among the greatest privileges of having worked on this book in three different countries were the people I got to know, who enriched this project through their knowledge of archival materials, their intellectual generosity, and their friendship. To them I owe deep gratitude.

This book took shape while I was a research fellow at the German Historical Institute in Washington, DC, which generously funded large proportions of the research for this book. It also provided a stimulating in- tellectual environment, and I am sure my former colleagues Philipp Gassert, Katharina Kloock, Jan Logemann, Anke Ortlepp, Ines Prodoehl, Corinna Unger, and Richard Wetzell will find our many conversations about Billy Graham reflected in this book. I would also like to thank the fantastic interns who conducted much of the newspaper research that went into this book, among them Birte Meinschien, who has turned into an excellent historian in her own right.

I am grateful for the intellectual input from and the time spent with my wonderful US-based colleagues John Corrigan, Darren Dochuk, Aaron Griffith, David King, Kathryn Lofton, Laurie Maffly-Kipp, Matthew Sutton, and Anne Wills. And I am particularly grateful to Grant Wacker, who adopted me and this project as part of his extended academic family, who always asked the right questions, and whose support I could always rely on. I am also indebted to Melani McAlister, who read large portions of the manuscript with an eye equally critical and kind and provided excellent ideas for improvement.

Melani was also integral to the stimulating discussions of the transatlantic research group A Global History of US Evangelicalism, which shaped this book in important ways. I can't thank enough Heather Curtis, Hans Krabbendam, John Maiden, Kendrick Oliver, Axel Schäfer, Tim Stoneman, and David Swartz, who generously shared with me their own thinking about transnational religious history. The intriguing and unique conversations we shared demonstrated again and again why research and knowledge know no borders.

Several German colleagues from different disciplines have provided me with the opportunity to discuss my ideas, and their questions, comments, and own work have profoundly shaped this book. I would like to especially thank Karl Ditt, Christiane Eisenberg, Thomas Großbölting, Klaus Große Kracht, Hubert Knoblauch, Inken Prohl, Katja Rakow, and Thomas Welskopp.

Scholars of British religious history have generously shared their knowledge with me, and I hope that David Bebbington, Callum Brown, Grace Davie, and David Hempton will see how much their thinking has shaped my own since we all met at the Radcliffe Institute for Advanced Studies. I would especially like to thank Hugh McLeod, who invited me to the workshops he organized there and who arranged for several other opportunities to discuss my work with him and others. His comments on my work were always thoughtful, probing, kind, and supportive. No less influential on my thinking about the project were the British historians of the United States, and I would especially like to thank Kendrick Oliver and Adam Smith for inviting me into the inspiring community of the Institute of Historical Research North American History seminar. This became an important intellectual home, and their support and friendship were all the more important for its timing, coming right after my move to the United Kingdom.

I have been privileged to benefit from the kindness of, support from, and conversations with my wonderful colleagues at King's College London. In the everyday of teaching and student support, my close collaborations with Clare Birchall and Dan Matlin have been as rewarding as they were inspiring, and both have been sources of strength and encouragement in more ways than they can know. Also at King's College London I learned so much from my own undergraduate and graduate students. Two of my former PhD students have shaped this book in profound ways, and I would like to thank Samuel Jeffery for sharing his own impressive knowledge of transnational religious history. Chris Birkett not only shared my interest in religion and sports, but was also an outstanding and insightful personal editor whose interventions strengthened this manuscript significantly.

Several archivists have shared their knowledge with me, and I would like to thank all of them. Our research as historians would not be possible without their hard work behind the scenes. Werner Beyer at the Archives of the German Evangelical Alliance in Bad Blankenburg guided me through uncataloged files and equally enhanced my knowledge of evangelical life in Germany. I owe my deepest gratitude to Bob Shuster and Paul Erikson at the Billy Graham Archives for their commitment to keeping Billy Graham's memory alive, for their hospitality and good humor, and for many shared meals and conversations. You made me feel at home at these archives where I spent so much of my time.

Theo Calderara at Oxford University Press embraced this book with open arms, and I can't thank him enough for that. Isabell Prince and the editorial team at Oxford University Press finalized the manuscript in a genuinely supportive and meticoulous way. The comments of the two anonymous reviewers gave this book additional breadth and depth and turned the manuscript into a better book. And I would like to thank Paul Betts, who over lunch, gave this book its title. I would also like to thank Oxford University Press for allowing me to reuse parts of a previously published chapter in Chapter 3: "Billy Graham's Cold War Crusades: Rechristianization, Secularization, and the Spiritual Creation of the Free World in the 1950s," in *Secularization and Religious Innovation in the North Atlantic World*, ed. David Hampton and Hugh McLeod (New York: Oxford University Press, 2017), 234–254.

Writing this book was also a spiritual journey for me. While I wrote about those exploring their faith, questioning it, and living it, I felt again and again invited to reflect on my own faith, my Catholic upbringing, and my current religious home in the Church of England. I am grateful for those who provided the intellectual and spiritual input to make these explorations more meaningful, probing, and fruitful for me, namely Fr. Jim Greenfield; Michael Suarez, SJ; Rev. Georgie Simpson (†), Rev. Andrew Bunch, and Rev. Daniel Walters. Many friends close by and further away provided support and distraction—whatever was needed more. This list will certainly be incomplete, and yet I would like to especially thank Liz Holmes, Louise Jarvis, Frances Bagnall-Oakeley, Diana McEwen, Eva Walters, Anke Ortlepp, Kathrin Melliwa, and Richard Wetzell.

Those who move a lot often face the question where home is. My home is my family. I firmly believe that this book would have remained unfinished if it had not been for the unconditional faith in my work by my godmother, Ursula Ott. It would have been written with less laughter and smiles if it had not been for my sister Barbara Emanuel and her wonderful family, Thomas, Lara, Helena, and Emilia, and the precious times we spent together. This book would have been written differently if my parents Ralf und Antonia Balbier had not stood by their word to provide their children with roots and wings. There are no words to express my gratitude to them. While working on *Altar Call* I formed my own family. Jan Palmowski did not just read the full manuscript, but also lived with it all these years and shaped it with sharp comments, probing questions, and his unmatched intellectual generosity and kindness. I enjoyed every single one of our conversations about this book, but even more so our son Max's cheeky attempts to make these conversations increasingly impossible. Nothing matters more to me than the two of you, and I dedicate this book to you with love and deepest gratitude.

Notes

Introduction

1. https://www.wheaton.edu/media/billy-graham-center-archives/Chronology-1934-2018.pdf.

2. See the two outstanding academic biographies on Graham: Grant Wacker, *America's Pastor: Billy Graham and the Shaping of a Nation*, Cambridge, MA: Harvard University Press, 2014 and William Martin, *A Prophet with Honor: The Billy Graham Story*, New York: William Morrow, 1991.

3. James Enns, *Saving Germany: North American Protestants and Christian Mission to Germany, 1945–1974*, Montreal: McGill University Press, 2017; John Corrigan and Frank Hinkelmann, *Return to Sender: American Evangelical Missions to Europe in the 20th Century*, Berlin: Lit Verlag, 2019; Hans Krabbendam, *Saving the Overlooked Continent: American Protestant Missions in Western Europe, 1940–1975*, Leuven: Leuven University Press, 2021. See also Uta Balbier, "Youth for Christ in England und Deutschland: Religiöser Transnationalismus und christliche Nachkriegsordnung 1945–1948," *Archiv für Sozialgeschichte* 51 (2011): 209–224.

4. Joel Carpenter, *Revive Us Again: The Reawakening of American Fundamentalism*, New York: Oxford University Press, 1997.

5. Callum G. Brown, *Religion and Society in Twentieth-Century Britain*, London: Routledge, 2014, 188–202. See also Alana Harris and Martin Spence, "'Disturbing the Complacency of Religion'? The Evangelical Crusades of Dr Billy Graham and Father Patrick Peyton in Britain, 1951–54," *Twentieth Century British History* 18, no. 4 (2007): 481–513. The most detailed contemporary account of the events at Harringay is Frank Colquhoun, *Harringay Story: The Official Record of the Billy Graham Greater London Crusade, 1954*, London: Hodder and Stoughton, 1955.

6. Thomas Grossbölting, *Losing Heaven: Religion in Germany since 1945*, trans. Alex Skinner, New York: Berghahn, 2016, 160.

7. Richard Carwardine, *Transatlantic Revivalism: Popular Evangelicalism in Britain and America, 1790–1865*, Westport, CT: Greenwood Press, 1978; David Hempton, *Methodism: Empire of the Spirit*, New Haven: Yale University Press, 2005; David Bebbington, *Victorian Religious Revivals: Culture and Piety in Local and Global Contexts*, New York: Oxford University Press, 2012; Mark A. Noll, David Bebbington, and George A. Rawlyk, *Evangelicalism: Comparative Studies of Popular Protestantism in North America, the British Isles, and Beyond, 1700–1990*, New York: Oxford University Press, 1994.

8. Randall Herbert Balmer, *Evangelicalism in America*, Waco, TX: Baylor University Press, 2016; David Bebbington, *Evangelicalism in Modern Britain: A History from*

the 1730s to the 1980s, London: Unwin Hayman, 1989; Gisa Bauer, *Evangelikale Bewegung und evangelische Kirche in der Bundesrepublik Deutschland: Geschichte eines Grundsatzkonflikts (1945–1989)*, Göttingen: Vandenhoeck & Ruprecht, 2012; Friedhelm Jung, *Die deutsche evangelikale Bewegung: Grundlinien ihrer Geschichte und Theologie*, 3rd ed., Bonn: Verlag für Kultur und Wissenschaft, 2001; Frederik Elwert, Martin Radermacher, and Jens Schlamelcher, *Handbuch Evangelikalismus*, Bielefeld: Transcript Verlag, 2017.

9. This speaks to the important sociological framework developed in Grace Davie, *Religion in Britain since 1945: Believing without Belonging*, Oxford: Blackwell, 1994.

10. Simon J. D. Green, *The Passing of Protestant England: Secularisation and Social Change, c.1920–1960*, Cambridge: Cambridge University Press, 2011, 254. For the historiographical context see Jeremy Morris, "Secularization and Religious Experience: Arguments in the Historiography of Modern British Religion," *Historical Journal* 55, no. 1 (2012): 195–219.

11. Green, *Passing of Protestant England*, 272.

12. Hugh McLeod, *The Religious Crisis of the 1960s*, Oxford: Oxford University Press, 2007, 249. See also the important transatlantic studies collected in David Hempton and Hugh McLeod, *Secularization and Religious Innovation in the North Atlantic World*, New York: Oxford University Press, 2017. A case against "American exceptionalism" in the field of religious history is also made by Mark Ruff, "Religious Transformation since 1945: Is There an American Religious Exceptionalism?," in *Schweizerische Zeitschrift für Religions- und Kulturgeschichte* 107 (2013): 33–48. For the European-American divide in the field of religion see Peter L. Berger, Grace Davie, and Effie Fokas, *Religious America, Secular Europe? A Theme and Variations*, Aldershot: Ashgate, 2008.

13. A critical assessment along the same lines was made by Mark Ruff, "Integrating Religion into the Historical Mainstream: Recent Literature on Religion in the Federal Republic of Germany," *Central European History* 42 (2009): 307–337. Ruff points out as well the lack of works that cross confessional boundaries and identifies a "seeming alienation of religious history from the historical mainstream" (p. 308).

14. Bauer, *Evangelikale Bewegung*.

15. Meredith McGuire, *Lived Religion: Faith and Practice in Everyday Life*, New York: Oxford University Press, 2008, 21; see also Nancy Ammerman, *Everyday Religion: Observing Modern Religious Lives*, New York: Oxford University Press, 2006.

16. David T. Hall, "Introduction," in David Hall, *Lived Religion in America: Toward a History of Practice*, Princeton, NJ: Princeton University Press, 1997, vii. Methodologically I am building on Robert A. Orsi, *Between Heaven and Earth: The Religious Worlds People Make and the Scholars Who Study Them*, Princeton, NJ: Princeton University Press, 2005; Robert A. Orsi, *The Madonna of 115th Street*, 2nd ed., New Haven: Yale University Press, 2002.

17. Michael O'Sullivan, "From Catholic Milieu to Lived Religion: The Social and Cultural History of Modern German Catholicism," *History Compass* 7, no. 3 (2009): 837–861; and most recently Michael O'Sullivan, *Disruptive Power: Catholic Women, Miracles, and Politics in Modern Germany, 1918–1965*, Toronto: University of Toronto Press,

2018; and for British Catholicism Alana Harris, *Faith in the Family: A Lived Religious History of English Catholicism, 1945–82*, Manchester: Manchester University Press, 2013. However, the tremendous potential of such an approach to British Protestantism is demonstrated for an earlier period by Sarah Williams, *Religious Belief and Popular Culture in Southwark, c 1880–1939*, Oxford: Oxford University Press, 1999.

18. Jason W. Stevens, *God-Fearing and Free: A Spiritual History of America's Cold War*, Cambridge, MA: Harvard University Press, 2010; Jonathan P. Herzog, *The Spiritual-Industrial Complex: America's Religious Battle against Communism in the Early Cold War*, New York: Oxford University Press, 2011; Raymond Haberski Jr., *God and War: American Civil Religion since 1945*, New Brunswick, NJ: Rutgers University Press, 2012; William Inboden, *Religion and American Foreign Policy, 1945–1960: The Soul of Containment*, New York: Cambridge University Press, 2008. See also the earlier work: Stephen J. Whitfield, *The Culture of the Cold War*, Baltimore: Johns Hopkins University Press, 1991, 77–91. For the broader historical context see Andrew Preston, *Sword of the Spirit, Shield of Faith: Religion in American War and Diplomacy*, 1st ed., New York: Alfred A. Knopf, 2012.

19. Keith Robbins, *History, Religion, and Identity in Modern Britain*, London: Hambledon Press, 1993.

20. Martin Greschat, "'Rechristianisierung' und 'Säkularisierung': Anmerkungen zu einem europäischen interkonfessionellen Interpretationsmodell," in *Christentum und politische Verantwortung: Kirchen im Nachkriegsdeutschland*, ed. Jochen-Christoph Kaiser and Anselm *Doering-Manteuffel*, Stuttgart: Kohlhammer Verlag, 1990, 1–24; Axel Schildt, *Zwischen Abendland und Amerika: Studien zur westdeutschen Ideenlandschaft der 50er Jahre*, Munich: R. Oldenbourg Verlag, 1999; Martin Greschat, *Protestantismus im Kalten Krieg: Kirche, Politik und Gesellschaft im geteilten Deutschland 1945–1963*, Paderborn: Verlag Ferdinant Schoeningh, 2010.

21. Darren E. Grem, *The Blessings of Business: How Corporations Shaped Conservative Christianity*, New York: Oxford University Press, 2016; Sarah Hammond, *God's Businessmen: Entrepreneurial Evangelicals in Depression and War*, ed. Darren Dochuk, Chicago: University of Chicago Press, 2017; Kevin Kruse, *One Nation under God. How Corporate America Invented Christian America*, New York: Basic Books, 2015; Darren Dochuk, *Anointed with Oil: How Christianity and Crude Made Modern America*, New York: Basic Books, 2019. This recent historiographical turn is captured in Amanda Porterfield, John Corrigan, and Darren E. Grem, *The Business Turn in American Religious History*, New York: Oxford Scholarship Online, 2017.

22. Bethany Moreton, *To Serve God and Wal-Mart: The Making of Christian Free Enterprise*, Cambridge, MA: Harvard University Press, 2009.

23. Lieven Boeve and Kristien Justaert, *Consuming Religion in Europe? Christian Faith Challenged by Consumer Culture*, Münster: LIT Verlag, 2006.

24. For an overview on the interplay between business, wealth, and Christianity in British history, see David J. Jeremy, "Introduction: Debates about Interactions between Religion, Business and Wealth in Modern Britain," in *Religion, Business and Wealth in Modern Britain*, ed. David J. Jeremy, New York: Routledge, 1998, 1–34. See also his

in-depth study David J. Jeremy, *Capitalists and Christians: Business Leaders and the Churches in Britain, 1900–1960*, Oxford: Clarendon Press, 1990.

25. I am building here on the arguments by Vincent Jude Miller, *Consuming Religion: Christian Faith and Practice in a Consumer Culture*, New York; London: Continuum, 2005 and Kathryn Lofton, *Consuming Religion*, Chicago: University of Chicago Press, 2018.

26. Kurt Lang and Gladys Lang, "Decisions for Christ: Billy Graham in New York," in *Identity and Anxiety: Survival of the Person in Mass Society*, ed. Maurice R. Stein, Arthur J. Vidich, and David M. White, New York: Free Press, 1960, 415–427.

27. James Hudnut-Beumler, *Looking for God in the Suburbs: The Religion of the American Dream and Its Critics, 1945–1965*, New Brunswick, NJ: Rutgers University Press, 1994.

28. I am building here on Hugh McLeod's important reflections on the impact of "affluence" on the way Europeans practice their religion and live their religious lives. McLeod, *Religious Crisis*, 102–123. See also Grace Davie, *Religion in Britain: A Persistent Paradox*, 2nd ed., Chichester: John Wiley and Sons, 2015, 133–174. ProQuest Ebook Central, https://ebookcentral.proquest.com/lib/oxford/detail.action?docID=1887762.

29. "Man muß ihn hören," *Berliner Sonntagsblatt, die Kirche*, Sonderausgabe, June 27, 1954, 2.

30. "Daher ist anzunehmen, dass die amerikanischen Evangelikalen um Billy Graham während des Berliner Kongresses unbeabsichtigt die deutschen (aus dem Bereich der Ev. Allianz kommenden) Konferenzteilnehmer anregten, sich selbst als in der evangelikalen Tradition stehend zu erkennen und durch die Übernahme des Begriffes auch terminologisch den Anschluß an die im angelsächsischen Raum schon zu einem breiten Strom angeschwollene evangelikale Bewegung zu vollziehen." Peter Beyreuther, quoted in Jung, *Die deutsche evangelikale Bewegung*, 24–25.

31. See also for the fascinating history of transnational engagement of American missionaries abroad during the early American republic: Emily Conroy-Krutz, *Christian Imperialism: Converting the World in the Early American Republic*, Ithaca, NY: Cornell University Press, 2015.

32. David R. Swartz, *Facing West: American Evangelicals in an Age of World Christianity*, New York: Oxford University Press, 2020, 5.

33. Heather Curtis, "Depicting Distant Suffering: Evangelicals and the Politics of Pictorial Humanitarianism in the Age of American Empire," *Material Religion* 8, no. 2 (2012): 154–183.

34. Heather Curtis, *Holy Humanitarians: American Evangelicals and Global Aid*, Cambridge. MA: Harvard University Press, 2018; David P. King, *God's Internationalists: World Vision and the Age of Evangelical Humanitarianism*, Philadelphia: University of Pennsylvania Press, 2019.

35. Melani McAlister, *The Kingdom of God Has No Borders: A Global History of US Evangelicals*, New York: Oxford University Press, 2018, 11.

36. My interpretation of the function of prayer builds on the work of scholars on charismatic religiosity: R. Marie Griffith, "Submissive Wives, Wounded Daughters, and Female Soldiers: Prayer and Christian Womanhood in Women's Aglow Fellowship,"

in *Lived Religion in America: Toward a History of Practice*, ed. David D. Hall, Princeton: Princeton University Press, 1997, 160–195; Yannick Fer, "Pentecostal Prayer as Personal Communication and Invisible Institutional Work," in *A Sociology of Prayer*, ed. Guiseppe Giordan and Linda Woodhead, 49–65, Farnham: Ashgate, 2015.

37. Guiseppe Giordan, "You Never Know: Prayer as Enchantment," in *A Sociology of Prayer*, ed. Guiseppe Giordan and Linda Woodhead, Farnham: Ashgate, 2015, 2.

38. Birgit Meyer, "Introduction. From Imagined Communities to Aesthetic Formations: Religious Mediations, Sensational Forms, and Styles of Binding," in *Aesthetic Formations: Media, Religion, and the Senses*, ed. Birgit Meyer, New York: Palgrave Macmillan, 2010, 5.

Chapter 1

1. "Crusade for Britain," *Time*, March 8, 1954, 73.

2. Countless accounts of the opening night at Harringay appeared in the religious and secular press. See, for example, "Evangelism of Mr. Graham," *The Times*, March 2, 1954, 3; "What It Looked Like at Harringay," *British Weekly*, March 4, 1954, 5. From the organizers' perspective: Colquhoun, *Harringay Story*, 87–95.

3. Davie, *Religion in Britain*, 7.

4. For the complicated spectrum of evangelical organizations in Germany inside and outside the Evangelical Church see Bauer, *Evangelikale Bewegung*. Bauer's main argument is that the history of the evanglical movement in Germany was shaped predominantly by its interaction with the Evangelical Church, in particular through its constitutive critique of the church. See esp. 82–85.

5. Wacker, *America's Pastor*. The exception is Brown's in-depth assessment of Harringay as part of his history of religion in 1950s Britain: Brown, *Religion and Society*, 188–202. Grossbölting's comprehensive religious history of Germany post-1945 mentions Graham only once in passing. Grossbölting, *Losing Heaven*, 160.

6. William G. McLaughlin, *Modern Revivalism: Charles Grandison Finney to Billy Graham*, reprinted Eugene, OR: Wipf & Stock Publishers, 2005, 8 (originally published by the Ronald Press Company, 1959). Robert Wuthnow builds compellingly on McLaughlin's interpretation of the 1950s revival in *The Restructuring of American Religion: Society and Faith since World War II*, Princeton, NJ: Princeton University Press, 1988.

7. Callum Brown, *The Death of Christian Britain: Understanding Secularization, 1800–2000*, Routledge: London, 2009, 173.

8. Grossbölting, *Losing Heaven*, 23.

9. On the Los Angeles revival see Martin, *Prophet with Honor*, 106–120.

10. Wuthnow, *Restructuring of American Religion*, 17; see also Hudnut-Beumler, *Looking for God*, 29–84.

11. Wuthnow, *Restructuring of American Religion*, 140–145.

12. Hudnut-Beumler, *Looking for God*, 31.

13. Martin, *Prophet with Honor*, 106.

14. Matthew A. Sutton, *American Apocalypse: A History of Modern Evangelicalism*, Cambridge, MA: Harvard University Press, 2014, xiv. World War II as a transformative point in US evangelicalism is a focus of the groundbreaking study by Carpenter, *Revive Us Again*.

15. For a selection of campaign posters see all folders in Box 7, CN 1, BGCA. On the listeners in their cars: "Tent Revival to Continue," *Los Angeles Times*, October 24, 1949, A8.

16. "Tent Revival to Close with Famous Sermon," *Los Angeles Times*, November 12, 1949, A3.

17. "That Old Time Religion Goes Modern," *Daily News*, September 30, 1949, 3. Image of kneeling people in prayer is a nice contrast to the rather lurid article accompanying the image on the conversion of television star: Harvey Fritts, "Revival Steers Colonel Zack," *Los Angeles Examiner*, November 3, 1949, 1.

18. "Watchman in Night Prays with Strays," *Los Angeles Times*, November 5, 1949, A2.

19. Billy Graham, *Revival in Our Time: The Story of the Billy Graham Evangelistic Campaigns*, Wheaton, IL: Von Kampen Press, 1950, 73. Quoted from his first sermon delivered in Los Angeles: *Revival in Our Time*, 69–80.

20. Reinhold Niebuhr, "Religiosity and Christian Faith," *Christianity and Crisis*, January 24, 1955, 1.

21. For a critique of the state of religion in the 1950s United States see Will Herberg, *Protestant, Catholic, Jew: An Essay in American Religious Sociology*, Garden City, NY: Doubleday, 1955; Peter Berger, *The Noise of Solemn Assemblies: Christian Commitment and the Religious Establishment in America*, Garden City, NY: Doubleday, 1961; Gibson Winter, *The Suburban Captivity of the Churches: An Analysis of Protestant Responsibility in the Expanding Metropolis*, Garden City, NY: Doubleday, 1961. There is a masterly analysis in Hudnut-Beumler, *Looking for God*, 109–174. See also Andrew Finstuen, *Original Sin and Everyday Protestants: The Theology of Reinhold Niebuhr, Billy Graham, and Paul Tillich in an Age of Anxiety*, Chapel Hill: University of North Carolina Press, 2009, 13–46, on Graham as a proponent of the so-called captive revival, 3.

22. Graham, *Revival in Our Time*, 106. Quoted form his sermon: "How to Be Filled with the Spirit," 105–121.

23. Data as given by the Billy Graham Center Archives: https://www.wheaton.edu/media/billy-graham-center-archives/Chronology-1934-2018.pdf.

24. Graham, *Revival in Our Time*, 70.

25. Harold Ockenga, "Berlin a Symbol of Conquered Germany," *United Evangelical Action*, September 1, 1947, 5–6, 9; Harold Ockenga, "The Source of Future German Democracy," *United Evangelical Action*, September 15, 1947, 5–6.

26. Torrey M. Johnson, "Will the German Nation Be Lost for God?," *United Evangelical Action*, October 15, 1947, 5–6.

27. T. Christie Innes, "Britain's Spiritual State an American Concern," *United Evangelical Action*, April 15, 1946, 11–12.

28. Torrey Johnson, "Out Your Way," *Youth for Christ Magazine*, June 1946, 4.

29. "Evangelist Will Remain Silent on Cohen Matter," *Los Angeles Times*, November 16, 1949, 28.

30. Ian Randall and David Hilborn, *One Body in Christ: The History and Significance of the Evangelical Alliance*, Carlisle: Paternoster Press, 2001, 182 and 224.

31. Adrian Hastings, *A History of English Christianity, 1920–1990*, 3rd ed., Philadelphia: Trinity Press International, 1991, 453–454. For the particular religious atmosphere of the 1950s see also 403–504.

32. Brown, *Death of Christian Britain*, 188; also Hastings, *History*, 444.

33. For a renaissance of British evangelicalism after World War II see Bebbington, *Evangelicalism in Modern Britain*, 249–263; and Kenneth Hylson-Smith, *Evangelicals in the Church of England, 1734–1984*, Edinburgh: T & T Clark, 1988, 287–293.

34. Alister Chapman, *Godly Ambition: John Stott and the Evangelical Movement*, Oxford: Oxford University Press, 2014, 79–84.

35. Hylon-Smith, *Evangelicals*, 288.

36. According to Bebbington, Inter-Varsity Fellowship is "probably the most important single factor behind the advance of conservative evangelicalism in the postwar period." Bebbington, *Evangelicalism in Modern Britain*, 259.

37. Chapman, *Godly Ambition*, 40.

38. The evangelical fever of the decade is captured in Bebbington, *Evangelicalism in Modern Britain*, 249–263; Randall and Hilborn, *One Body in Christ*, 217–221; and from a personal perspective in Jean A. Rees, *His Name Was Tom: The Biography of Tom Rees*, London: Hodder and Stoughton, 1971.

39. Other members include Lieutenant Colonel D. C. D. Munro and the businessmen Lindsay Klegg and Alfred Owen; Rev. Frank Colquhoun, editor of the *London Crusade News*; Maurice Rowlandson, a British evangelical who would become Graham's representative in Britain; and Roy Cattell of the British Evangelical Alliance. Memberships are listed in "First Short Report by Rev. Blinco," Minutes of the Executive Committee held at 30, Bedford Place, August 17, 1953, Minute Book Executive Committee Billy Graham Greater London Crusade, 12, Archives of the Evangelical Alliance UK (AEAUK).

40. Minutes of the First Meeting of the Executive Committee held at 30, Bedford Place, on January 29, 1953, Minute Book Executive Committee Billy Graham Greater London Crusade, 1, AEAUK.

41. Rev. Hugh R. Gough, "My Impressions of Billy Graham," *London Crusade News*, November 1953, 2.

42. Minutes of the First Meeting of the Executive Committee held at 30, Bedford Place, on January 29, 1953, Minute Book Billy Graham Executive Committee, 2, AEAUK.

43. "Billy Graham and the Greater London Crusade," *The Times*, February 25, 1954, 8.

44. "Billy Graham—the Man and His Ministry," *Christian Herald and Sign of Our Times*, February 27, 1954, 131 and 140.

45. "Billy's Britain," *Time*, March 22, 1954, 67. On his welcome and the press: "The Crusade for Britain," *Time*, March 8, 1954, 72–74; "34,586 Decisions," *Time*, May 31, 1954, 44.

46. "Evangelist Billy Graham London's Top Attraction: Young American Overcomes the First Wave of Cynical and Critical Appraisal," *New York Times*, March 7, 1954, E6.

47. "USA-Apostel Billy bekehrt die Engländer," *Hamburger Abend*, May 25, 1954, Magazine and Newspaper Clippings Collection, Reel 8, CN 360, BGCA.

48. "Mit Bibel, Mikrophon und Cowboy," *Frankfurter Allgemeine Zeitung*, April 2, 1954, 2; "Der Evangelist," *Frankfurter Allgemeine Zeitung*, June 1, 1954, 2.

49. Wilhelm Brauer, *Billy Graham, ein Evangelist der neuen Welt*, Giessen: Brunnen Verlag, 1954.

50. Paul Deitenbeck, *Eine Weltstadt horcht auf: Begegnung mit Billy Graham*, no date, no place, copy held at the Stadtbibliothek Wuppertal (KAPS.23.25).

51. Billy Graham, *Friede mit Gott*, Wuppertal: R. Brockhaus Verlag, 1954.

52. Prospectus Billy Graham Continental Tour, June 12–30, 1954, no date or author, Folder 3, Box 5, CN 622, BGCA.

53. Zentralausschuss-Arbeitstagung in Patmos, 17.1.1955, ADEA.

54. Deutsche Evangelistenkonferenz, Besuch des Evangelisten Pfarrer Dr. Billy Graham i. Deutschland im Juni 1954, Weihnachten 1953, ADEA.

55. Brauer to Zilz, June 16, 1954, ADEA.

56. Brauer, *Billy Graham*, 97–98.

57. For Lilje's and Dibelius's life and thinking see Hanns Lilje, *Memorabilia: Schwerpunkte eines Lebens*, Nuremberg: Laetere Verlag, 1973; Robert Stupperich, *Otto Dibelius: Ein evangelischer Bischof im Umbruch der Zeiten*, Göttingen: Vandenhoek & Ruprecht, 1989.

58. Martin Greschat, *Die evangelische Christenheit und die deutsche Geschichte nach 1945: Weichenstellungen in der Nachkriegszeit*, Stuttgart: W. Kohlhammer Verlag, 2002, 71.

59. Grossbölting, *Losing Heaven*, 27.

60. Bauer, *Evangelikale Bewegung*, 178–180.

61. Bauer, *Evangelikale Bewegung*, 179.

62. On the *Kirchentage* see Benjamin Pearson, "The Pluralization of Protestant Politics: Public Responsibility, Rearmament, and Division at the 1950s *Kirchentage*," *Central European History* 43 (2010): 270–300. On the Akademien: Thomas Mittmann, *Kirchliche Akademien in der Bundesrepublik: Gesellschaftliche, politische und religiöse Selbstverortungen*, Göttingen: Wallstein Verlag, 2011. On new religious forms in and visibility of German Catholicism see Michael E. O'Sullivan, "West German Miracles: Catholic Mystics, Church Hierarchy, and Postwar Popular Culture," *Zeithistorische Forschungen / Studies in Contemporary History* 6 (2009): article 1, http://www.zeithistorische-forschungen.de/16126041-OSullivan-1-2009.

63. Nicolai Hannig, *Die Religion der Öffentlichkeit: Medien, Religion und Kirche in der Bundesrepublik 1945–1980*, Göttingen: Wallstein Verlag, 2010; Frank Bösch and Lucian Hölscher, *Kirchen-Medien-Öffentlichkeit: Transformationen kirchlicher Selbst- und Fremddeutungen seit 1945*, Göttingen: Wallstein Verlag, 2009.

64. "Kreuzritter im flotten Dreireiher," *Ruhr Nachrichten*, June 25, 1954, Magazine and Newspaper Clippings Collection, Reel 8, CN 360, BGCA.

65. "50,000 kamen, um Billy Graham sprechen zu hören," *Westdeutsche Rundschau*, June 25, 1954, Magazine and Newspaper Clippings Collection, Reel 8, CN 360, BGCA. See also the vast number of articles from the German national and regional press, which allow one to reconstruct the contours of the event. Note that numbers regarding attendance shifted between twenty-five thousand and fifty thousand, as well as the fact that only one article speaks exactly of five hundred inquirers, while many just speak of several hundred.

66. Programm der Veranstaltung im Olympiastadion Dr Billy Graham am 27. Juni 1954, Folder 3, Box 5, CN 622, BGCA.

67. "Graham Exhorts Berliners," *New York Times*, June 28, 1954, 14.

68. "80000 Menschen," *Berliner Sonntagsblatt, die Kirche*, no. 27, 1954, 5.

69. John Cogley, "Billy Graham at the Garden," *Commonweal*, June 21, 1957, 302.

70. "That Old Time Religion Goes Modern," *Daily News*, September 30, 1949, 3.

71. "Mr Graham Sets to Work," *Manchester Guardian*, March 2, 1954, 4.

72. "Statistics of a Crusade," *The Times*, May 30, 1954, 2.

73. "Das Nüchterne," *Frankfurter Allgemeine Zeitung*, June 24, 1955, 2.

74. "Ein Missionar unter Christen," *Tagesspiegel*, June 29, 1954, 4.

75. Dorothy C. Haskin, "Spiritual Awakening in California," *Moody Monthly*, January 1950, 328–329.

76. "Letters to the Editor by Barrington Baptist David L. Madeira and Louis A. Petersen, United Presbyterian Church, U.S.A." *Christianity Today*, June 23, 1958, 27.

77. "Catholic Paper Lauds Dr. Graham," *Washington Post*, February 3, 1952, M13.

78. "Graham Ban Ruling Given to Catholics," *Reporter Dispatch*, June 1, 1957, Folder 1, Box 3, CN 1, BGCA.

79. "Priest Explains Ban on Revival Meetings," *World Telegram and Sun*, May 31, 1957, Folder 21, Box 2, CN 1, BGCA.

80. On the Graham-McIntire controversy see Markku Ruotsila, *Fighting Fundamentalist: Carl McIntire and the Politicization of American Fundamentalism*, New York: Oxford University Press, 2016, esp. 133 and 139–140.

81. Bebbington, *Evangelicalism in Modern Britain*, 267.

82. In the early 1950s, German evangelicals had their home in the German holiness movement (*Gemeinschaftsbewegung*) organized in the Gnadauer Gemeinschaftverband, in the revival movement composed of evangelists and missionaries (for example, the Deutsche Evangelistenkonferenz), in missionary seminars and Bible colleges, and in the Deutsche Evangelische Allianz, which emerged from the international Evangelical Alliance founded in 1846. See Bauer, *Evangelikale Bewegung*, 40; also Jung, *Die deutsche evangelikale Bewegung*; Siegfried Hermle, "Die Evangelikalen als Gegenbewegung," in *Umbrüche: Der deutsche Protestantismus und die sozialen Bewegungen in den 1960er und 70er Jahren*, ed. Siegfried Hermle, Claudia Lepp, and Harry Oelke, Göttingen: Vandenhoeck & Ruprecht, 2007, 325–352. See also earlier studies produced from within the movement: Erich Beyreuther, *Der Weg der Evangelischen Allianz in Deutschland*, Wuppertal: R. Brockhaus Verlag, 1969; Fritz Laubach, *Aufbruch der Evangelikalen*, Wuppertal: R. Brockhaus Verlag, 1972.

83. Walther Zilz to Paul Deitenbeck, Berleburg, May 26, 1954; Walther Zilz an die Brüder des Vorstandes unserer Deutschen Evangelischen Allianz, June 10, 1955, AGEA, Bad Blankenburg.

84. Walther Zilz an die Brüder des Vorstandes unserer Deutschen Evangelischen Allianz, June 10, 1955, ADEA. See also Sitzung des Zentralausschusses für die Vorbereitung und Ausführung der Billy-Graham-Evangelisationen in Deutschland am Freitag, 18. März 1955, im Haus des C.V.J.M. in Frankfurt/M, ADEA.

85. "Youth and the Billy Graham Campaign," *Methodist Recorder*, March 11, 1954, 12. Graham stirred similar debates in American Methodist circles, Finstuen, *Original Sin*, 131.

86. "Dr Soper and Moral Rearmament," *Methodist Recorder*, March 18, 1954, 5.

87. Rev. A. William Hopkins, "Billy Graham—Some Observations," *Methodist Recorder*, April 1, 1954, 9.

88. For Reed's critique see "Youth and the Billy Graham Campaign," *Methodist Recorder*, March 11, 1954, 12; Soper and Weatherhead are quoted in *Mood Monthly*, Special Issue, 1954, 88.

89. Editorial letter box, *Methodist Recorder*, March 18, 1954, 13. Very supportive also is the article "Heaven at Harringay," *Methodist Recorder*, April 8, 1954, 3.

90. Quoted in "God Bless Billy Graham," *Manchester Guardian*, March 26, 1954, 3.

91. Bebbington, *Evangelicalism in Modern Britain*, 267.

92. Rev. Dr. Townley Lord, "Will London Respond?," *London Crusade News*, February 1954, 3.

93. "Billy Graham among His Fellow Baptists," *Baptist Times*, March 18, 1954, 1.

94. Rev. Dr. Townley Lord, "Will London Respond?," *London Crusade News*, February 1954, 3.

95. "Billy Graham ist eine Frage an die Kirche." Heinrich Giesen, "Zum Thema 'Billy Graham,'" *Kirche und Mann*, August 1954, 7.

96. Giesen, "Zum Thema 'Billy Graham,'" 7.

97. "Mr. Graham's Campaign," *Church Times*, March 12, 1954, 200.

98. "Was sagen Sie zu Graham, erste Stimmen," *Berliner Sonntagsblatt, die Kirche*, no. 28, 1954, 4.

99. "Was sagen Sie zu Graham: Weitere Stimmen," *Berliner Sonntagsblatt, die Kirche*, no. 29, 1954, 5. "Es war eine Evangelisation in der Art der alten Welt mit den Mitteln der neuen durch einen Mann der neuen Welt."

100. "Talk of the Week," *Church of England Newspaper*, March 5, 1954, 4.

101. Finstuen, *Original Sin*, 131.

102. Finstuen, *Original Sin*, 63.

103. Finstuen, *Original Sin*, 60. Along similar lines argues Steven, *God-fearing and Free*, 29–63.

104. "Differing Views on Billy Graham," *Life*, July 1, 1957, 92.

105. Gollwitzer to Giesen, November 7, 1955, EZA, 71/1827.

106. It was only when Thielicke attended Graham's crusade in Los Angeles in 1963 that he changed his mind about Graham's style and mission. Now he was impressed by Graham's sincerity and modesty, even at the moment when thousands came

forward to accept Christ as their Savior. The German theologian was so impressed
that he published an open letter in the English church periodical *The Christian* in
German and English in which he apologized for his earlier theological judgments
about Graham's mission. He emphasized that the personal contact with the preacher
and the atmosphere during the crusade had altered his opinion. Self-critically, he
asked what he and his colleagues lacked that made Graham's mission necessary.
Helmut Thielicke, Brief an Billy Graham, Abschrift aus Die Gemeinde, 5. Januar
1964, ADEA.
107. Walter Dirks, "Trommler des lieben Gottes: Bermekungen zu Billy Graham und
Genossen," *Frankfurter Hefte* 10 (1955): 544.
108. "Editorial: Theology, Evangelism, Ecumenism," *Christianity Today*, January 20,
1958, 20.
109. Jerry Bevan to R. T. Ketcham, November 6, 1950, reprinted as part of Graham-
Ketcham Correspondence, 1, Folder 21, Box 11, CN 318, BGCA. This conflict would
deepen during future campaigns when Graham's team repeatedly invited "liberal"
or "modernist" ministers to join organizing committees. It would escalate further
during Graham's New York Crusade in 1957, when well-known modernists such
as John Sutherland Bonnell, Henry Van Dunsen, and Norman Vincent Peale were
asked to join the crusade team, enraging leading fundamentalists.
110. Steven P. Miller, *Billy Graham and the Rise of the Republican South*,
Philadelphia: University of Pennsylvania Press, 2009, 21–31.
111. Sutton, *American Apocalypse*, 290; on the racial implications of the NAE's founding
see also 286–287. Sutton also highlights the xenophobic rages that tainted the history of white conservative evangelicals. On anti-immigration sentiments after
World War I, see 123–125; on the difficult stance toward the Ku Klux Klan, 128–130;
and on racial integration during World War II, 278–279.
112. Quoted in Curtis Mitchell, *God in the Garden: The Amazing Story of Billy Graham's
First New York Crusade*, Garden City, NY: Doubleday, 2005 [1957], 50.
113. John Corrigan, *Business of the Heart: Religion and Emotion in the Nineteenth
Century*, Berkeley: University of California Press, 2002, 232. Later, in the context of
the New York Crusade in 1957, Graham would actively make his religious revival
work more attractive for African Americans by signing up the African American
pastor Howard Jones as associate evangelist and by sharing the crusade stage with
African American artists such as Ethel Walters. See Wacker, *America's Pastor*, 126.
114. Anthea Butler, *White Evangelical Racism: The Politics of Morality in America*, Chapel
Hill: University of North Carolina Press, 2021, 60. On Graham's revival work and
race see especially 33–55.
115. Witness statements in Colquhoun, *Harringay Story*, 238.
116. "Editorial Letter Box," *Methodist Recorder*, March 25, 1954, 11.
117. Protokoll der Sitzung des erweitertes Vertrauensrates der Deutschen
Evangelistenkonferenz in Fragen der stattgefundenen Billy-Graham-
Versammlungen in Deutschland, Donnerstag, 30. Juni 1955, im Heim des
C.V.J.M. in Frankfurt/M., 5. ADEA. And: Bericht über den Billy-Graham-Abend in
Mannheim. ADEA.

118. Bericht über den Billy-Graham-Abend in Mannheim. ADEA; "Der Evangelist im Stadion," *Frankfurter Allgemeine Zeitung*, July 2, 1955, 2.

119. Reprinted in Charles T. Cook, *London Hears Billy Graham*, London: Marshall, Morgan and Scott, 1954, 97.

120. "Letter to the Editors," *Baptist Times*, April 1, 1954, 7.

121. Deutsche Evangelistenkonferenz an die Leiter und Mitarbeiter in den Ortskomités für den Grahambesuch 1955, Dillbrecht über Haiger/Dillkreis, Himmelfahrt 1955, ADEA.

122. Wilhelm Brauer: Evangelisation Dr. Billy Graham in Deutschland im Sommer 1955, ADEA. Original "die verschiedensten christlichen Kreise sich zu einer aktiven evangelischen Allianz zusammenfanden."

123. Protokoll der "Brüderlichen Besprechung" in Fragen der Billy Graham Versammlung in Deutschland, am Pfingstmontag, 30. Mai 1955, im Parkhotel, Düsseldorf, 1–2, ADEA; Zentralausschuss-Arbeitstagung in Patmos, 17.1.1955, 2, ADEA.

124. Bericht über den Billy-Graham Abend in Mannheim, ADEA.

125. "Friendly neutrality" is the term used by Archbishop Geoffrey Fisher in Fisher to John Weaver, Detroit, February 2, 1954, Fisher Papers, Vol. 141, 1954, fol. 322, LPL. This position is also expressed in "Mr. Graham's Campaign," *Church Times*, March 12, 1954, 200.

126. Graham to Fisher, May 5, 1954, Fisher Papers, Vol. 141, 1954, fol. 348, LPL.

127. Fisher to Wilson-Haffenden, March 17, 1954, Fisher Papers, Vol. 141, 1954, fol. 327, LPL.

128. The fact was also noted in the United States: "Billy Graham's Biggest British Conquest," *Life*, June 7, 1954, 159.

129. Der evangelische Bischof von Berlin, An die Herren Geistlichen in Berlin, Berlin, den 9. April 1960, Landesarchiv Berlin (LAB), B Rep. 002, Nr. 1765. The German original reads: "Im ökumenischen Zeitalter sollten unsere Herzen dafür offen sein, wenn einmal ein Anstoß aus einem anderen Land und einer anderen Kirche kommt."

130. Wilhelm Brauer, "Was hat uns das zu sagen? Schlusswort," *Europas Goldene Stunde: Stimmen zum Besuch Billy Grahams aus Kirche, Presse und Gemeinde*, ed. Wilhelm Brauer, Wuppertal: Brockhaus Verlag, 1955, 90. The original reads: "Das ist nicht Amerikanismus, sondern christliche Allianz, Ökumene im allerinnigsten Sinne."

131. Seelig to Wilson, March 9, 1954, Folder 21, Box 1, CN 1, BGCA.

132. Cook, *London Hears Billy Graham*, 54.

133. Brown, *Death of Christian Britain*, 173.

Chapter 2

1. For details on marketing materials and scale see Mitchell, *God in the Garden*, 32.

2. "New Evangelist," *Time*, October 25, 1954, 56. On Graham as a brand see Grem, *The Blessings of Business*, 63.

3. Quoted in Mitchell, *God in the Garden*, 57.

4. For a concise overview of the relationship between religion and business in the United States and its historiography see Amanda Porterfield, John Corrigan, and Darren E. Grem, "Introduction," in *The Business Turn in American Religious History*, ed. Amanda Porterfield, John Corrigan, and Darren E. Grem, New York: Oxford Scholarship Online, 2017, http://www.oxfordscholarship.com/view/10.1093/oso/9780190280192.001.0001/oso-9780190280192-chapter-1.

5. Corrigan, *Business of the Heart*.

6. Darren Dochuk, "Moving Mountains: The Business of Evangelicalism and Extraction in a Liberal Age," in *What's Good for Business: Business and Politics since World War II*, ed. Julian Zelizer and Kimberly Phillips-Fein, New York: Oxford University Press, 2012, 72–90; Dochuk, *Anointed with Oil*; Dochuk, *God's Businessmen;* Kruse, *One Nation under God*.

7. Kruse, *One Nation under God*, 7.

8. Quoted in Hastings, *A History*, 422.

9. For an overview on the interplay between business, wealth, and Christianity in British history, see Jeremy, "Introduction."

10. Stathis Kalyvas, *The Rise of Christian Democracy in Europe*, Ithaca, NY: Cornell University Press, 1996.

11. Martin, *Prophet with Honor*, 113.

12. On the history of the Christian Business Men Committees see Grem, *Blessings of Business*, 36–42.

13. Martin, *Prophet with Honor*, 139.

14. The business community's support for the New York Crusade was quite striking: Stanley High, senior editor at *Readers Digest*; bestselling author Norman Vincent Peale; and media moguls Henry Luce and William Randolph Hearst, both supporters of Graham's mission since the Los Angeles crusade, joined the crusade's organizing committee. Edwin F. Chinlund, a top executive with experience as director of Western Union, General Telephone Co., General Public Utilities Corp., and Scandinavian Airline Systems, took over the post of treasurer in the committee. See Martin, *Prophet with Honor*, 225–226; and "City Businessmen Work for Crusade," *World-Telegram & Sun*, May 20, 1957, Folder 21, Box 2, CN 1, BGCA.

15. Martin, *Prophet with Honor*, 225–226.

16. Grem, *Blessings of Business*, 62.

17. On Graham and free enterprise, see Grem, *Blessings of Business*, 57–58.

18. "Differing Views on Billy Graham," *Life*, July 1, 1957, 92.

19. Reinhold Niebuhr, "After Comment, the Deluge," *Christian Century*, September 4, 1957, 1034–1035.

20. Graham, *Revival in Our Time*, 49.

21. "Editorially Speaking," *New York Crusade News*, December 1956, 2, Folder 18, Box 2, CN 1, BGCA.

22. Curtis Mitchell, *Those Who Came Forward: An Account of Those Whose Lives Were Changed by the Ministry of Billy Graham*, Kingswood: World's Works 1913, 1966, 116.

23. Martin, *Prophet with Honor*, 129–139. A compelling economic history of the BGEA can be found in Grem, *Blessings of Business*, 64–70. On Graham as an entrepreneur see also Wacker, *America's Pastor*, 137–167.
24. "Washington Is Ready," *Youth for Christ Magazine*, January 1952, 66.
25. Jeremy, *Capitalists and Christians*, 402. See also Proposed Estimated Budget, Billy Graham London Crusade, Folder 21, Box 1, CN 1, BGCA.
26. Bishop of Barking to Billy Graham, October 24, 1953, Folder 21, Box 1, CN 1, BGCA.
27. Prayer Partner-Newsletter, No. 5, no date, 2, Folder 5, Box 2, CN 9, BGCA.
28. Prayer Partner-Newsletter, No. 5, no date, 2, Folder 5, Box 2, CN 9, BGCA.
29. Clement to Ford Foundation, October 26, 1953 and Horace H. Hull to Ford Foundation, October 26, 1953, Folder 21, Box 1, CN 1, BGCA.
30. Whitaker to Wilson, January 13, 1954, Folder 21, Box 1, CN 1, BGCA.
31. Jeremy, *Capitalists and Christians*, 401.
32. "The Question of Finance," *London Crusade News*, November 1953, 3.
33. A comprehensive study of the interplay between business and Christianity in the United Kingdom is provided by Jeremy, *Capitalists and Christians*.
34. Godfrey C. Robinson, "After Harringay," *Baptist Times*, May 27, 1954, 9.
35. "What It Looked Like at Harringay," *British Weekly*, March 4, 1954, 5; "Letters to the Editors," *British Weekly*, March 25, 1954, 9.
36. The committee was formed in October 1953 and took on the responsibility for the negotiations surrounding the rent of Harringay Arena, the discussions about financial agreements with the Billy Graham organization, and the fundraising campaign in the United Kingdom. Jeremy, *Capitalists and Christians*, 400–401.
37. Jeremy, *Capitalists and Christians*, 402–404.
38. Jeremy, *Capitalists and Christians*, 405.
39. Jeremy, *Capitalists and Christians*, 408.
40. Jeremy, *Capitalists and Christians*, 404. See also Billy Graham Greater London Crusade, Statement of Income and Expenditure, Folder 3, Box 5, CN 9, BGCA.
41. Rev. F. T. Ellis, "Reaching London's Millions," *London Crusade News*, December 1953, 3.
42. Ellis, "Reaching London's Millions," 3.
43. Colquhoun, *Harringay Story*, 42–43; Cook, *London Hears Billy Graham*, 25–26.
44. "Oil Town U.S.A.," *London Crusade News*, November 1953, 4.
45. Colquhoun, *Harringay Story*, 46.
46. Martin, *Prophet with Honor*, 140.
47. https://www.youtube.com/watch?v=hPJmYbF3Duo.
48. "Mr Graham on the Beam at Burtonwood," *Manchester Guardian*, May 12, 1954, 9.
49. "Film Folk Attending Tent Meets," *Citizen News*, October 15, 1949, 7, Magazine and Newspaper Clippings Collection, Scrapbook 5, CN 360, BGCA.
50. Preparation Folder of Willis G. Haymaker, Billy Graham London Crusade, page 3 of Section 2, Folder 21, Box 1, CN 1, BGCA.
51. Protokoll der "Brüderlichen Besprechung" in Fragen der Billy Graham Versammlung in Deutschland, am Pfingstmontag, 30. Mai 1955, im Parkhotel, Düsseldorf, 4, ADEA.

52. Deitenbeck, *Eine Weltstadt horcht auf*, no page numbers. "Für den christusfernen Menschen sind Gott und Christus keine Realitäten. Sie wissen oft wenig damit anzufangen. Dürfen wir ihnen, die ganz visuell eingestellt sind, keine Brücke bauen, ihnen etwas für sie Reales vor Augen führen?"

53. Letter Zilz to Deitenbeck, Herrn Pastor Deitenbeck, Lüdenscheid, Berlenburg, den 26. Mai 1954, ADEA.

54. Circular by Heidi Meister, Liebe Freunde, Berlin, 15, Juni 1954, ADEA.

55. The Billy Graham Evangelistic Team, Dear Brother Brauer, London, May 12, 1955, Abschrift, ADEA.

56. Protokoll der "Brüderlichen Besprechung" in Fragen der Billy Graham Versammlung in Deutschland, am Pfingstmontag, 30. Mai 1955, im Parkhotel, Düsseldorf, 4, ADEA.

57. The original reads: "Das mag im Himmel so sein, aber nicht auf Erden!" Zilz an die Brüder des Vorstandes der Deutschen Evangelischen Allianz, Berleburg, den 9. Mai 1955, 1, ADEA. For earlier conflicts regarding locations and Evans's particular business rhetoric see Erich Bass to Friedrich Müller, Briefabschrift, 10.5.1955, 2, ADEA.

58. "Wir sind Verkäufer des größten Schatzes der Welt. Die besten Mittel müssen angewand werden, um ans Ziel zu kommen." Billy Graham, "Dies ist Gottes Stunde!" Ansprache, gehalten auf einer Mitarbeiterkonferenz am 24. Juni 1954 in Düsseldorf, in Brauer, *Billy Graham*, 51–57, 56.

59. Graham, "Dies ist Gottes Stunde!"

60. Protokoll der Sitzung des erweiterten Vertrauensrates der Deutschen Evangelistenkonferenz in Fragen der stattgefundenen Billy-Graham-Versammlungen in Deutschland, Donnerstag, 30. Juni 1955, im Heim des C.V.J.M. in Frankfurt/M., 2–4, ADEA. For further details on marketing and participants, see Wilhelm Brauer, "Wenn Gottes Winde wehen . . . ," in *Europa's Goldene Stunde: Stimmen zum Besuch Billy Grahams*, ed. Wilhelm Brauer, Wuppertal: R. Brockhaus Verlag, 1956, 50–54.

61. Peter Scheider, Aktennotiz betr.: Besprechung mit Jerry Beavan and Charlie Riggs in Berlin, Hamburg und Essen am 3. bis 5. Dezember 1959, ADEA.

62. Protokoll der ersten Sitzung des Zentralausschusses für die geplante Groß-Evangelisation mit Billy Graham, am Freitag, 6. November 1959 in Hamburg, 8, ADEA.

63. Protokoll der Sitzung der Exekutive des Zentralkomitees am 9.8.1960 auf dem Flugplatz Düsseldorf, 3, ADEA.

64. Bericht an das Zentralkomitee über die Evangelisationen Billy Grahams in Deutschland, 3, ADEA.

65. Circular, An die Mitglieder des Zentralkomitees für die Großstadt-Evangelisationen mit Billy Graham, circular, Berlin-Steglitz, Ende Juni 1960, 2, ADEA.

66. "Deutschland ist wichtig in der Welt," *Westdeutsche Allgemeine Zeitung*, September 10, 1960, 7.

67. Protokoll der fünften Sitzung des Zentralkomitees für "Großstadt-Evangelisationen mit Billy Graham," am Donnerstag, 23. Februar 1961, im Amtszimmer von Superintendent Bachmann, Essen, 3, ADEA.

68. Porterfield et al., *The Business Turn*.

69. Jung, *Die deutsche evangelikale Bewegung*, 24–25; Bauer, *Evangelikale Bewegung*, 29.

70. Dochuk, *God's Businessmen*, esp. 175–180; Grem, *Blessings of Business*, esp. 59–64.

71. Billy Graham answers his critics. Reprint from the February 7, 1956, issue of *Look*, 2, Folder 46, Box 1, CN 1, BGCA.

72. "Billy Graham: A New Kind of Evangelist," *Time*, October 25, 1954, 8.

73. Martin, *Prophet with Honor*, 126.

74. "Heaven, Hell, and Judgement Day," *Time*, March 20, 1950, 56.

75. *Decision*, Vol. 1, no. 2, June 1956. Folder 46, Box 1, CN 1, BGCA.

76. Sermon: "God's Promise of a New Heart," New York City, June 29, 1957, 11, Folder 94, Box 10, CN 285, BGCA. Darren Grem noted how Graham established a rhetoric of conversion that reflected the 1950s secular marketing rhetoric in trying to establish a personal relationship between the consumer of faith, with Jesus being the consumable product. Grem, *Blessings of Business*, 63.

77. "New York Has 1,000 Gods and You Must Make a Choice," *New York Crusade News*, May 28, 1957, 1, Folder 18, Box 2, CN 1, BGCA.

78. Cecil Northcott, "Graham at the Gate," *Christian Century*, October 19, 1960, 1208.

79. "Wie ich Billy Graham erlebte," *Hamburger Anzeiger*, July 10, 1960, Magazine and Newspaper Clippings Collection, Reel 8, CN 360, BGCA.

80. "Billy Graham: A New Kind of Evangelist," *Time*, October 25, 1954, 54–56, 54.

81. "Resting Up to Save Souls," *Life*, December 26, 1955, 100–103.

82. Grem states as well that "in the 1950s, Graham affirmed sexual hierarchies and domestic expectations for women." Grem, *Blessings of Business*, 62. The interconnectedness of home, gender, and Graham's anticommunism is explored in more detail and discussed in the broader context of US Cold War culture in K. A. Cuordileone, *Manhood and American Political Culture in the Cold War*, New York: Routledge 2005, 37–96.

83. "Great Religious Revival to Continue Sixth Week," *Los Angeles Examiner*, October 31, 1949, part 2, p. 1, Magazine and Newspaper Clippings Collection, Scrapbook 5, CN 360, BGCA.

84. Mitchell, *Those Who Came Forward*, 14.

85. Lang and Lang, "Decisions for Christ," 422, 424.

86. Lang and Lang, "Decisions for Christ," 426.

87. David E. Kucharsky, "Broken Barriers around the Bay," *Christianity Today*, July 7, 1958, 26–27, 27. In New York City, for example, they remained among themselves: the economic and social identity of Graham's religious offer clearly excluded ethnically and racially diverse groups. This became especially obvious during the New York Crusade in 1957. Despite the large Puerto Rican and African American population of the city, neither of those groups was represented at the Garden in significant numbers. See "Protestants on Broadway, Editorial Correspondence," *Christian Century*, September 18, 1957, 1095–1096.

88. Paige Glotzer, *How the Suburbs Were Segregated: Developers and the Business of Exclusionary Housing, 1890–1960*, New York: Columbia University Press, 2020.

89. Grem, *Blessing of Business*, 65.

90. Wacker, *America's Pastor*, 140.

91. "What It Looked Like at Harringay," 5; "Graham Campaign Cries 'Back to the Church,'" *Church of England Newspaper*, March 5, 1954, 3.

92. "Mit Bibel, Mikrophon und Cowboy," *Frankfurter Allgemeine Zeitung*, April 2, 1954, 2.

93. "Das Nüchterne," *Frankfurter Allgemeine Zeitung*, June 24, 1955, 2.

94. E.g., "Billy Graham, Missionar im Neon-Licht," *Siegener Zeitung*, June 19, 1954, Magazine and Newspaper Clippings Collection, CN 360, Reel 8, BGCA.

95. "An Evening at Harringay," *Baptist Times*, March 11, 1954, 8.

96. Colquhoun, *Harringay Story*, 20.

97. For a description of the local crusade machinery see "Großstadt Evangelisation mit Billy Graham," *Kirche in Hamburg*, October 2, 1960, 3, 11, 12, esp. 3.

98. Graham, *Revival in Our Time*, 38.

99. "Statistics of a Crusade," *The Times*, May 30, 1954, 2.

100. Ruth Adams, "Some Tales from the Harringay Pilgrims," *Church of England Newspaper*, March 26, 1954, 14.

101. See also the description in John Pollock, *Crusade '66: Britain Hears Billy Graham*, London: Hodder and Stoughton, 1966, 38.

102. "Evangelism, but No 'Foaming at the Mouth,'" *Manchester Guardian*, February 26, 1954, 8.

103. "Talk of the Week," *Church of England Newspaper*, March 5, 1954, 4.

104. Quoted in "34,586 Decisions," *Time*, May 31, 1954, 44.

105. "Millionen Menschen hören Billy Graham," *General-Anzeiger Oberhausen*, June 25, 1954; "Kreuzritter im flotten Zweireiher," *Ruhr Nachrichten*, June 25, 1954, Magazine and Newspaper Clippings Collection, Reel 8, CN 360, BGCA.

106. "Meet Mrs. Billy Graham," *British Weekly*, April 8, 1954, 5.

107. Arthur H. Chapple, *Billy Graham*, London: Marshall, Morgan and Scott, 1954.

108. "Billy Graham at Home: 20 Lovely Pictures of a Happy Christian Family Published by the Sunday Companion," Folder 5, Box 5, CN 9, BGCA.

109. "Nicht Graham ruft Euch, sonder Gott," *Berliner Sonntagsblatt, die Kirche*, special edition, June 27, 1954, 3.

110. "Billy Graham and Harringay: An Assessment," *Methodist Recorder*, May 20, 1954, 1. This point is also made in Bebbington, *Evangelicalism in Modern Britain*, 259.

111. "Mr. Graham Ends His Mission," *The Times*, May 24, 1954, 4.

112. "A Sermon at Harringay," *British Weekly*, March 18, 1954, 8.

113. As a study conducted by Clifford Hill in 1963 showed, of the 69 percent of immigrants from the British Caribbean who had been practicing Anglicans at home, only 4 percent continued to be after their arrival in London. Needless to say, there were many reasons for these immigrants to set up their own churches or to leave church altogether, but one reason was undeniably the strong white identity of many Anglican churches in Britain. See Clifford S. Hill, *West Indian Migrants and the London Churches*, Oxford: Oxford University Press, 1963. For an excellent summary on the simmering racism in English Anglican churches see Alister Chapman, "What Evangelical Anglicans Learned from the World, 1945–2000," in *Evangelicalism and*

the Church of England in the Twentieth Century, ed. Andrew Atherstone and John Maiden, Woodbridge: Boydell, 2014, 248–267, esp. 256–258.

114. McLeod, *Religious Crisis*, 103.

115. The German original reads: "Nimm eine Bibel im Handschuhfach mit." Curtis Mitchell, *Die nach vorne kamen: Evangelisation mit Billy Graham und ihre Ergebnisse*, Kassel: J.G. Oncken Verlag, 1967, 111–116.

116. Colquhoun, *Harringay Story*, 216.

117. "Der Stabschef Gottes," *Frankfurter Allgemeine Zeitung*, June 24, 1954, 2. Original: "Das deutsche Wirtschaftswunder sei ihm wie ein sichtbarer Lohn für die gläubige christliche Haltung der gesamten Bevölkerung."

118. Giesen, "Zum Thema 'Billy Graham,' " 7.

119. "Evangelist Economics," *Manchester Guardian*, June 26, 1954, 4.

120. "Zwölf Ernten im Jahr," *Der Spiegel*, June 23, 1954, 21–26.

121. Reuebekenntnis der Epikuräer, *Deutsche Zeitung und Wirtschaftszeitung*, June 25, 1955. "Diese Mischung von marktschreierischer Übertreibung, direkter Attacke und geschäftlicher Höflichkeit ist uneuropäisch und läßt sich nur aus dem amerikanischen Lebensgefühl begreifen." 55.1/190, Evangelisches Landesrachiv Berlin (ELAB).

122. "Rabbis Commend, Criticize Graham," *New York Times*, May 19, 1957, 53.

123. "Billy Graham in New York," *Manchester Guardian*, March 11, 1955, 5.

124. "Differing Views on Billy Graham," *Life*, July 1, 1957, 92.

125. "Die Gnadenverheißung wird als einfacher Geschäftsakt erklärt: 'Gott sagt: Ich habe meinen Sohn hergegeben, gib du deine Sünden her. Dann werde ich dir vergeben.' " "Der Prediger auf dem Fußballplatz," *Süddeutsche Zeitung*, June 4, 1955, 35.

126. Charles Templeton, "Evangelism for Tomorrow," *Christianity Today*, January 20, 1958, 87.

127. On rationality and secular culture: Alan D. Gilbert, *The Making of Post-Christian Britain: A History of the Secularization of Modern Society*, New York: Longman, 1980, 63–66.

Chapter 3

1. Cecil Northcott, "Graham at the Gate," *Christian Century*, October 19, 1960, 1208.

2. On America's spiritual Cold War see Stevens, *God-Fearing and Free*; Herzog, *The Spiritual-Industrial Complex*; Haberski, *God and War*; Inboden, *Religion and American Foreign Policy*.

3. Herzog, *The Spiritual-Industrial Complex*, 6.

4. Quoted in Greschat, "Rechristianisierung," 1. Greschat makes the courageous attempt in this important essay to compare re-Christianization discourses in several Western societies, and this chapter builds on this idea.

5. Quoted in Axel Schildt, *Moderne Zeiten: Freizeit, Massenmedien und "Zeitgeist" in der Bundesrepublik der 1950er Jahre*, Hamburg: Hans Christians Verlag, 1995, 337.

6. On the "Christian Civilization" discourse in war time Britain see Keith Robbins, "Britain, 1940, and Christian Civilization,'" in *History, Society and the Churches: Essays in Honour of Owen Chadwick*, ed. Derek Beales and Geoffrey Best, Cambridge: Cambridge University Press, 1985, 279–300.

7. Arnold Toynbee, *Christianity and Civilization: Burge Memorial Lecture; 1940*, London: Student Christian Movement Press, 1940.

8. Quoted in Richard Wright, *Patriots: National Identity in Britain, 1940–2000*, Oxford: Pan Books, 2002, 224.

9. Robbins, *History, Religion, and Identity*, 224.

10. Wire copy of an editorial, November 4, 1949. Published as part of the online exhibition of the Billy Graham Center Archives on Graham's Los Angeles revival campaign: http://www2.wheaton.edu/bgc/archives/exhibits/LA49/06media15.html.

11. "Bowron Backs Young Evangelist's Revival," *Los Angeles Times*, September 25, 1949, 2.

12. Quoted in Whitfield, *Culture of the Cold War*, 81.

13. Haberski, *God and War*, 21.

14. Proclamation, The City of Greenville, SC, Major J. Kenneth Cass, March 17, 1950, Folder 1, Box 1, CN 1, BGCA.

15. Article in the Bob Jones University Alumni News, March–April 1950, Folder 1, Box 1, CN 1, BGCA.

16. "Washington Is Ready," *Youth for Christ Magazine*, January 1952, 66. See also the preparation material in Folder 6, Box 1, CN 1, BGCA.

17. "Washington Is Ready," 66.

18. "Graham to Preach from Capitol Today," *Washington Post*, February 3, 1952, M13; "America's Most Prayed for Campaign," *Moody Monthly*, March 1952, 476, 483; "Rockin' the Capitol," *Time*, March 3, 1952, 76.

19. "Letter to the Editors," *Washington Post*, January 20, 1952, B4; and *Washington Post*, January 25, 1952, 20.

20. "Billy Graham Tours National Shrines, Asks Moral Awakening," *Washington Post*, January 13, 1952, M11.

21. "An Evangelistic Meeting on the Steps of the Capitol," *New York Times*, February 4, 1952, 4; "Billy Graham Preaches to Thousands with Capitol Steps as His Pulpit," *Los Angeles Times*, February 4, 1952, 5; "40,000 Hear Billy Graham's Sermon in Drizzle at Capitol," *Chicago Daily Tribune*, February 4, 1952, 1; a good impression of the meeting is also given in "Washington Crusade Extended," *Youth for Christ Magazine*, March 1952, 64–70.

22. "40,000 Hear Billy Graham's Sermon," 1.

23. Kirstin Kobes Du Mez compellingly showed Graham's role in establishing a highly patriarchal Christian nationalism during his early crusades that paved the way not just for the rise of the Religious Right but also for Donald Trump's presidency, which received overwhelming support from white evangelicals. Kristin Kobes Du Mez, *Jesus and John Wayne: How White Evangelicals Corrupted a Faith and Fractured a Nation*, New York: Liveright Publishing, 2020, esp. 22–39.

24. "Crusader in the Capital," *Time*, February 11, 1952, 83.

25. "Billy Graham," *Der Spiegel* 16 (1952): 26.

26. "Washington Is Ready," 66.
27. On the history of the special relationship: Kathleen Burk, *Old World, New World: The Story of Britain and America*, London: Little, Brown, 2007, esp. 560–659.
28. Colquhoun, *Harringay Story*, 21.
29. Willis Haymaker, Billy Graham London Crusade, Reasons for Project, 1–3, Folder 21, Box 1, CN 1, BGCA.
30. Minutes of the Executive Committee held at 30, Bedford Place, September 11, 1953, Minute Book Billy Graham Executive Committee, 15, AEAUK.
31. Minutes of the Executive Committee held at 30, Bedford Place, November 2, 1953, Minute Book Billy Graham Executive Committee, 20, AEAUK.
32. Chapple, *Billy Graham*; on the trip to Korea, see Martin, *Prophet with Honor*, 149–151.
33. *London Crusade News*, October 1953, 1.
34. D. J. Wilson-Haffenden, "I Long and Pray for Revival in London," *London Crusade News*, October 1953, 2. Graham emphasizes the importance of the coronation as well during an interview with *Moody Monthly*. "Crusade Questions, Replies by Billy Graham," *Moody Monthly*, Special Issue on Harringay, 1954, 32. For the context see Edward Shils and Michael Young, "The Meaning of the Coronation," *Sociological Review* 1 (1953): 63–81. A compelling summary on the coronation within British contemporary religious and political culture is given by Chapman, *Godly Ambition*, 38–40.
35. Brown, *Death of Christian Britain*, 6.
36. "The Greatest Revival in History?," *London Crusade News*, October 1953, 2–3.
37. "Crusade Questions," 32.
38. Colquhoun, *Harringay Story*, 78.
39. Colquhoun, *Harringay Story*, 87–88. See also "Billy Graham Launches Greater London Crusade," *Methodist Recorder*, March 4, 1954, 6; "What It Looked Like at Harringay," *British Weekly*, March 4, 1954, 5.
40. Colquhoun, *Harringay Story*, 140.
41. Cook, *London Hears*, 73.
42. "180,000 Attend Final Crusade Rallies," *London Crusade News*, July 1954, 1.
43. "Greater London Crusade; To the Editor of the Times," *The Times*, May 22, 1954, 7.
44. John Henderson on Dr. Graham and Political Leaders, quoted in Cook, *London Hears*, 107.
45. "Record 120,000 at London Arena Hear Billy Graham End Crusade," *New York Times*, May 23, 1954, 1.
46. An in-depth analysis of the ideas and ideals of East and West German Protestants during the first decades of the Cold War is provided by Greschat, *Protestantismus im Kalten Krieg*.
47. Brauer, *Europas Goldene Stunde*, 8.
48. Dirks, „Trommler des lieben Gottes," 538.
49. A concise summary of the debates about the Occident can be found in Schildt, *Moderne Zeiten*, 333–336; for more detail see Schildt, *Zwischen Abendland*.
50. For the debates in German Protestantism surrounding the question of an alliance with the West, which was contested because of its close cultural affiliation with the

United States and its implications for a future unification of Germany, see Thomas Sauer, *Westorientierung im deutschen Protestantismus: Vorstellungen und Tätigkeit des Kronberger Kreises*, Munich: R. Oldenbourg, 1999.

51. Schildt, *Zwischen Abendland*, 31–32.
52. On the first German crusade briefly: Martin, *Prophet with Honor*, 187–188.
53. "Fünftausend hören Billy Graham," *Frankfurter Allgemeine Zeitung*, June 24, 1954, 2.
54. "Billy Graham Predigt Waffenbrüderschaft," *Bild*, June 24, 1954, Magazine and Newspaper Clippings Collection, Reel 8, CN 360, BGCA.
55. "Billy in Germany," *Time*, July 5, 1954, 48.
56. "Dr Graham on Germany," *Manchester Guardian*, June 25, 1954, 7; "Billy Graham in Germany: Evangelist's Success in Duesseldorf," *Manchester Guardian*, June 26, 1954, 5.
57. "Weil in Berlin das Herz der Welt schlägt, weil von hier aus—mehr als von jedem anderen Platz der Welt—der Angst die Stirn geboten wird, deshalb spricht Billy Graham in Berlin." "Ein Mann gegen die große Weltangst," B.Z., June 26, 1954, Magazine and Newspaper Clippings Collection, Reel 8, CN 360, BGCA. These events surrounding the 1954 Berlin crusade are discussed in Uta Balbier, "Billy Graham in West Germany: German Protestantism between Americanization and Rechristianization," *Zeithistorische Forschungen / Studies in Contemporary History* 7 (2010): article 3, http://www.zeithistorische-forschungen.de/16126041-Balbier-3-2010.
58. Pressestelle der evangelischen Kirchenleitung Berlin-Brandenburg, Pressebericht vom 27. Juni 1954, 28. Juni 1954, 1, 55.1/190, ELAB.
59. "Ein Missionar unter Christen," *Tagesspiegel*, supplement, June 29, 1954, 4.
60. "Billy Graham in New York," *Manchester Guardian*, March 11, 1955, 5.
61. "'Glaring Inadequacy' of Many Methodist Sermons," *Manchester Guardian*, July 5, 1955, 5.
62. "Free Church Moderator's Suggestion," *The Times*, April 26, 1955, 7.
63. Giesen, "Zum Thema 'Billy Graham,'" 7. "Insbesondere werden wir hellhörig, wenn ausgerechnet ein Prediger des Evangeliums und nun gar ein Amerikaner Kreuzzugsparolen vorträgt unter Anspielung auf die militärischen Fähigkeiten der Deutschen."
64. Redaktion *Kirche und Mann*, "Noch einmal: Zum Thema Billy Graham," November 1954, 5.
65. "Unsere Leser schreiben, Hermann Soth, Kettwig (Ruhr)," *Kirche in Hamburg*, October 23, 1960, 8.
66. Such as in Grossbölting, *Losing Heaven*, 43–76.
67. "Europe Seeks God, Evangelist Holds," *New York Times*, July 7, 1954, 28.
68. Herzog, *Spiritual-Industrial Complex*, 95.
69. "Vice President Nixon Speaks Enthusiastically of New York Crusade," *New York Crusade News*, March 1957, 3, Folder 18, Box 2, CN 1, BGCA.
70. "Text of Billy Graham's Sermon Opening His Crusade in Madison Square Garden," *New York Times*, May 16, 1957, 22.
71. Quoted in Mitchell, *God in the Garden*, 180.

72. George Dugan, "Throng Sets Arena Record Richard Nixon Is Platform Guest," *New York Times*, July 21, 1957, 48.

73. Robert Ferm, *Persuaded to Live: Conversion Stories from the Billy Graham Crusades*, Ada, MI: Fleming H. Revell, 1958, 159.

74. Dugan, "Throng Sets Arena Record," 48.

75. "Editorial Page. Is Graham's Revival a Circus Or a Spiritual Awakening?," *Mirror*, June 24, 1957, folder 1, Box 3, CN 1, BGCA.

76. Billy Graham in Berlin von Miss.-Insp. P. Walter Golze, Vorsitzender der Evangelischen Allianz in Berlin, no date, ADEA. See also Cecil Northcott, "Graham at the Gate," *Christian Century*, October 19, 1960, 1208.

77. BM II/3717, Herrn Bürgermeister Major Amrehn, betr.: Großstadt-Evangelisation mit Billy Graham/Zuwendungsantrag der Deutschen Evangelischen Allianz, Berlin, den 9.8.1960, B Rep. 002/1765, LAB. Regarding further funding through the Bureau of the Affairs of Greater Berlin, see Bm II A, Herrn Bürgermeister Amrehn, betr. Großstadt-Evangelisationen mit Billy Graham—Verwendungsdnachweis zum Bewilligungsbescheid vom 13.9.d.J. und Nachbewilligungsantrag, Berlin, 16.12.1960, B Rep. 002/1765, LAB.

78. "Die Großstadtevangelisationen mit Dr. Billy Graham," Herausgegeben von Wilhelm Brauer im Auftrag der deutschen Evangelistenkonferenz, Broschüre, no date, no place, 6 and 19, Broschüre Nr. 1040, Oncken Archiv.

79. Brauer, "Die Großstadtevangelisationen mit Dr. Billy Graham," 7.

80. Staatssekretär für Kirchenfragen an den Magistrat von Groß-Berlin, betr.: NATO-Veranstaltung mit Billy Graham vom 26.9. bis 2.10.1960 in Westberlin, C Rep. 104-678, LAB.

81. "SED beschwert sich über Graham," *Frankfurter Rundschau*, September 29, 1960, 2.

82. Especially: "New Restrictions on W. Berliners," *The Times*, September 29, 1960. Also: "Berlin's Status Reaffirmed by the West," *The Times*, September 28, 1960, 12; "A Tent in the Tiergarten," *The Guardian*, September 29, 1960, 11; "Graham Defies Reds," *New York Times*, September 29, 1960, 3; "Graham Draws East Berliners," *New York Times*, September 28, 1960, 3.

83. Schmidt und Kludas an den Bürgermeister von Berlin, Büro für Gesamtberliner Fragen zu Händen von Herrn Dr. Legien, betr.: Zuschußantrag vom 1.7.1960, Geschäftszeichen Bm II, Berlin, August 6, 1960, 1, B Rep. 002-1765, LAB.

84. Presseinformation, Peter Schneider, Berlin, 1. Oktober 1960, 3, 55.1/190, ELAB.

85. "Evangelist Will Remain Silent on Cohen Matter," *Los Angeles Times*, November 16, 1949, 28.

86. The fight against communism understood as a religion in itself and therefore a spiritual thread rather than a political one dates back to the fundamentalist movements of the early 1920s: see George Marsden, *Fundamentalism and American Culture*, 2nd ed., New York: Oxford University Press, 2006, 206–211.

87. Colquhoun, *Harringay Story*, 21.

88. Sermon reprinted in Mitchell, *Those Who Came Forward*, 27.

89. Quoted in Lang and Lang, "Decisions for Christ," 423.

90. Billy Graham Greater London Crusade, Report of the Special Meeting of the Executive Committee held on 22nd of April 1953 to meet Mr. Horace Hull, Minute Book Billy Graham Executive Committee, 6, AEAUK.

91. Quoted in Jeremy, *Capitalists and Christians*, 403.

92. Bebbington, *Evangelicalism in Modern Britain*, 253–254.

93. Edward England, *Afterwards; a Journalist Sets out to Discover What Happened to Some of Those Who Made a Decision for Christ during the Billy Graham Crusades in Britain in 1954 and 1955*, London: Victory, 195, 11–34. See also Cook, *London Hears*, 114–115; Colquhoun, *Harringay Story*, 206–207.

94. England, *Afterwards*, 23.

95. Colquhoun, *Harringay Story*, 207. In the collection of conversion stories entitled "Persuaded to Live," Robert Ferm tells the story of a young student at the University of London who heard Graham speak when he returned to the city in 1955. Ferm quotes her saying: "All the time I studied the communistic philosophy, I knew there was something better. I did not expect to hear it from an American evangelist." See, Ferm, *Persuaded to Live*, 61.

96. Alan Wilkinson, *Christian Socialism: Scott Holland to Tony Blair*, Norwich: SCM Press, 2012; Herbert Wehner, *Christentum und demokratischer Sozialismus*, Freiburg: Dreisam Verlag, 1986.

97. Cook, *London Hears*, 123.

98. Quoted in Colquhoun, *Harringay Story*, 74. A detailed account of the incident is given in Martin, *Prophet with Honor*, 175–176.

99. "Crusade for Britain," *Time*, March 8, 1954, 72–74.

100. Protokoll der "Brüderlichen Besprechung" in Fragen der Billy Graham Versammlung in Deutschland, am Pfingstmontag, 30. Mai 1955, im Parkhotel, Düsseldorf, 4, ADEA.

101. Mirjam Loos, "Antikommunistische und anti-antikommunistische Stimmen im evangelischen Kirchenmilieu: Die Debatte um Wiedervereinigung, Westbindung und Wiederbewaffnung," in *"Geistige Gefahr" und "Immunisierung der Gesellschaft": Antikommunismus und politische Kultur in der frühen Bundesrepublik*, ed. Stefan Creuzberger and Dierk Hoffmann, Munich: Oldenburg Verlag, 2014, 199–213.

102. "Billy Graham in Germany," *United Evangelical Action*, August 15, 1955, 5.

103. Protokoll der gemeinsamen Sitzung des Zentralausschusses für Billy Graham-Evangelisationen in Deutschland und des Vorstandes der Deutschen evangelischen Allianz, April 27, 1955, ADEA.

104. "Wir haben zweimal in Massen ja gesagt, einmal in Langemarck und nach Stalingrad im Sportpalast. Ein so verwundetes Volk wie das deutsche darf nicht der Gefahr des Rausches ausgesetzt werden und muß Zeit finden, damit seine Wunden heilen können." "Umstrittener Graham," *Frankfurter Allgemeine Zeitung*, July 2, 1955, 3.

105. "Was sagen Sie zu Graham, erste Stimmen," *Berliner Sonntagsblatt, die Kirche*, no. 28, 1954, 4.

106. "Der Feldprediger aus der Neuen Welt," *Kirche in Hamburg*, September 1960, NEKA.

107. Miller, *Billy Graham*, 21.

108. Miller, *Billy Graham*, 28.
109. Wacker, *America's Pastor*, 124; Miller, *Billy Graham*, 29. Miller underlines, however, that Graham made the decision "reluctantly" and that late-comers would be allowed to sit anywhere in the stadium.
110. Miller, *Billy Graham*, 22–24.
111. Quoted in Miller, *Billy Graham*, 29. For the broader interplay between the civil rights struggle and the Cold War see Mary L. Dudziak, *Cold War Civil Rights: Race and the Image of American Democracy*, Princeton, NJ: Princeton University Press, 2000.
112. "Record Crowd at Dallas Crusade," *London Crusade News*, October 1953, 4; "Asheville Crusade," *London Crusade News*, January 1954, 1.
113. Shaun Herron, "Billy Graham," *British Weekly*, March 4, 1954, 1.
114. Donald Soper, "South Africa. Action Now," *Tribune (Blackpool)*, July 8, 1955, 4–5.
115. Kenneth Leech, *Race, Changing Society and the Churches*, London: SPCK, 2005, 104.
116. Leech, *Race*, 104. For the living situation of black immigrants in Britain in 1954, see, for example, Robin D. G. Kelley and Stephen G. N. Tuck, *The Other Special Relationship: Race, Rights, and Riots in Britain and the United States*, New York, Palgrave, 2015, 13.
117. Kelley and Tuck, *The Other Special Relationship*, 3.
118. Even though this overlay still-existing racial prejudices in German society, especially regarding children of color, as shown by Heide Fehrenbach, *Race after Hitler: Black Occupation Children in Postwar Germany and America*, Princeton, NJ: Princeton University Press, 2005.
119. Maria Höhn and Martin Klimke, *A Breath of Freedom: The Civil Rights Struggle, African American GIs, and Germany*, New York: Palgrave Macmillan, 2010.

Chapter 4

1. Maurice Rowlandson, *Life with Billy*, London: Hodder & Stoughton, 1992, 46.
2. Oral history interview with Rev. Armin Gesswein conducted by Dr. Lois Ferm, July 13, 1971, 4, Folder 55, Box 3, CN 141, BGCA.
3. Gesswein, interview.
4. Billy Graham Evangelistic Association, *Revival in Our Time*, 17.
5. Gesswein, interview, 4.
6. "Atlantians Prepare to Greet Graham," *Atlanta Journal*, September 7, 1950, no page, Folder 2, Box 1, CN 1, BGCA.
7. The Greater Atlanta Evangelistic Crusade Cottage Prayer Meetings, no date, 3, Folder 2, Box 1, CN 1, BGCA.
8. "It's Prayer Time in New York," Draft from the desk of W.G. Haymaker, p. D, Folder 9, Box 2, CN 1, BGCA.
9. This is stated in Colquhoun, *Harringay Story*, 36. See also "Prayer Groups," *London Crusade News*, February 1954, 2.

10. Prayer Partner News-Letter no. 2, no date, 1, Folder 2, Box 5, CN 9, BGCA.

11. Prayer Partner News-Letter no. 2, 1.

12. Cook, *London Hears*, 24–25; Colquhoun, *Harringay Story*, 34–36.

13. Oral history interview with Dr. Stephen Olford conducted by Dr. Lois Ferm, December 10, 1970, 31, Folder 27, Box 5, CN 141, BGCA.

14. Prayer Partner News-Letter no. 2, 1.

15. Prayer Partner News-Letter, no. 6, no date, 2, Folder 5, Box 2, CN 9, BGCA.

16. "Harringay Arena for London Crusade," *London Crusade News*, November 1953, 1.

17. Rev. Geoffrey R. King, "Underground Movement," *London Crusade News*, October 1953, 3.

18. All London prayer newsletters can be found in Folder 5, Box 2, CN 9, BGCA. For prayer on space and planning see, for example: Roy Cattell, Prayer Partner News-Letter, no. 3 Special, no date, Folder 5, Box 2, CN 9, BGCA.

19. "Die Großstadtevangelisationen mit Dr. Billy Graham," Herausgegeben von Wilhelm Brauer im Auftrag der deutschen Evangelistenkonferenz, Broschüre, no date, no place, 15, Broschüre Nr. 1040, Oncken Archiv.

20. "Liebe Freunde," Letter by Heidi Meister, Berlin, June 15, 1954, ADEA.

21. The German original reads: "Wenn wir immer so hart arbeiten würden, dann bräuchte kein Billy Graham zu kommen!" Meister, letter.

22. Points of Discussion with Dr. Graham, no date, 2, Folder 13, Box 5, CN 622, BGCA.

23. The German original reads: "Wir spürten es immer wieder, daß Schwierigkeiten hinweggebetet und Wege geebnet wurden." Brauer, "Die Großstadtevangelisationen mit Dr. Billy Graham," 5.

24. Letter by the German Evangelical Alliance and others to Dr Billy Graham, 206 Saukehall Street, Glasgow, Scotland, handwritten date, April 1955, ADEA.

25. Brauer, *Europas Goldene Stunde*, 52.

26. J. F. Laun, "Stehen wir vor einer Erweckung," in *Billy Graham: Ein Evangelist der Neuen Welt*, ed. Wilhelm Brauer, Basel: Brunnen Verlag, 1955, 70.

27. Protokoll der Sitzung der Exekutive des Zentralkomitees am 9.8.1960 auf dem Flugplatz Düsseldorf, 2, ADEA.

28. Circular, An die Mitglieder des Zentralkomitees für die Großstadt-Evangelisationen mit Billy Graham, Berlin-Steglitz, Ende Juni 1960, 2, ADEA.

29. Brauer, "Die Großstadtevangelisationen mit Dr. Billy Graham," 15.

30. Peter Scheider, Aktennotiz betr.: Besprechung mit Jerry Beavan and Charlie Riggs in Berlin, Hamburg und Essen am 3. bis 5. Dezember 1959, 3, ADEA.

31. "Prayer Conference Emphasizes New Areas," *New York Crusade News*, December 1956, 4, Folder 18, Box 2, CN 1, BGCA. A summary of the prayer activities during the New York Crusade is given in Mitchell, *God in the Garden*, 78–81.

32. "November Prayer Card Request Set New Record," *New York Crusade News*, December 1956, Folder 18, Box 2, CN 1, BGCA.

33. "Prayer Chains Start around the World," *New York Crusade News*, January 1957, 4, Folder 18, Box 2, CN 1, BGCA.

34. Memorandum from W. G. Haymaker to Members of the Executive Committee, April 21, 1957, Folder 1, Box 2, CN 1, BGCA.

35. General Prayer Chairman, Circular to all prayer partners, no date, Folder 9, Box 2, CN 1, BGCA. See also the organigram: The Billy Graham New York Crusade Area-Wide Prayer Groups, no author, no date, Folder 9, Box 2, CN 1, BGCA.

36. "Thousands of Prayer Meetings on Eve of Crusade," *New York Crusade News*, May 1957, 1, Folder 18, Box 2, CN 1, BGCA.

37. "Suggestions for conducting your prayer period," no author, no date, Folder 9, Box 2, CN 1, BGCA.

38. Giordano, "You Never Know," 2.

39. Haymaker, "It's Prayer Time," p. E.

40. Re. Floyd E. George et al to prayer partners, no date, Folder 9, Box 2, CN 1, BGCA.

41. Haymaker, "It's Prayer Time," p. E.

42. "Rev. David Head Conducting One of the 5,000 Crusade Prayer Groups," *New York Crusade News*, June 25, 1957, 1, Folder 18, Box 2, CN 1, BGCA.

43. On the importance of objects to create religious spaces and meanings see Colleen McDannell, *Material Christianity: Religion and Popular Culture in America*, New Haven: Yale University Press, 1998.

44. "Prayer Reminders for Telephone Ready," *New York Crusade News*, December 1956, 4, Folder 18, Box 2, CN 1, BGCA.

45. Haymaker to J. Woodrow Fuller, December 1, 1950, Folder 3, Box 1, CN 1, BGCA.

46. "Radio Station WABC to Carry Prayer Broadcast Beginning April 1," *New York Crusade News*, March 1957, 1, Folder 18, Box 2, CN 1, BGCA.

47. To the members of the Executive Committee of the Billy Graham New York Crusade Inc., April 2, 1957, 3, Folder 1, Box 2, CN 1, BGCA.

48. Billy Graham Greater London Crusade 1966, Prayer Committee Minutes of a meeting held on February 10, 1965, 1, Folder 8, Box 7, CN 9, BGCA. Later the committee considered airing a prayer bulletin via Radio Caroline or Radio London in support of the women's house meetings. See Prayer Committee Minutes of a meeting held on October 26, 1965, 1, Folder 8, Box 7, CN 9, BGCA.

49. "Sanctity on the Assembly Line," A Report furnished through the courtesy of the Committee for Industrial Prayer Meetings in connection with the Billy Graham Crusade, Folder 9, Box 2, CN 1, BGCA.

50. Haymaker, "It's Prayer Time," p. G.

51. Haymaker, "It's Prayer Time," p. G.

52. Joseph Overkamp to Haymaker, July 24, 1957 (*sic*: probably a typo in the date and written in June 1957), Folder 46, Box 1, CN 1, BGCA.

53. Overkamp to Haymaker.

54. Colquhoun, *Harringay Story*, 37.

55. Report of the final Prayer Committee of the Great London Crusade held on June 2nd, 1955, fol. 31 and Miss Scarles' Report, fol. 32, Minute Book Billy Graham Executive Committee, 1955, AEAUK.

56. Oral history interview with Rev. Thomas Livermore conducted by Dr. Robert O. Ferm, August 1971 (no exact date given), 11, Folder 9, Box 10, CN 141, BGCA.

57. Prayer Partner News-Letter, no. 10, March 1954, 2, Folder 5, Box 2, CN 9, BGCA.

58. Prayer groups provide an excellent lens to explore several deeper issues relating to the complex relationship between gender and evangelical Christianity discussed in Margaret Bendroth, *Fundamentalism and Gender, 1875 to the Present*, New Haven: Yale University Press, 1993.

59. Anne Braude, "Women's History Is American Religious History," in *Retelling U.S. Religious History*, ed. Thomas Tweed, Berkeley: University of California Press, 1996, 92. The historiographical shifts in the field are discussed in Joanna De Groot and Sue Morgan, "'Beyond the 'Religious Turn': Past, Present and Future Perspectives in Gender History," "Sex, Gender and the Sacred: Reconfiguring Religion in Gender History," *Gender and History*, Special Issue, 25, no. 3 (2014): 1–30; see also Ute Gause, *Kirchengeschichte und Genderforschung: Eine Einführung in protestantischer Perspektive*, Tübingen: Mohr Siebeck, 2006, who states that German religious historiography at that time lagged behind Anglo-American research in its focus on male-dominated organizational structures.

60. On Ruth's life and her role in her husband's ministry see the forthcoming biography: Anne Blue Wills, *An Odd Cross to Bear: A Life of Ruth Bell Graham*, Grand Rapids: Eerdmans, forthcoming. See also Ruth's autobiography: Ruth Bell Graham, *Footprints of a Pilgrim: The Life and Loves of Ruth Bell Graham*, Edinburgh: Thomas Nelson, 2001.

61. She made this statement, for example, during one of her rare public appearances on the New York Crusade platform. "Crusade Extended to August 31," *New York Crusade News*, August 1957, 1, Folder 18, Box 2, CN 1, BGCA.

62. Letter by Wilis Haymaker to Walter Smyth, February 11, 1957, Folder 9, Box 2, BGCA; Letter by Grady Wilson to Willis Haymaker, March 4, 1957, Folder 9, Box 2, BGCA.

63. Billy Graham Greater London Crusade 1966, Crusade Bulletin, January–February 1966, 2, Folder 3, Box 7, CN 9, BGCA.

64. Agenda for the Executive Committee meeting, November 5, 1956, 5, Folder 1, Box 2, CN 1, BGCA.

65. Mrs. Richard P. Sentz to Haymaker, February 21, 1957, Folder 9, Box 2, CN 1, BGCA.

66. Prayer Committee Minutes of a meeting on March 31, 1965, 1, Folder 8, Box 7, CN 9, BGCA.

67. Curtis Mitchell, *Billy Graham London Crusade*, Minneapolis: World Wide Publications, 1966, 68.

68. "London Women Are Praying," *Decision*, February 1966, 16.

69. Prayer Committee Minutes of a meeting held on June 23, 1965, 2, Folder 7, Box 9, CN 9, BGCA.

70. Prayer Committee Minutes.

71. Prayer Committee Minutes.

72. "London Women Are Praying," *Decision*, February 1966, 16.

73. Prayer Committee Minutes of a meeting held on March 4, 1966, 1, Folder 8, Box 7, CN 9, BGCA.

74. Griffith, "Submissive Wives," 186.

75. "Rev. J.D. Blinco, British Methodist Leader, Tells Challenge of N.Y. Crusade," *New York Crusade News*, February 1957, 1, Folder 18, Box 2, CN 1, BGCA.

76. Excerpts from New York Crusade Prayer Partners and Prayer Groups around the World, Folder 9, Box 2, CN 1, BGCA.

77. Fer, "Pentecostal Prayer."

78. Roy Cattell, Prayer Letter no. 4, no date, Folder 2, Box 5, CN 9. BGCA.

79. Over a hundred of these letters and telegrams are collected in scrapbooks in Box 4, CN 9, BGCA.

80. Frank A. Fox to Billy Graham, March 16, 1954, Scrapbook, Box 4, CN 9, BGCA. Many letters arrived from the First Baptist Church of Dallas, the church Graham held membership with.

81. Alice Simmons to Billy Graham, March 8, 1954, Scrapbook, Box 4, CN 9, BGCA.

82. "Prayer Partners Write . . . ," *New York Crusade News*, February 1957, 4, Folder 18, Box 2, CN 1, BGCA.

83. Mitchell, *God in the Garden*, 79.

84. Letter by Jerry Beavan, December 4, 1956, Folder 9, Box 2, CN 1, BGCA.

85. "Prayer Chain Starts around the World," *New York Crusade News*, January 1957, 4, Folder 18, Box 2, CN 1, BGCA.

86. Excerpts from New York Crusade Prayer Partners and Prayer Groups around the World, Folder 9, Box 2, CN 1, BGCA.

87. Memorandum from W. G. Haymaker to Members of the Executive Committee, April 21, 1957, Folder 1, Box 2, CN 1, BGCA.

88. Prayer Groups around the World, no date, no author, Folder 9, Box 2, CN 1, BGCA.

89. Excerpts from New York Crusade Prayer Partners and Prayer Groups around the World, 2, Folder 9, Box 2, CN 1, BGCA.

90. "Man muß ihn hören," *Berliner Sonntagsblatt, die Kirche*, Sonderausgabe, June 27, 1954, 2.

91. Sitzung des Zentralausschusses für die Vorbereitung und Ausführung der Billy-Graham-Evangelisationen in Deutschland am Freitag, 18. März 1955, im Haus des C.V.J.M. in Frankfurt/M, ADEA.

92. Report of the final Prayer Committee of the Greater London Crusade held on June 2, 1955, fol. 31, Minute Book Billy Graham Executive Committee, 1955, AEAUK.

93. Peter Scheider, Aktennotiz betr.: Besprechung mit Jerry Beavan and Charlie Riggs in Berlin, Hamburg und Essen am 3. bis 5. Dezember 1959, ADEA.

94. "Am Orte der Veranstaltung vereinigte sich das Gebet mit all jenen Betern, die in allen Erdteilen des Dienstes unseres Evangelisten an dem betreffenden Ort gedachten." Brauer, "Die Großstadtevangelisationen mit Dr. Billy Graham," 15.

95. Billy Graham Greater London Crusade, Prayer Partner Newsletter no. 7, Attachment: Operation Andrew, Folder 5, Box 2, CN 9, BGCA.

96. Prayer Partner Newsletter no. 7, Attachment: Operation Andrew.

97. Vision for the North Midlands, no. 2, March–April 1966, 1, Folder 7, Box 7, CN 9, BGCA.

98. "Mr. Graham Ends His Mission," *The Times*, May 24, 1954, 4.

99. Olford, interview, 29.

100. Olford, interview, 29.

101. "Heaven and Harringay," *Methodist Recorder*, April 8, 1954, 3.

102. Agenda for the Executive Committee meeting, January 7, 1957, 3, Folder 1, Box 2, CN 1, BGCA.

103. "Operation Andrew: Your Church's Most Vital Link to 20th Century Evangelism," Folder 9, Box 2, CN 1, BGCA.

104. "Group Reservations Offer Unique Opportunity for Personal Evangelism," *New York Crusade News*, May 1957, 1, 3, Folder 18, Box 2, CN 1, BGCA.

105. Walter Smyth, circular to New York churches, no date, Folder 9, Box 2, CN 1, BGCA.

106. "Virginians Sing Way to Crusade," *New York Times*, June 16, 1957, 68.

107. Mitchell, *They Met God*, 83–86, 84; "Virginians Sing Way to Crusade," 68.

108. "'Operation Andrew' Attracts Scores to Graham Crusade," *Journal* (Elizabeth, NJ), June 19, 1957, Folder 1, Box 3, CN 1, BGCA.

109. "Virginians Sing Way to Crusade," 68.

110. "Crusade Sidelights," *New York Crusade News*, May 1957, 1, Folder 18, Box 2, CN 1, BGCA.

111. Ferm, *Persuaded to Live*, 160. Joy, another teenager, described the importance of joint singing on the bus back to New Jersey after having accepted Christ (Ferm, 153).

112. "Crusade Sidelights," *Moody Monthly*, October 1954, 82.

113. No title, *Decision*, December 1962, 4.

114. See, for just one example, "Virginians Sing Way to Crusade," 68.

115. Colquhoun, *Harringay Story*, 107.

116. "How the Crusade Linked Two Churches," *Baptist Times*, July 7, 1966, 7.

117. Leech, *Race, Changing Society*, 32.

118. Peter Scheider, Aktennotiz betr.: Besprechung mit Jerry Beavan and Charlie Riggs in Berlin, Hamburg und Essen am 3. bis 5. Dezember 1959, 3, ADEA.

119. Brauer, "Die Großstadtevangelisationen mit Dr. Billy Graham," 12.

120. Circular, An die Mitglieder des Zentralkomitees für die Großstadt-Evangelisationen mit Billy Graham, Berlin-Steglitz, Ende Juni 1960, 2, ADEA.

121. Circular, An die Mitglieder des Zentralkomitees für die Großstadt-Evangelisationen mit Billy Graham, Berlin-Steglitz, Mai 1960, 71/1827, EZA.

122. Bericht an das Zentralkomitee über die Evangelisationen Billy Grahams in Deutschland, 3, ADEA; "Billy Graham und der Andreasplan," *Sonntagsblatt* 36 (1960): 36.

123. Brauer, "Die Großstadtevangelisationen mit Dr. Billy Graham," 12.

124. "Evangelisation beginnt im Bus," *Westfälische Allgemeine Zeitung*, September 9, 1960, 13.

125. "Billy Graham und der Andreasplan Plan," 36.

126. Billy Graham Information für die Gemeindeblätter (not dated, but published in the preparation of the 1966 Berlin crusade), ADEA.

127. "Der Andreasplan," *Berliner Sonntagsblatt, die Kirche* 42 (1960): 3.

128. Prayer Partner News-Letter no. 2, no date, 1, Folder 5, Box 2, CN 9, BGCA.

129. Brown, *Religion and Society*, 195.

130. Responses from local churches to the New York Crusade, no date, no place, 8, Folder 8, Box 3, CN 1, BGCA.

131. Robert Orsi, "Everyday Miracles: The Study of Lived Religion," in *Lived Religion in America: Toward a History of Practice*, ed. David D. Hall, Princeton, NJ: Princeton University Press, 1997, 6–7.

Chapter 5

1. "The Sound of Hymns over Broadway," *Press* (Jamaica, NY), May 17, 1957, Folder 21, Box 2, CN 1, BGCA.
2. "An Observer's Impression," *Methodist Recorder*, March 4, 1954, 6.
3. In the words of Birgit Meyer: "Imaginations are required to become tangible outside the realm of mind, by creating a social environment that materializes through the structuring of space, architecture, ritual performance, and by inducing bodily sensations." Meyer, "Introduction," 5.
4. Based on Meyer, "Introduction," 6–7.
5. Ole Rjis and Linda Woodhead, *A Sociology of Religious Emotion*, Oxford: Oxford University Press, 2012, 182.
6. Meyer, "Introduction," 21.
7. Christoph Ribbat, *Religiöse Erregung: Protestantische Schwärmer im Kaiserreich*, Frankfurt am Main: Campus Verlag, 1996.
8. Bebbington, *Victorian Religious Revivals*, 269.
9. Ribbat speaks of "funktionierende, lebendige religiöse Institutionen." Ribbat, *Religiöse Erregung*, 237.
10. "Die goldene Stunde der Entscheidung," *Frankfurter Allgemeine Zeitung*, June 29, 1954, 2.
11. "120,000 People at Final Graham Rally," *Church of England Newspaper*, May 28, 1954, 3.
12. "Billy Graham bekehrt 20,000 Berliner," *Die Zeit*, July 1, 1954, https://www.zeit.de/1954/26/billy-graham-bekehrt-20000-berliner; "Das Nüchterne," *Frankfurter Allgemeine Zeitung*, June 24, 1955, 2; Mitchell, *God in the Garden*, 47.
13. "Catering Arrangements," *London Crusade News*, March 1954, 2.
14. "Billy Graham bekehrt 20,000 Berliner."
15. "Dr Graham's Return," *Manchester Guardian*, October 4, 1954, 6.
16. Mitchell, *God in the Garden*, 47–48.
17. Bericht an das Zentralkomitee über die Evangelisationen Billy Grahams in Deutschland, signed by Paul Schmidt, handwritten date 1960, 3, ADEA.
18. George Target, "A Few Questions for Billy Graham: Crusade Assessment IV," *British Weekly*, August 4, 1966, 7, 11.
19. Colquhoun, *Harringay Story*, 84–85.
20. "God in the Garden," *Time*, May 27, 1957, 46.
21. "Crusade Sidelights," *New York Crusade News*, May 1957, 1, Folder 18, Box 2, CN 1, BGCA.
22. Mitchell, *Billy Graham London Crusade*, 37.

23. "Billy Graham bekehrt 20,000 Berliner."

24. "With Billy Graham Madison Square Garden a Cathedral," *Paterson (NJ) News*, May 17, 1957, Folder 21, Box 2, CN 1, BGCA.

25. Colquhoun, *Harringay Story*, 85.

26. "Mr Graham Claws Doubt Out of the Air," *Manchester Guardian*, May 16, 1955, 5.

27. Ferm, *They Met God*, 61.

28. The German original reads: "Kommet her zu mir alle, die ihr mühselig und beladen seid, ich will euch erquicken." "Billy Graham bekehrt 20.000 Berliner." The choice seemed rather odd, considering the importance of John 14:6 in the evangelical mindset. But then again, Germany did not have an evangelical tradition comparable to the Anglo-American one.

29. Colquhoun, *Harringay Story*, 92.

30. "Billy in the Ring," *Time*, March 14, 1955, 56.

31. Cartoon described in Mitchell, *God in the Garden*, 52.

32. For the conceptual framing of this point see Laurence R. Moore, *Selling God: American Religion in the Marketplace of Culture*, New York: Oxford University Press, 1995.

33. Graham, *Revival in Our Time*, 39.

34. Cook, *London Hears*, 39–40.

35. "With Billy Graham Madison Square Garden a Cathedral."

36. "What It Looked Like at Harringay," *British Weekly*, March 4, 1954, 5.

37. Mitchell, *God in the Garden*, 98.

38. E.g., "Makes Decision after Hearing Choir," Folder 8, Box 3, CN 1, BGCA.

39. "Impressions at Harringay," *Methodist Recorder*, April 8, 1954, 3.

40. Edith Blumhofer, "Singing to Save: Music in the Billy Graham Crusades," in *Billy Graham: American Pilgrim*, ed. Andrew Finstuen, Grant Wacker, and Anne Blue Wills, New York: Oxford University Press, 2017, 76.

41. "What It Looked Like at Harringay," 5.

42. On the global journey of "How Great Thou Art" see Blumhofer, "Signing to Save," 77.

43. Blumhofer, "Signing to Save," 71.

44. Lang and Lang, "Decisions for Christ," 421. The Langs' study has a slightly dismissive undertone, but their findings regarding the social and religious composition of the audience are still of importance, as not many organized observations were conducted during the earlier Graham crusades. Later surveys and studies took place during the Knoxville crusade of 1970. See Donald A. Clelland et al., "In the Company of the Converted: Characteristics of a Billy Graham Crusade Audience," *Sociological Analysis* 35, no. 1 (1974): 45–56, with some interesting findings regarding the education, southern identity, and family values of the audience. See also Ronald C. Wimberley et al., "Conversion in a Billy Graham Crusade: Spontaneous Event or Ritual Performance?," *Sociological Quarterly* 16, no. 2 (1975): 162–170.

45. Cook, *London Hears*, 41.

46. Madison Square Garden Opening Sermon by Dr Billy Graham (Evangelist), May 15, 1957, 4, Folder 46, Box 1, CN 1, BGCA.

47. "Special Report Billy Graham in New York—II," *Christianity and Crisis*, September 16, 1957, 119. His focus on the end of the world being in imminent reach, and the

urgency derived from that fact, grounded Graham firmly in the millennial preaching tradition of American fundamentalism. See Sutton, *American Apocalypse*. See also Angela M. Lahr, *Millennial Dreams and Apocalyptic Nightmares*, New York: Oxford University Press, 2007.

48. Cook, *London Hears*, 42; Madison Square Garden Opening Sermon by Dr Billy Graham (Evangelist), 15 May 1957, 4, Folder 46, Box 1, CN 1, BGCA.
49. "Billy Graham bekehrt 20,000 Berliner."
50. For an example of Graham's preaching in New York see Mitchell, *God in the Garden*, 152–161.
51. Ferm, *They Met God*, 17.
52. "Life Long Church Member Finds Christ," Testimonies and Incidents from the New York Crusade, Folder 8, Box 3, CN 1, BGCA; Ferm, *Conversion Stories*, 49.
53. Mitchell, *Those Who Came Forward*, 32.
54. "What Mr. Graham Has Proved," *The Manchester Guardian*, May 24, 1954, 11. Number for first night from Colquhoun, *Harringay Story*, 91.
55. Some of these numbers are just estimates; the only confirmed number is that of the total of filled-in decision cards. See Wilhelm Brauer, *Billy Graham*, 68, 72. He makes reference to the substantial number of Catholics who filled in decision cards (72).
56. Mitchell, *God in the Garden*, 177, 56. These numbers can also be found in "The Sound of Hymns over Broadway." Numbers for the opening night: "Billy Graham Opens Crusade; Best First Night Response," *Herald Tribune*, May 16, 1957, Folder 21, Box 2, CN 1, BGCA.
57. "Augenzeugenbericht," *Berliner Sonntagsblatt, die Kirche*, Sonderausgabe, June 27, 1954, 4.
58. In Wilhelm Brauer, *Europa's Goldene Stunde*, 24–25.
59. Part of the German translation of the sermon printed in Deutsche Evangelische Allianz, *Noch ruft Gott: Billy Graham in Essen, Hamburg und Berlin*, Wuppertal: Brockhaus Verlag, 1961, 78–80, 79.
60. Greater London Crusade statistics covering the first twelve weeks, March 1–May 22, 1954, Folder 3, Box 5, CN 9, BGCA.
61. This gender ration is mentioned in, for example, "Billy's Britain," *Time*, March 22, 1954, 67. A sharp analysis of how the Graham team responded to the challenge of converting men through rhetoric and performance can be found in James Gilbert, *Men in the Middle: Searching for Masculinity in the 1950s*, Chicago: University of Chicago Press, 2005, 106–134.
62. "Die Großstadtevangelisationen mit Dr. Billy Graham," Herausgegeben von Wilhelm Brauer im Auftrag der deutschen Evangelistenkonferenz, Broschüre, no date, no place, 13, Broschüre Nr. 1040, Oncken Archiv.
63. Greater London Crusade statistics covering the first twelve weeks, March 1–May 22, 1954, Folder 3, Box 5, CN 9, BGCA. The spectrum of age was rather similar in both gender groups: 8 percent of the inquirers were children between five and eleven; around 30 percent were adults between nineteen and forty-nine, and only 6 percent of the female inquirers and 8 percent of the male inquirers registered as fifty-plus.

Among those stepping forward, 40 percent indicated that they were church members, 60 percent that they did not belong to a church.

64. Brauer, "Die Großstadtevangelisationen mit Dr. Billy Graham," 13.

65. Bebbington, *Victorian Religious Revivals*, 272.

66. "A Mighty City Hears Billy's Mighty Call," *Life*, May 27, 1957, 20–27.

67. "A Sermon at Harringay," *British Weekly*, March 18, 1954, 8.

68. "Billy Graham Crusade Takes on the Big City," *New York Times*, May 19, 1957, E11.

69. The German original reads: "Frauen mit Kindern an der Hand, Männer in jedem Alter, alte Leute, Menschen, wie man sie an jedem Samstag durch die Straßen ziehen sieht, und allenfalls durch etwas weniger elegante Kleidung von den Kinogängern des Wochenendes unterschieden." "Der Prediger auf dem Fußballplatz," *Süddeutsche Zeitung*, June 4, 1955, 35.

70. Colquhoun, *Harringay Story*, 194.

71. Mitchell, *God in the Garden*, 50.

72. Ribbat, *Religiöse Erregung*. 237.

73. As documented in the conversion stories: Testimonies and Incidents from the New York Crusade, Folder 8, Box 3, CN 1, BGCA; and "Intellectual Assent at Harringay," *Methodist Recorder*, May 20, 1954, 3.

74. "Owner of Modelling School Accepts Christ," Testimonies and Incidents from the New York Crusade, Folder 8, Box 3, CN 1, BGCA.

75. Colquhoun, *Harringay Story*, 214.

76. "The Story of Three Girls," Testimonies and Incidents from the New York Crusade, Folder 8, Box 3, CN 1, BGCA.

77. "Intellectual Assent at Harringay," 3. See also "Typical Testimony of a Housewife," Testimonies and Incidents from the New York Crusade, Folder 8, Box 3, CN 1, BGCA.

78. Mitchell, *Those Who Came Forward*, 140.

79. Ferm, *Persuaded to Live*, 36.

80. Ferm, *Persuaded to Live*, 44.

81. Bericht über den Billy-Graham Abend in Mannheim, no place, no date, ADEA. The German original reads, "Es war für viele ein überwältigendes Erlebnis, diese ergriffene Menge vor der Tribüne heilsverlangend, bußfertig und bekenntnisfreudig zu beobachten. Jünglingen und Greisen liefen die Tränen über die Wangen, und sicherlich gab es an diesem Abend echte Entscheidungen und Bekehrungen unter einem unzweideutigen Wirken des hl. Geistes."

82. "Heaven and Harringay," *Methodist Recorder*, April 8, 1954, 3.

83. Michell, *Those Who Came Forward*, 122.

84. "Owner of Modelling School Accepts Christ."

85. Ferm, *Persuaded to Life*, 26.

86. "Heaven and Harringay," 3.

87. "Was uns dann im Laufe der Veranstaltung so innerlich bewegte, daß sich einem, ohne daß man es wollte, das Herz auftat, das kann nur Gottes hl. Geist gewesen sein, der gegenwärtig war." Maria Redemaker an Giesen, 22. August 1955, 71/1827, EZA.

88. Ferm, *They Met God*, 22.

89. Ferm, *They Met God*, 22.

90. Ferm, *They Met God*, 28.

91. Ferm, *They Met God*, 51. A similar story is reported in Mitchell, *Those Who Came Forward*, 163.

92. "Mr. Graham Ends His Mission," *The Times*, May 24, 1954, 4.

93. "Mr. Graham Ends His Mission," 4.

94. Lang and Lang, "Decisions for Christ," 418.

95. Ferm, *They Met God*, 56.

96. For just one example of a person attending the New York Crusade several times, see Mitchell, *Those Who Came Forward*, 138–145.

97. The German original reads, "Billy Graham steht vorne und betet. Er sagt nicht: 'Kommt zu mir.' Er sagt 'Kommt zu Gott!' Ich fühlte den starken Schlag meines Herzens, als ich vor ihnen aufstand. Ich mied ihre Blicke voller Scham. Aber dann ging ich nach vorne, und viele gingen noch mit mir, sehr viele. Es war nicht mehr so schwer." "Ein Teenager über Billy Graham," *Westdeutsche Allgemeine Zeitung*, September 20, 1960, 12.

98. Ferm, *They Met God*, 47.

99. Ferm, *They Met God*, 33.

100. "The Counselling Room at Harringay," *Methodist Recorder*, May 20, 1954, 3.

101. Colquhoun, *Harringay Story*, 91.

102. Singing during the return from the Olympic Stadium is documented in "Billy Graham bekehrt 20,000 Berliner."

103. Bebbington, *Victorian Religious Revivals*, 268.

104. "Man muß ihn hören," *Berliner Sonntagsblatt, die Kirche*, Sonderausgabe, June 27, 1954, 2.

105. "Augenzeugenbericht," 4.

106. Helmut Thielicke, *Auf Kanzel und Katheder: Aufzeichnungen aus Arbeit und Leben*, Hamburg: Furche-Verlag H. Rennebach, 1965, 200–201.

107. Cook, *London Hears*, 47.

108. "Heaven at Harringay," *Methodist Recorder*, April 8, 1954, 8.

109. "81 Million See Graham on Three Weekend TV Shows," *New York Crusade News*, June 1957, 1, Folder 18, Box 2, CN 1, BGCA.

110. Ferm, *Persuaded to Live*, 97.

111. Examples can be found in Ferm, *They Met God*.

112. Cook, *London Hears*, 110.

113. Interesting Facts, Testimonies and Incidents from the New York Crusade, Folder 8, Box 3, CN 1, BGCA.

114. "Reporter's Exclusive Look at Graham's 'Inquiry Tent,'" Folder 21, Box 2, CN, 1, BGCA.

115. The number can't be verified, but it indicates what message the organizers wanted to convey. Cook, *London Hears*, 40.

116. "A Sermon at Harringay," 8.

117. "Billy Graham bekehrt 20,000 Berliner."

118. See, for example, Andrew Chambers, "Reading, the Godly, and Self-Writing in England, circa 1580–1720," *Journal of British Studies* 46, no. 4 (2007): 796–825.

119. Ferm, *Persuaded to Live*.

120. Mitchell, *Die nach vorne kamen*. Original: Mitchell, *Those Who Came Forward*.

121. E.g., Mitchell, *Those Who Came Forward*, 147.

122. John Corrigan, *Emptiness: Feeling Christian in America*, Chicago: University of Chicago Press, 2015.

123. Mitchell, *Those Who Came Forward*, 67–74, 126–130.

124. "Report from the People," *Decision*, September 1966, 15.

125. Pollock, *Crusade '66*, 35.

126. Rjis/Woodhead, Sociology of Religious Emotion, 182.

127. Wacker, *America's Pastor*, 28.

128. Ferm, *They Met God*, 28.

Epilogue

1. On the Earl's Court crusade see Martin, *Prophet with Honor*, 318–325; on Graham's arrival see Pollock, *Crusade '66*, 15–22; on the atmosphere at Waterloo Station, see "Billy Graham Arrives," *Church of England Newspaper*, May 27, 1966, 1.

2. Pollock, *Crusade '66*, 15.

3. "What Does a City Do with a Blessing?," *Decision*, August 1962, 8–9.

4. "Los Angeles Crusade Begins," *Decision*, August 1963, 16.

5. Pollock, *Crusade '66*, 23.

6. "90,000 hören Billy Graham," *Der Tagesspiegel*, October 25, 1966, 8.

7. McLeod, *Religious Crisis*, 1–2.

8. On secularization processes in Germany in the 1960s see Grossbölting, *Losing Heaven*, 105–166.

9. Pollock, *Crusade '66*, 11. On secular culture in Britain in the 1960s: McLeod, *Religious Crisis*; Brown, *Death of Christian Britain*; Gilbert, *Making of Post-Christian Britain*.

10. Estimated numbers in Mitchell, *Billy Graham London Crusade*, 7–8. This is also confirmed in an oral history interview with Rev. John L. Bird, who observed the same for Duke Baptist Church. Oral history interview with Rev. John L. Bird conducted by Dr. Robert O. Ferm, 5, Folder 30, Box 2, CN 141, BGCA.

11. Pollock, *Crusade '66*, 30.

12. Peter Schneider: Bericht über die Großstadtevangelisation mit Dr. Billy Graham vom 16.–23. October 1966 in Berlin, 21.11.1966, 4, ADEA.

13. Peter Schneider: Ergebnis-Protokoll über die Sitzung des Kuratoriums am Montag, dem 17. Oktober 1966, in Berlin, 24.11.1966, 1, ADEA.

14. "Demos and the Absent Crusaders," *Methodist Recorder*, June 9, 1966, 3.

15. "Prepare, Believe, Expect," *Decision*, February 1964, 7.

16. Even though Britain did witness a similar trend with particularly conservative churches and denominations growing in the 1970s. McLeod, *Religious Crisis*, 210.

17. "The Evangelical Undertow," *Time*, December 20, 1963, 38.

18. On the Bultmann controversy and its role in the shaping of the evangelical movement in Germany see Bauer, *Evangelikale Bewegung*, 259–423.
19. "Towards a Hidden God," *Time*, April 8, 1966, 50–51.
20. "A Public Discussion at the Harvard Law Forum: Evangelism and the Intellectual," *Decision*, October 1962, 8.
21. "Is God Then Dead?," *Decision*, May 1966, 1, 14–15.
22. Mitchell, *Billy Graham London Crusade*, 14.
23. "Billy Battles On," *Church of England Newspaper*, June 10, 1966, 3.
24. "Billy's Crusade 'Is Not Going Well,'" *The Guardian*, June 5, 1966, 3.
25. Canterbury Diocesan Notes April 1966, No. 442, Ramsey Papers 91, 1966, f. 219, LPL.
26. Pollock, *Crusade '66*, 82.
27. "What Did Dr. Ramsey Say?," *Church of England Newspaper*, October 7, 1966, 1.
28. "What Did Dr. Ramsey Say," 2.
29. "Lord Soper on 'Authoritarian Evangelism,'" *Methodist Recorder*, June 2, 1966, 2.
30. Quoted in Bauer, *Evangelikale Bewegung*, 212–213.
31. "Geistig in der Hocke: Die Welt aus der Perspektive Billy Grahams," *Sonntagsblatt*, no. 27, July 3, 1966, 13.
32. "God's Word in Berlin," *Decision*, October 1966, 16.
33. Otto Dibelius, "Billy Graham: Seine Lebensarbeit gehört der modernen Welt," *Berliner Sonntagsblatt, die Kirche*, June 12, 1966, 3.
34. "Der Prediger in der Deutschlandhalle," *Der Tagesspiegel*, October 18, 1966, 7.
35. McLeod, *Religious Crisis*, 72 and 241.
36. Quoted in Martin, *Prophet with Honor*, 320.
37. "The Griller Grilled," *The Guardian*, June 30, 1966, 8.
38. This was acknowledged by the German organizers themselves: Peter Schneider: Bericht über die Großstadtevangelisation mit Dr. Billy Graham vom 16.–23. October 1966 in Berlin, 21.11.1966, 5, ADEA.
39. Grossbölting, *Losing Heaven*, 111.
40. Martin, *Prophet with Honor*, 293.
41. Martin, *Prophet with Honor*, 250.
42. Martin, *Prophet with Honor*, 306–307.
43. Martin, *Prophet with Honor*, 286.
44. This is revealed by Lois Ferm in an oral history interview with Viscount L. W. Brentford conducted by Dr. Lois Ferm on July 7, 1974, 12, Folder 36, Box 2, CN 141, BGCA.
45. "Galvanized by Graham," *Church of England Newspaper*, June 10, 1966, 16.
46. "'It's Tough' Says Graham: Recorder Earl's Court Assessment," *Methodist Recorder*, June 9, 1966, 3.
47. Oral history interview with Henry Hole conducted by Dr. Robert O. Ferm, no date, 7–8, Folder 28, Box 4, CN 141, BGCA.
48. Oral history interview with Oliver Stott conducted by Dr. Robert O. Ferm, July 6, 1974, 10, Folder 24, Box 42, CN 141, BGCA.
49. Pollock, *Crusade '66*, 85.
50. "Crusade Points," *Church of England Newspaper*, June 24, 1966, 3.
51. Pollock, *Crusade '66*, 88.

52. This figure is given in an article in the *Berliner Kurier*, October 24, 1966 in Die Großstadtevangelisation mit Billy Graham im Spiegel der Presse, 5, 55.1/190, ELAB.

53. News Release from the Billy Graham Greater London Crusade 1966, June 12, 1966, 1–2, Folder 7, Box 8, CN 9, BGCA. Also, "London Writes More History," *Decision*, August 1966, 8–9.

54. "Billy Battles On," *Church of England Newspaper*, June 10, 1966, 3.

55. "East Londoner's Reactions," *Church of England Newspaper*, June 17, 1966, 3.

56. "Massenspeisung mit 'Biblischem Brot,'" *Süddeutsche Zeitung*, October 21, 1966, 3.

57. Brown, *Death of Christian Britain*, 185.

58. Pollock, *Crusade '66*, 88.

59. Pollock, *Crusade '66*, 37.

60. Brian Cooper, "Has the Christian Situation Altered?," *British Weekly*, July 21, 1966, 5.

61. Mitchell, *Billy Graham London Crusade*, 75–76.

62. "Ich war von meiner Ware überzeugt! Billy Grahams Evangelisation in Berlin," *Sonntagsblatt*, October 30, 1966, 14.

63. "Degutted and Individualized," *Church of England Newspaper*, July 1, 1966, 9. Leech is quoting the part "degutted and individualized" from a criticism expressed by Canon Stanley Evans in 1964.

64. Shaun Herron, "Bill Graham," *British Weekly*, March 4, 1954, 1.

65. This strong judgment is made by Leech, *Race, Changing Society*, 104.

66. Großevangelisation der Deutschen Evangelischen Allianz, Kommuniqué, März 1966, 1–2, ADEA.

67. "Billy Graham Meets the Press," *Church of England Newspaper*, May 27, 1966, 2; "Race Prejudice Here, Dr Graham Says," *The Times*, May 26, 1966, 14.

68. Wacker, *America's Pastor*, 128.

69. Quoted in Pollock, *Crusade '66*, 41.

70. "Billy in Brixton," *Church of England Newspaper*, June 17, 1966, 2.

71. "Der Prediger in der Deutschlandhalle," *Der Tagesspiegel*, October 18, 1966, 7.

72. The German original reads: "Menschen nicht ernsthaft dazu führt, ihre Verantwortung in der Welt, als Christen, wahrzunehmen." "Wer kritisiert Billy?," *Christ und Welt*, September 23, 1966, 38.

73. Cooper, "Has the Christian Situation Altered?," 5.

74. "Christians Speak on Vietnam," *Church of England Newspaper*, July 8, 1966, 10.

75. "Johnson Flies to Houston for Graham Sermon," *New York Times*, November 29, 1965, 28. *Decision* magazine gave a detailed report on the Houston crusade, making no reference to the controversial remarks regarding the antiwar protesters: "The President Visits the Crusade," *Decision*, February 1966, 8–9, 13.

76. "Die Habichte und die Tauben," *Die Zeit*, December 17, 1965, https://www.zeit.de/1965/51/die-habichte-und-die-tauben/.

77. George Target, "A Few Questions for Billy Graham," *British Weekly*, August 4, 1966, 11.

78. "A Measure of the Revelations," *The Guardian*, May 26, 1966, 6.

79. "Letters to the Editors," *The Guardian*, June 3, 1966, 12. See also for other comments: "Letters to the Editors," *The Guardian*, June 26, 1966, 6.

80. Martin, *Prophet with Honor*, 322. Also, Pollock, *Crusade '66*, 80.

81. Andrew Finstuen, "Professor Graham: Billy Graham's Mission to Colleges and Universities," in *Billy Graham: American Pilgrim*, ed. Andrew Finstuen, Grant Wacker, and Anne Blue Wills, New York: Oxford University Press, 2017, 32–33.

82. Martin, *Prophet with Honor*, 369. See also the detailed analysis in Randall E. King, "When Worlds Collide: Politics, Religion, and Media at the 1970 East Tennessee Billy Graham Crusade," *Journal of Church and State 39*, no. 2 (1997): 273–295.

83. Martin, *Prophet with Honor*, 376–377.

84. "Billy Graham 'befeuert' Berlin," *Frankfurter Rundschau*, October 19, 1966, 8.

85. "Die Habichte und die Tauben," *Die Zeit*, December 17, 1965. https://www.zeit.de/1965/51/die-habichte-und-die-tauben/.

86. "Berlin," *Decision*, June 1966, 11.

87. Gustav Roth (Unterwegskreis in West-Berlin) an Kirchenleitung in Berlin-West, Kurt Scharf, 13.1. 1966. 201/6, EZA. For the history of the Unterwegskreis see Gerhard Altenburg, "'Junge Draufgänger' unterwegs. Erbe der 'Illegalen,' Keimzelle der Bonhoeffer-Rezeption und Entwicklungsraum theologischer Persönlichkeiten: Die Anfänge des Berliner Unterwegskreises," *Berliner Theologische Zeitschrift 27*, no. 2 (2010): 351–373.

88. Der Generalsuperintendent von Berlin an alle Pfarrer und Pastorinnen, Hilfsprediger und Vikare in Westberlin und an alle Amtsträger innerhalb der Freikirchen und der Gemeinschaft innerhalb der Landeskirche, Berlin, December 19, 1965, 55.1/190, ELAB.

89. Der Generalsuperintendent von Berlin, Rundschreiben, 2. September 1966. 55.1/190, ELAB.

90. Peter Schneider, Kommuniqué, March 1966, ADEA.

91. "Billy Graham 'befeuert' Berlin," *Frankfurter Rundschau*, October 19, 1966, 8.

92. "Stand Fast in Freedom," *Decision*, December 1966, 10–11.

93. "Don't Rock the Ark," *Washington Post*, June 23, 1969, B1.

94. "The Christian Conscience," *British Weekly*, January 6, 1966, 1.

95. Target, "A Few Questions for Billy Graham," 7, 11. See by the same author: "The Griller Grilled," *The Guardian*, June 30, 1966, 8.

96. Results of the survey were published in the *Church of England Newspaper*, December 30, 1966. On commercialization aspects: 7.

97. "Massenspeisung mit 'Biblischem Brot,'" *Süddeutsche Zeitung*, October 21, 1966, 3.

98. Cecil Northcott, "The Billy Graham Crusade: Is the Evangelism for Our Time?," *Church Times*, May 27, 1966, 11.

99. "Kenneth Leech Argues That Billy Graham's Gospel Is Degutted and Individualized," *Church of England Newspaper*, July 1, 1966, 9.

100. "Pfarrer Werner: Feldzug gegen die erwachsenen Gewissen der Christen," in epd ZA, Nb. 69, April 8, 1970, 55.1/191, ELAB. The German original reads, "die religiöse Verbrämung eines unchristlichen Antikommunismus und die Aufplusterung des 'American Way of Life' zum Modell christlichen Lebens."

101. "Eine weltumspannende Gemeinde rückt ihren internationalen Star ins Scheinwerferlicht," quoted from *Der Abend*, October 17, 1966. In Die

Großstadtevangelisation mit Billy Graham im Spiegel der Presse, 3, Press clipping collection 190, ELAB.

102. Melani McAlister, *The Kingdom of God Has No Borders: A Global History of US Evangelicals*, New York: Oxford University Press, 2018.

Bibliography

Archives Consulted

Billy Graham Center Archives, Wheaton, Illinois (BGCA)
CN 1 Papers of Willis Graham Haymaker
CN 9 Billy Graham Evangelistic Association Ltd.
CN 141 Oral History and Manuscripts Project
CN 265 Billy Graham Sermons
CN 318 Papers of L. Nelson Bell
CN 360 Magazine and Newspaper Clippings Collection
CN 622 Papers of Cliff Barrows

Archive of the Evangelical Alliance UK, London (AEAUK)
Minute Book of the Greater London Crusade Executive Committee, 1954
Minute Book of the Greater London Crusade Subcommittees, 1954
Minute Book of the Executive Committee of the London Crusade 1955
Minute Book of the Subcommittees of the London Crusade 1955

Archive der Deutschen Evangelischen Allianz, Bad Blankenburg (ADEA)
Uncataloged items on Billy Graham's German crusades in 1954, 1955, 1960, and 1966

Evangelisches Zentralarchiv (EZA)
Bestand 71/1827: Teilnahme Billy Grahams am 7. DEKT in Frankfurt 1956
Bestand 201/6: Kirchliche Gremien, Staatliche Stellen, Verlage und Vereine (1962–1968)

Evangelisches Landeskirchliches Archiv in Berlin (ELAB)
55.1/190 Billy Graham I (1954–1966)
55.1/191 Billy Graham II (1967–1983)

Lambeth Palace Library, London (LPL)
Fisher Papers, Volume 141, 1954
Ramsey Papers, Volume 91, 1966

Landesarchiv, Berlin (LAB)
B Rep. 002 Der Regierende Bürgermeister von Berlin/Senatskanzlei
B Rep. 020 Der Polizeipräsident in Berlin
C Rep. 104 Magistrat von Berlin, Bereich Inneres

Nordelbisches Kirchenarchiv, Kiel (NEKA)
Die Kirche in Hamburg

Periodicals

Baptist Times
Berliner Sonntagsblatt, die Kirche
British Weekly
Chicago Daily Tribune
Christ und Welt
Christian Century
Christian Herald and Sign of Our Times
Christianity and Crisis
Christianity Today
Church of England Newspaper
Church Times
Commonweal
Decision
Der Spiegel
Die Zeit
Frankfurter Allgemeine Zeitung
Kirche in Hamburg
Kirche und Mann
Life
London Crusade News
Los Angeles Times
Manchester Guardian
Methodist Recorder
Moody Monthly
New York Crusade News
New York Times
Sonntagsblatt
Süddeutsche Zeitung
Tagesspiegel
Time
The Guardian
The Times
United Evangelical Action
Washington Post
Westdeutsche Allgemeine Zeitung
Youth for Christ Magazine

Books and Articles

Altenburg, Gerhard. "'Junge Draufgänger' unterwegs. Erbe der 'Illegalen,' Keimzelle der Bonhoeffer-Rezeption und Entwicklungsraum theologischer Persönlichkeiten: Die Anfänge des Berliner Unterwegskreises." *Berliner Theologische Zeitschrift* 27, no. 2 (2010): 351–373.

Ammerman, Nancy. *Everyday Religion: Observing Modern Religious Lives.* New York: Oxford University Press, 2006.

Balbier, Uta. "Billy Graham in West Germany: German Protestantism between Americanization and Rechristianization." *Zeithistorische Forschungen / Studies in Contemporary History* 7 (2010): article 3, http://www.zeithistorische-forschungen.de/16126041-Balbier-3-2010.

Balbier, Uta. "Youth for Christ in England und Deutschland: Religiöser Transnationalismus und christliche Nachkriegsordnung, 1945–1948." *Archiv für Sozialgeschichte* 51 (2011): 209–224.

Balmer, Randall Herbert. *Evangelicalism in America.* Waco, TX: Baylor University Press, 2016.

Bauer, Gisa. *Evangelikale Bewegung und evangelische Kirche in der Bundesrepublik (1945–1989).* Göttingen: Vandenhoeck & Ruprecht, 2012.

Bebbington, David. *Evangelicalism in Modern Britain: A History from the 1730s to the 1980s.* London: Unwin Hyman, 1989.

Bebbington, David. *Victorian Religious Revivals: Culture and Piety in Local and Global Contexts.* New York: Oxford University Press, 2012.

Bendroth, Margaret. *Fundamentalism and Gender, 1875 to the Present.* New Haven: Yale University Press, 1993.

Berger, Peter. *The Noise of Solemn Assemblies: Christian Commitment and the Religious Establishment in America.* Garden City, NY: Doubleday, 1961.

Berger, Peter L., Grace Davie, and Effie Fokas. *Religious America, Secular Europe? A Theme and Variations.* Aldershot: Ashgate, 2008.

Beyreuther, Erich. *Der Weg der Evangelischen Allianz in Deutschland.* Wuppertal: R. Brockhaus Verlag, 1969.

Blumhofer, Edith. "Singing to Save: Music in the Billy Graham Crusades." In *Billy Graham: American Pilgrim*, edited by Andrew Finstuen, Grant Wacker and Anne Blue Wills, 64–82. New York: Oxford University Press, 2017.

Bösch, Frank, and Lucian Hölscher. *Kirchen-Medien-Öffentlichkeit: Transformationen kirchlicher Selbst- und Fremddeutungen seit 1945.* Göttingen: Wallstein Verlag, 2009.

Boeve, Lieven, and Kristien Justaert. *Consuming Religion in Europe? Christian Faith Challenged by Consumer Culture.* Münster: Lit Verlag, 2006.

Braude, Anne. "Women's History Is American Religious History." In *Retelling U.S. Religious History*, edited by Thomas Tweed, 87–107. Berkeley: University of California Press, 1996.

Brauer, Wilhelm. *Billy Graham, ein Evangelist der neuen Welt.* Giesen: Brunnen Verlag, 1954.

Brauer, Wilhelm. *Europas Goldene Stunde: Stimmen zum Besuch Billy Grahams aus Kirche, Presse und Gemeinde.* Wuppertal: Brockhaus Verlag, 1955.

Brown, Callum G. *Religion and Society in Twentieth-Century Britain.* London: Routledge, 2014.

Brown, Callum G. *The Death of Christian Britain: Understanding Secularization, 1800–2000.* London: Routledge, 2009.

Burk, Kathleen. *Old World, New World: The Story of Britain and America.* London: Little, Brown, 2007.

Butler, Anthea. *White Evangelical Racism: The Politics of Morality in America.* Chapel Hill: University of North Carolina Press, 2021.

Carpenter, Joel. *Revive Us Again: The Reawakening of American Fundamentalism.* New York: Oxford University Press, 1997.

Carwardine, Richard. *Transatlantic Revivalism: Popular Evangelicalism in Britain and America, 1790–1865.* Westport, CT: Greenwood Press, 1978.

Chambers, Andrew. "Reading, the Godly, and Self-Writing in England, circa 1580–1720." *Journal of British Studies* 46, no. 4 (2007): 796–825.

Chapman, Alister. *Godly Ambition: John Stott and the Evangelical Movement.* Oxford: Oxford University Press, 2014.

Chapman, Alister. "What Evangelical Anglicans Learned from the World, 1945–2000." In *Evangelicalism and the Church of England in the Twentieth Century*, edited by Andrew Atherstone and John Maiden, 248–267. Woodbridge: Boydell, 2014.

Chapple, Arthur H. *Billy Graham.* London: Marshall, Morgan and Scottt, 1954.

Clelland, Donald A., et al. "In the Company of the Converted: Characteristics of a Billy Graham Crusade Audience." *Sociological Analysis* 35, no. 1 (1974): 45–56.

Colquhoun, Frank. *Harringay Story: The Official Record of the Billy Graham Greater London Crusade, 1954.* London: Hodder & Stoughton, 1955.

Conroy-Krutz, Emily. *Christian Imperialism: Converting the World in the Early American Republic.* Ithaca, NY: Cornell University Press, 2015.

Cook, Charles T. *London Hears Billy Graham.* London, Marshall, Morgan and Scott Lt., 1954.

Corrigan, John. *Business of the Heart: Religion and Emotion in the Nineteenth Century.* Berkeley: University of California Press, 2002.

Corrigan, John. *Emptiness: Feeling Christian in America.* Chicago: University of Chicago Press, 2015.

Corrigan, John, and Frank Hinkelmann. *Return to Sender: American Evangelical Missions to Europe in the 20th Century.* Berlin: Lit Verlag, 2019.

Cuordileone, K. A. *Manhood and American Political Culture in the Cold War.* New York: Routledge 2005.

Curtis, Heather. "Depicting Distant Suffering: Evangelicals and the Politics of Pictorial Humanitarianism in the Age of American Empire." *Material Religion* 8, no. 2 (2012): 154–183.

Curtis, Heather. *Holy Humanitarians: American Evangelicals and Global Aid.* Cambridge, MA: Harvard University Press, 2018.

Davie, Grace. *Religion in Britain: A Persistent Paradox.* 2nd ed. Chichester: John Wiley and Sons, 2015. https://ebookcentral.proquest.com/lib/oxford/detail.action?docID=1887762.

Davie, Grace. *Religion in Britain since 1945: Believing without Belonging.* Oxford: Blackwells, 1994.

De Groot, Joanna, and Sue Morgan. "'Beyond the "Religious Turn": Past, Present and Future Perspectives in Gender History.'" In "Sex, Gender and the Sacred: Reconfiguring Religion in Gender History," *Gender and History*, Special Issue, 25, no. 3 (2014): 1–30.

Deitenbeck, Paul. *Eine Weltstadt horcht auf: Begegnung mit Billy Graham.* No date, no place.

Deutsche Evangelische Allianz. *Noch ruft Gott: Billy Graham in Essen, Hamburg und Berlin.* Wuppertal: Brockhaus Verlag, 1961.

Dirks, Walter. "Trommler des lieben Gottes: Bemerkungen zu Billy Graham und Genossen." *Frankfurter Hefte* 10 (1955): 537–544.

Dochuk, Darren. *Anointed with Oil: How Christianity and Crude Made Modern America.* New York: Basic Books, 2019.

Dochuk, Darren. "Moving Mountains: The Business of Evangelicalism and Extraction in a Liberal Age." In *What's Good for Business: Business and Politics since World War II*, edited by Julian Zelizer and Kimberly Phillips-Fein, 72–90. New York: Oxford University Press, 2012.

Du Mez, Kristin Kobes. *Jesus and John Wayne: How White Evangelicals Corrupted a Faith and Fractured a Nation*. New York: Liveright Publishing, 2020.

Dudziak, Mary L. *Cold War Civil Rights: Race and the Image of American Democracy*. Princeton, NJ: Princeton University Press, 2000.

Elwert, Frederik, Martin Radermacher, and Jens Schlamelcher. *Handbuch Evangelikalismus*. Bielefeld: Transcript Verlag, 2017.

England, Edward. *Afterwards: A Journalist Sets Out to Discover What Happened to Some of Those Who Made a Decision for Christ during the Billy Graham Crusades in Britain in 1954 and 1955*. London: Victory, 1956.

Enns, James. *Saving Germany: North American Protestants and Christian Mission to Germany, 1945–1974*. Montreal: McGill University Press, 2017.

Fehrenbach, Heide. *Race after Hitler: Black Occupation Children in Postwar Germany and America*. Princeton, NJ: Princeton University Press, 2005.

Fer, Yannick. "Pentecostal Prayer as Personal Communication and Invisible Institutional Work." In *A Sociology of Prayer*, edited by Guiseppe Giordan and Linda Woodhead, 49–65. Farnham: Ashgate, 2015.

Ferm, Robert. *Persuaded to Live: Conversion Stories from the Billy Graham Crusades*. Ada, MI: Fleming H. Revell, 1958.

Ferm, Robert. *They Met God at the New York Crusade*. Minneapolis: Billy Graham Evangelistic Association, 1957.

Finstuen, Andrew. *Original Sin and Everyday Protestants: The Theology of Reinhold Niebuhr, Billy Graham, and Paul Tillich in an Age of Anxiety*. Chapel Hill: University of North Carolina Press, 2009.

Finstuen, Andrew. "Professor Graham: Billy Graham's Mission to Colleges and Universities." In *Billy Graham: American Pilgrim*, edited by Andrew Finstuen, Grant Wacker, and Anne Blue Wills, 23–38. New York: Oxford University Press, 2017.

Gause, Uta. *Kirchengeschichte und Genderforschung: Eine Einführung in protestantischer Perspektive*. Tübingen: Mohr Siebeck, 2006.

Gilbert, Alan D. *The Making of Post-Christian Britain: A History of the Secularization of Modern Society*. New York: Longman, 1980.

Gilbert, James. *Men in the Middle: Searching for Masculinity in the 1950s*. Chicago: University of Chicago Press, 2005.

Giordan, Guiseppe. "You Never Know. Prayer as Enchantment." In *A Sociology of Prayer*, edited by Guiseppe Giordan and Linda Woodhead, 1–8. Farnham: Ashgate, 2015.

Glotzer, Paige. *How the Suburbs Were Segregated: Developers and the Business of Exclusionary Housing, 1890–1960*. New York: Columbia University Press, 2020.

Graham, Ruth Bell. *Footprints of a Pilgrim: The Life and Loves of Ruth Bell Graham*. Edinburgh: Thomas Nelson, 2001.

Graham, Billy. *Friede mit Gott*. Wuppertal: R. Brockhaus Verlag, 1954.

Graham, Billy. *Revival in Our Time: The Story of the Billy Graham Evangelistic Campaigns*. Wheaton, IL: Von Kampen Press, 1950.

Green, Simon J. D. *The Passing of Protestant England: Secularisation and Social Change, c.1920–1960*. Cambridge: Cambridge University Press, 2011.

Grem, Darren E. *The Blessings of Business: How Corporations Shaped Conservative Christianity*. New York: Oxford University Press, 2016.

Greschat, Martin. *Die evangelische Christenheit und die deutsche Geschichte nach 1945: Weichenstellungen in der Nachkriegszeit*. Stuttgart: W. Kohlhammer Verlag, 2002.

Greschat, Martin. *Protestantismus im Kalten Krieg. Kirche, Politik und Gesellschaft im geteilten Deutschland 1945-1963*. Paderborn: Verlag Ferdinant Schoeningh, 2010.

Greschat, Martin. "'Rechristianisierung' und 'Säkularisierung': Anmerkungen zu einem europäischen interkonfessionellen Interpretationsmodell." In *Christentum und politische Verantwortung: Kirchen im Nachkriegsdeutschland*, edited by Jochen-Christoph Kaiser and Anselm Doering-Manteuffel, 1-24. Stuttgart: Kohlhammer Verlag, 1990.

Griffith, R. Marie. "Submissive Wives, Wounded Daughters, and Female Soldiers: Prayer and Christian Womanhood in Women's Aglow Fellowship." In *Lived Religion in America: Toward a History of Practice*, edited by David D. Hall, 160-195. Princeton. NJ: Princeton University Press, 1997.

Grossbölting, Thomas, and Alex Skinner. *Losing Heaven: Religion in Germany since 1945*. New York: Berghahn, 2016.

Haberski, Raymond, Jr. *God and War: American Civil Religion since 1945*. New Brunswick, NJ: Rutgers University Press, 2012.

Hall, David T. "Introduction." In *Lived Religion in America: Toward a History of Practice*, edited by David D. Hall, vii-xiii. Princeton, NJ: Princeton University Press, 1997.

Hammond, Sarah. *God's Businessmen: Entrepreneurial Evangelicals in Depression and War*. Edited by Darren Dochuk. Chicago: University of Chicago Press, 2017.

Hannig, Nicolai. *Die Religion der Öffentlichkeit: Medien, Religion und Kirche in der Bundesrepublik 1945-1980*. Göttingen: Wallstein Verlag, 2010.

Harris, Alana. *Faith in the Family: A Lived Religious History of English Catholicism, 1945-82*. Manchester: Manchester University Press, 2013.

Harris, Alana, and Martin Spence. "'Disturbing the Complacency of Religion'? The Evangelical Crusades of Dr Billy Graham and Father Patrick Peyton in Britain, 1951-54." *Twentieth Century British History* 18, no. 4 (2007): 481-513.

Hastings, Adrian. *A History of English Christianity, 1920-1990*. 3rd ed. London: Trinity Press International, 1991.

Hempton, David. *Methodism: Empire of the Spirit*. New Haven: Yale University Press, 2005.

Hempton, David, and Hugh McLeod. *Secularization and Religious Innovation in the North Atlantic World*. New York: Oxford University Press, 2017.

Herberg, Will. *Protestant, Catholic, Jew: An Essay in American Religious Sociology*. Garden City, NY: Doubleday, 1955.

Hermle, Siegfried. "Die Evangelikalen als Gegenbewegung." In *Umbrüche: Der deutsche Protestantismus und die sozialen Bewegungen in den 1960er und 70er Jahren*, edited by Siegfried Hermle, Claudia Lepp, and Harry Oelke, 325-352. Göttingen: Vandenhoeck & Ruprecht, 2007.

Herzog, Jonathan P. *The Spiritual-Industrial Complex: America's Religious Battle against Communism in the Early Cold War*. New York: Oxford University Press, 2011.

Hill, Clifford S. *West Indian Migrants and the London Churches*. Oxford: Oxford University Press, 1963.

Höhn, Maria, and Martin Klimke. *A Breath of Freedom: The Civil Rights Struggle, African American GIs, and Germany*. New York: Palgrave Macmillan, 2010.

Hudnut-Beumler, James. *Looking for God in the Suburbs: The Religion of the American Dream and Its Critics, 1945–1965*. New Brunswick, NJ: Rutgers University Press, 1994.

Hylson-Smith, Kenneth. *Evangelicals in the Church of England, 1734–1984*. Edinburgh: T & T Clark, 1988.

Inboden, William. *Religion and American Foreign Policy, 1945–1960: The Soul of Containment*. New York: Cambridge University Press, 2008.

Jeremy, David J. *Capitalists and Christians: Business Leaders and the Churches in Britain, 1900–1960*. Oxford: Clarendon Press, 1990.

Jeremy, David J. *Religion, Business and Wealth in Modern Britain*. New York: Routledge, 1998.

Jung, Friedhelm. *Die deutsche evangelikale Bewegung: Grundlinien ihrer Geschichte und Theologie*. 3rd. ed. Bonn: Verlag für Kultur und Wissenschaft, 2001.

Kalyvas, Stathis. *The Rise of Christian Democracy in Europe*. Ithaca, NY: Cornell University Press, 1996.

Kelley, Robin D. G., and Stephen G. N. Tuck. *The Other Special Relationship: Race, Rights, and Riots in Britain and the United States*. New York: Palgrave, 2015.

King, David P. *God's Internationalists: World Vision and the Age of Evangelical Humanitarianism*. Philadelphia: University of Pennsylvania Press, 2019.

King, Randall E. "When Worlds Collide: Politics, Religion, and Media at the 1970 East Tennessee Billy Graham Crusade." *Journal of Church and State* 39, no. 2 (1997): 273–295.

Krabbendam, Hans. *Saving the Overlooked Continent: American Protestant Missions in Western Europe, 1940–1975*. Leuven: Leuven University Press, 2021.

Kruse, Kevin. *One Nation under God: How Corporate America Invented Christian America*. New York: Basic Books, 2015.

Lahr, Angela M. *Millennial Dreams and Apocalyptic Nightmares*. New York: Oxford University Press, 2007.

Lang, Kurt, and Gladys Lang. "Decisions for Christ: Billy Graham in New York." In *Identity and Anxiety: Survival of the Person in Mass Society*, edited by Maurice R. Stein, Arthur J. Vidich, and David M. White, 415–427. New York: Free Press, 1960.

Laubach, Fritz. *Aufbruch der Evangelikalen*. Wuppertal: R. Brockhaus Verlag, 1972.

Laun, J. F. "Stehen wir vor einer Erweckung?" In *Billy Graham: Ein Evangelist der Neuen Welt*, edited by Wilhelm Brauer, 69–73. Basel: Brunnen Verlag, 1955.

Leech, Kenneth. *Race, Changing Society and the Churches*. London: SPCK, 2005.

Lilje, Hanns. *Memorabilia: Schwerpunkte eines Lebens*. Nuremberg: Laetere Verlag, 1973.

Lofton, Kathryn. *Consuming Religion*. Chicago: University of Chicago Press, 2018.

Loos, Mirjam. "Antikommunistische und anti-antikommunistische Stimmen im evangelischen Kirchenmilieu: Die Debatte um Wiedervereinigung, Westbindung und Wiederbewaffnung." In *"Geistige Gefahr" und "Immunisierung der Gesellschaft": Antikommunismus und politische Kultur in der frühen Bundesrepublik*, edited by Stefan Creuzberger and Dierk Hoffmann, 199–213. Munich: Oldenburg Verlag, 2014.

Marsden, George. *Fundamentalism and American Culture*. 2nd ed. New York: Oxford University Press, 2006.

Martin, William. *A Prophet with Honor: The Billy Graham Story*. New York: William Morrow, 1991.

McAlister, Melani. *The Kingdom of God Has No Borders: A Global History of US Evangelicals*. New York: Oxford University Press, 2018.

McDannell, Colleen. *Material Christianity: Religion and Popular Culture in America*. New Haven: Yale University Press, 1998.

McGuire, Meredith. *Lived Religion: Faith and Practice in Everyday Life*. New York: Oxford University Press, 2008.

McLaughlin, William G. *Modern Revivalism: Charles Grandison Finney to Billy Graham*. Reprint ed. Eugene: Wipf & Stock Publishers, 2005. Originally published by the Ronald Press Company, 1959.

McLeod, Hugh. *The Religious Crisis of the 1960s*. Oxford: Oxford University Press, 2007.

Meyer, Birgit. "Introduction. From Imagined Communities to Aesthetic Formations: Religious Mediations, Sensational Forms, and Styles of Binding." In *Aesthetic Formations: Media, Religion, and the Senses*, edited by Birgit Meyer, 1–28. New York: Palgrave Macmillan, 2010.

Miller, Steven P. *Billy Graham and the Rise of the Republican South*. Philadelphia: University of Pennsylvania Press, 2009.

Miller, Vincent Jude. *Consuming Religion: Christian Faith and Practice in a Consumer Culture*. New York: Continuum, 2005.

Mitchell, Curtis. *The Billy Graham London Crusade*. Minneapolis: World Wide Publications, 1966.

Mitchell, Curtis. *Die nach vorne kamen: Evangelisation mit Billy Graham und ihre Ergebnisse*. Kassel: J.G. Oncken Verlag, 1967.

Mitchell, Curtis. *God in the Garden: The Amazing Story of Billy Graham's First New York Crusade*. Garden City, NY: Doubleday, 1957.

Mitchell, Curtis. *Those Who Came Forward: An Account of Those Whose Lives Were Changed by the Ministry of Billy Graham*. Kingswood: World's Works 1913, 1966.

Mittmann, Thomas. *Kirchliche Akademien in der Bundesrepublik: Gesellschaftliche, politische und religiöse Selbstverortungen*. Göttingen: Wallstein Verlag, 2011.

Moore, Laurence R. *Selling God: American Religion in the Marketplace of Culture*. New York: Oxford University Press, 1995.

Moreton, Bethany. *To Serve God and Wal-Mart: The Making of Christian Free Enterprise*. Cambridge, MA: Harvard University Press, 2009.

Morris, Jeremy. "Secularization and Religious Experience: Arguments in the Historiography of Modern British Religion." *Historical Journal* 55, no. 1 (2012): 195–219.

Noll, Mark A., David Bebbington, and George A. Rawlyk. *Evangelicalism: Comparative Studies of Popular Protestantism in North America, the British Isles, and Beyond, 1700–1990*. New York: Oxford University Press, 1994.

O'Sullivan, Michael E. *Disruptive Power: Catholic Women, Miracles, and Politics in Modern Germany, 1918–1965*. Toronto: University of Toronto Press, 2018.

O'Sullivan, Michael E. "From Catholic Milieu to Lived Religion: The Social and Cultural History of Modern German Catholicism." *History Compass* 7, no. 3 (2009): 837–861.

O'Sullivan, Michael E. "West German Miracles: Catholic Mystics, Church Hierarchy, and Postwar Popular Culture." *Zeithistorische Forschungen / Studies in Contemporary History* 6 (2009): article 1, http://www.zeithistorische-forschungen.de/16126041-OSullivan-1-2009.

Orsi, Robert A. *Between Heaven and Earth: The Religious Worlds People Make and the Scholars Who Study Them*. Princeton, NJ: Princeton University Press, 2005.

Orsi, Robert A. "Everyday Miracles: The Study of Lived Religion." In *Lived Religion in America: Toward a History of Practice*, edited by David D. Hall, 3–21. Princeton, NJ: Princeton University Press, 1997.

Orsi, Robert A. *The Madonna of 115th Street*. Faith and Community in Italian Harlem, 1880–1950. 2nd ed. New Haven: Yale University Press, 2002.

Pearson, Benjamin. "The Pluralization of Protestant Politics: Public Responsibility, Rearmament, and Division at the 1950s *Kirchentage*." *Central European History* 43 (2010): 270–300.

Pollock, John. *Crusade '66: Britain Hears Billy Graham*. London: Hodder & Stoughton, 1966.

Porterfield, Amanda, John Corrigan, and Darren E. Grem. *The Business Turn in American Religious History*. New York: Oxford Scholarship Online, 2017.

Preston, Andrew. *Sword of the Spirit, Shield of Faith: Religion in American War and Diplomacy*. New York: Alfred A. Knopf, 2012.

Randall, Ian, and David Hilborn. *One Body in Christ: The History and Significance of the Evangelical Alliance*. Waynesboro: Paternoster Press, 2001.

Rees, Jean A. *His Name Was Tom: The Biography of Tom Rees*. London: Hodder & Stoughton, 1971.

Ribbat, Christoph. *Religiöse Erregung: Protestantische Schwärmer im Kaiserreich*. Frankfurt am Main: Campus Verlag, 1996.

Rjis, Ole, and Linda Woodhead. *A Sociology of Religious Emotion*. Oxford: Oxford University Press, 2012.

Robbins, Keith. "Britain, 1940, and 'Christian Civilization.'" In *History, Society and the Churches: Essays in Honour of Owen Chadwick*, edited by Derek Beales and Geoffrey Best, 279–300. Cambridge: Cambridge University Press, 1985.

Robbins, Keith. *History, Religion, and Identity in Modern Britain*. London: Hambledon Press, 1993.

Rowlandson, Maurice. *Life with Billy*. London: Hodder & Stoughton, 1992.

Ruff, Mark. "Integrating Religion into the Historical Mainstream: Recent Literature on Religion in the Federal Republic of Germany." *Central European History* 42 (2009): 307–337.

Ruff, Mark. "Religious Transformation since 1945: Is There an American Religious Exceptionalism?" *Schweizerische Zeitschrift für Religions- und Kulturgeschichte* 107 (2013): 33–48.

Ruotsila, Markku. *Fighting Fundamentalist: Carl McIntire and the Politicization of American Fundamentalism*. New York: Oxford University Press, 2016.

Sauer, Thomas. *Westorientierung im deutschen Protestantismus: Vorstellungen und Tätigkeit des Kronberger Kreises*. Munich: R. Oldenbourg, 1999.

Schildt, Axel. *Moderne Zeiten: Freizeit, Massenmedien und "Zeitgeist" in der Bundesrepublik der 1950er Jahre*. Hamburg: Hans Christians Verlag, 1995.

Schildt, Axel. *Zwischen Abendland und Amerika: Studien zur westdeutschen Ideenlandschaft der 50er Jahre*. Munich: R. Oldenbourgh Verlag, 1999.

Shils, Edward, and Michael Young. "The Meaning of the Coronation." *Sociological Review* 1 (1953): 63–81.

Stevens, Jason W. *God-Fearing and Free: A Spiritual History of America's Cold War*. Cambridge, MA: Harvard University Press, 2010.

Stupperich, Robert. *Otto Dibelius: Ein evangelischer Bischof im Umbruch der Zeiten*. Göttingen: Vandenhoek & Ruprecht, 1989.

Sutton, Matthew A. *American Apocalypse: A History of Modern Evangelicalism*. Cambridge, MA: Harvard University Press, 2014.

Swartz, David R. *Facing West: American Evangelicals in an Age of World Christianity.* New York: Oxford University Press, 2020.

Thielicke, Helmut. *Auf Kanzel und Katheder: Aufzeichnungen aus Arbeit und Leben.* Hamburg: Furche-Verlag H. Rennebach, 1965.

Toynbee, Arnold. *Christianity and Civilization: Burge Memorial Lecture; 1940.* London: Student Christian Movement Press, 1940.

Wacker, Grant. *America's Pastor: Billy Graham and the Shaping of a Nation.* Cambridge: Harvard University Press, 2014.

Wehner, Herbert. *Christentum und demokratischer Sozialismus.* Freiburg: Dreisam Verlag, 1986.

Whitfield, Stephen J. *The Culture of the Cold War.* Baltimore: Johns Hopkins University Press, 1991.

Wilkinson, Alan. *Christian Socialism: Scott Holland to Tony Blair.* Norwich: SCM Press, 2012.

Williams, Sarah. *Religious Belief and Popular Culture in Southwark, c. 1880–1939.* Oxford: Oxford University Press, 1999.

Wills, Anne Blue. *An Odd Cross to Bear: A Life of Ruth Bell Graham.* Grand Rapids: Eerdmans, forthcoming.

Wimberley, Ronald C., et al. "Conversion in a Billy Graham Crusade: Spontaneous Event or Ritual Performance?" *Sociological Quarterly* 16, no. 2 (1975): 162–170.

Winter, Gibson. *The Suburban Captivity of the Churches: An Analysis of Protestant Responsibility in the Expanding Metropolis.* Garden City, NY: Doubleday, 1961.

Wright, Richard. *Patriots: National Identity in Britain, 1940–2000.* Oxford: Pan Books, 2002.

Wuthnow, Robert. *The Restructuring of American Religion: Society and Faith since World War II.* Princeton, NJ: Princeton University Press, 1988.

Index